PELICAN BOOKS

THE PELICAN HISTORY OF MUSIC
VOLUME TWO

The Pelican
History of Music

2

RENAISSANCE AND
BAROQUE

*

EDITED BY ALEC ROBERTSON
AND DENIS STEVENS

WITH THIRTY-TWO
PLATES

PENGUIN BOOKS

Penguin Books Ltd, Harmondsworth, Middlesex, England
Penguin Books, 625 Madison Avenue, New York, New York 10022, U.S.A.
Penguin Books Australia Ltd, Ringwood, Victoria, Australia
Penguin Books Canada Ltd, 41 Steelcase Road West, Markham, Ontario, Canada
Penguin Books (N.Z.) Ltd, 182–190 Wairau Road, Auckland 10, New Zealand

—

First published 1963
Reprinted 1965, 1967, 1969, 1971, 1973, 1974, 1976

—

Copyright © Penguin Books, 1963

—

Made and printed in Great Britain
by Cox & Wyman Ltd,
London, Reading and Fakenham
Set in Monotype Imprint

CONTENTS

IV · BAROQUE OPERA AND MASQUE
by Alec Harman

V · BAROQUE INSTRUMENTAL MUSIC
by Denis Stevens

LIST OF PLATES

Preface

THIS *History of Music*, although written by specialists, has been designed to satisfy the needs of intelligent and open-minded readers who know something about the history of art and literature yet lack the opportunity to link their knowledge with the more detailed aspects of musical art-forms. It cannot be, and is not intended to be, a comprehensive account of composers and their works, but rather an account of music seen against its various backgrounds – social, aesthetic, religious, and historical. The brief bibliographies are offered as a guide to further reading rather than an indication of works consulted in the compilation of individual chapters. The Editors extend their sincere thanks to the authorities of the Bodleian Library and the British Museum for help in providing illustrations, and also to Mr Edwin F. Gamble for his assistance in compiling the index. The quotations from *A History of Western Music* by Donald J. Grout in Part II are used by permission of the publishers, W. W. Norton & Co. Inc. and J. M. Dent.

ALEC ROBERTSON
DENIS STEVENS

1963

I · THE EARLY RENAISSANCE

Brian Trowell

1. The Transition to the Renaissance

MUSIC was certainly 'reborn' during the early Renaissance. If Richard Loqueville (d. 1418), who taught the young Dufay, could have returned to earth a century later, he would hardly have recognized a single familiar feature in the late works of Josquin des Prés (d. 1521). Josquin in his turn would probably have dismissed the music of Loqueville as so much incomprehensible gibberish. In describing the tonal revolution which separates these two masters, we have to deal not only with the lingering death of the Middle Ages and the equally gradual germination of Renaissance ideas, but with the birth of modern music itself. This is a large claim, and one which will probably surprise many readers. The origins of modern music have been traced back to various champions at various times: Monteverdi, Beethoven, Wagner, and Schoenberg are the most usual names. What early Renaissance composer can compare with any of these as an innovator?

The answer is: not one. There was no sudden break in the development of music; no bold revolutionary flouted accepted convention. Music was and remained an applied art, closely tied to its social and liturgical functions; the composer was normally an all-round practising musician who also happened to write new works in the course of his duties. He occupied quite an inferior rung on the social ladder (unless he also enjoyed a high position among the clergy), and did not meet with the sort of respect which a writer like Aretino or an artist like Michelangelo could command. The latter could 'treat the Pope as the King of France himself would not dare to treat him'; but we have to wait three centuries before we find a musician – Beethoven – breaking the bonds of convention in the same way, and reviling his chief patron in the streets of Vienna. Such romantic rebellion was out of the question for the early Renaissance composer, and could find no reflection in his works. The musical revolution of the fifteenth century was thus a slow affair, taking all of three generations to establish itself. It moved at different speeds in different countries. Mapping its course is rather like trying to plot the change from fresh water to salt where a river flows into the sea – with the added complication that the river is not the Severn but the Nile. There is no mainstream, no simple estuary, but a complex delta with all its cross-channels and backwaters. Nevertheless, the water is fresh at one end, salt at the other. The medium has changed, and with it the fauna and flora. The Middle Ages have become the Renaissance, and a new world has come into being: our world.

In what way is it 'our world'? At this point we run into some difficulty. If the intelligent listener could hear the music of the early Renaissance as easily as he can read its literature, walk around its buildings, and examine its statues and paintings, there would be no problem. But he enjoys very few chances of doing so. In spite of the efforts of scholars and enthusiasts over the past few decades, an immense amount of early music still remains unedited and therefore unperformable. The early Renaissance, up to and even beyond Josquin's time, has suffered particularly from this deadlock. The works of John Dunstable, for example, were not published in a practical, modern format until 1953, half a millennium after his death. The collected editions of such important masters as Guillaume Dufay and Johannes Ockeghem are not yet complete. It comes as rather a shock to realize that although Renaissance culture has been the subject of intense scrutiny ever since Michelet and Burckhardt printed their great studies over a century ago, the musical historian is still unable to write a comprehensive history of the period. However, the outlook is not entirely comfortless. A great deal has been done to survey the main landmarks in our territory, and a representative selection of works has been put before the public, both in print and in performance. The chances are that the reader of this volume will have been stimulated to buy it by listening to a broadcast or a recording of early music, executed in a reasonably authentic manner. He may even have been lucky enough to have heard a couple of works from the late fourteenth and the late fifteenth centuries performed one after the other in the same programme.

If so, he will need no historian to point out that the latter addresses him much more directly than the former. This is not to deny that the medieval world of sound presents a fascinating challenge; it offers its own rewards to the intelligent listener. Obrecht, Josquin, and Isaak, however, do not challenge us in this way; Josquin's music in particular does not seem strange or remote, but makes essentially the same appeal as Byrd, Bach, or even, be it said, Wagner. He speaks a language which we can readily understand, for it is a language which successive generations of composers have inherited, enriched, and handed on right down to our own times. No doubt the modern listener will occasionally stumble over an unfamiliar word or an unusual construction, but the basic grammar remains familiar enough. If, however, we start to travel backwards in time through the fifteenth century, sampling the music as we go, this feeling of contact with the musical language slowly becomes diluted. Ockeghem is already an equivocal figure; the later Dufay still has much to tell us; we can recognize what Binchois and Dunstable are saying. And then we are back in a strange land, the later Middle Ages, where our modern preconceptions can only hinder understanding.

So far we have tried to imagine the way in which an interested but uninstructed listener might react, in general terms, to early Renaissance music. It is now time to go into greater detail. How and why did the new music come into existence? Can we isolate the changes in the technique of composition as they occur? What relationship did music bear to the development of the Renaissance as a whole? In answering these and other questions, it will be best to start with a brief résumé of the most significant musical developments of the period; then to discuss the place of music and the musician in the broader context of his age; next, to give an account of the raw materials of his craft – voices, instruments, musical manuscripts and their interpretation; and finally, to examine the growth of new musical forms and styles as generation succeeded generation.

EARLY RENAISSANCE INNOVATIONS

The most important single innovation of the early Renaissance was undoubtedly the creation of choral polyphony. This was the essential prerequisite from which all later developments stemmed. In the Middle Ages, the chorus was never used for performing part-music. This was the preserve of soloists, since it had grown up as a kind of simultaneous troping of the soloist's portions of the chant. From the end of the fourteenth century, we notice a steady increase in the numbers of trained musicians in the choirs of the princely chapels and the wealthier cathedrals. From the 1420s the term 'chorus' begins to appear more and more frequently in manuscripts of sacred polyphony. Now, the idea of a family of blending, equally balanced voices had been quite foreign to the medieval composer, and the new medium radically changed the art of composition. Late Gothic polyphony was performed by a small chamber group of sharply contrasting timbres: the part-writing reflects this, and the aim was to make each voice as different as possible from its neighbours. With the change to a choral medium, the composer was faced with two related problems: he now had to blend the separate voices rather than make them stand out; and he had to be much more careful in his handling of dissonance.

A dissonance produced by two voices of the same colour sounds much harsher than the same dissonance produced by two voices of contrasting timbre. In writing for chorus, then, the composers of the 1420s abandoned the nervous ornamental dissonances of their forebears, and turned to the delights of euphony. We come across whole stretches of music which contain no dissonances at all, particularly in the works of English masters such as Dunstable and Pyamour. Obviously, however, unalloyed consonance can become a dull diet. So composers also began to consider how to tame dissonance. They started to use it structurally. The Gothic composer had enjoyed dissonance, but he had only employed it on the weaker beats of his music, between the perfect consonances of the strong beats. The counterpoint of the early Renaissance, on the other hand, harnessed the dissonance between preparation and resolution:

it could now appear on strong beats as a powerful motive force whose logical momentum propelled the contrapuntal harmony of the diatonic age until the time of Schoenberg and his school.

With the chorus established as a new medium, and with the problem of dissonance solved, Renaissance composers were free to break with other medieval traditions as well. If they used a Gregorian *cantus firmus*, for example, they no longer felt bound to place it in the tenor, disposed in long notes. The chant could now lie in any voice, or could travel from one part to another; its stark outline could be moulded into a more flexible rhythm, or could almost vanish under an exuberant profusion of ornament; towards the end of our period composers would break the chant into short phrases, which they used as thematic germs throughout the whole texture of their music. In choosing a *cantus firmus*, too, they were no longer governed by liturgical propriety: an antiphon from the Office – or even a secular song – could form the tenor of a Mass-setting; a composer would select a chant for an occasional motet, not because it came from the appropriate place in the liturgy, but because the words associated with the plainsong struck him as suitable. In secular song, the same attitude gradually led to the decay of the fixed forms of the medieval *chanson*, with its unvarying refrains.

By the time of Josquin's death, the composer could choose from a widely assorted armoury of new techniques. At one end of the spectrum lay the simple but plastic homophony of the *frottola*, with its emphasis on vertical chording and declamatory rhythms. At the other, we find one of the chief glories of Renaissance music, its imitative counterpoint. In this, the classic texture of 'democratic' part-writing, all the voices share equally in the musical material; each section of music is built up on a short theme which is passed from voice to voice after the manner of a fugal exposition. It is a texture which has fascinated composers down to the present day. To achieve it, the last link with the Middle Ages had to be broken. For the Gothic musician did not compose his music bar by bar as we do today. He started out with one part, normally the tenor, which he often derived from plainsong; he then proceeded to superimpose a second line of music above it, following the simple rules of two-part discant: after this, he – or indeed some other composer – went on to add a third whole part, still calculated from the tenor alone, so that this third voice might create quite harsh dissonances with the second. Like a Gothic building, his music was never complete, never a formal unity in the modern sense. It was of course possible to write occasional imitations using this method, but the opportunities became fewer and fewer as each successive voice was added to the complex. To write a canon, a strict imitation between two or more parts, the system had to be abandoned: the composer must work on all parts at once, fitting his music together bar by bar. It was no accident that the composers of Josquin's generation, who first made imitative counterpoint into an integrated and self-sufficient musical structure, had also mastered the most learned complexities of canonic writing.

The last significant innovation of the early Renaissance concerns the new respect with which composers came to treat the words that they set to music. The late medieval composer had not attempted to reproduce the accent and intonation of human speech when he set a text. The words were so many syllables, to be fitted to music which followed its own laws of construction. If musical logic demanded, he would end a section with a firm cadence half-way through a word, or split a word in two with a long rest. By the early sixteenth century, this attitude was rapidly changing. Both the humanists and the Reformers were closely concerned with words; and a new realism had come to dominate the fine arts. Composers, too, began to obey the prosody of natural speech in setting words to music. The 'just accent' which we can hear emerging in the vocal music of Josquin's time has been immensely important ever since.

This new feeling for words went beyond prosody. It extended to the emotional content of the words as well. The theorist Glareanus – who was also a humanist, friend of Erasmus, editor of Terence, and crowned poet of the Emperor Maximilian I – said of Josquin in 1547: 'no one has more effectively expressed the passions of the soul in music.' And indeed, we find in Josquin's music some of the first attempts at matching human emotions with an appropriate musical symbolism. This idea – the doctrine of the 'affects' – rapidly spread into the Italian madrigal, and eventually contributed to the downfall of Renaissance polyphony. It dominated Western musical thought down to the time of Richard Strauss.

This brief (and necessarily over-simplified) exposition of the new developments in early Renaissance music will stand us in good stead when we come to fill in some of the detail of the picture later on. It will have shown, perhaps, what a huge debt the music of succeeding centuries owes to this most exciting period.

2. Music and Musicians in Renaissance Life and Culture

THE POLITICAL SCENE – FRANCE AND BURGUNDY

OUR period opens with Henry V, victor of Agincourt, styling himself King of England and France. After his sudden death in 1422, his brother John of Bedford stayed on in Paris as regent for the young Henry VI. Large areas of France had been under English rule at one time or another during the Hundred Years War, and it was not until 1435 that the invaders were finally expelled. Bedford maintained the state of a king, with his own chapel, which included the composers Dunstable and Pyamour and perhaps others too. During the Wars of the Roses, England withdrew from the European scene and did not resume contact until the time of Henry VIII.

Henry V had subdued France with the active assistance of the Dukes of Burgundy. The rise and fall of this dukedom was one of the most remarkable features of fifteenth-century Europe. The original territory was the gift of a grateful father, John the Good of France, to his youngest son Philip the Hardy. Through his marriage with Margaret of Flanders, Philip inherited much of the rich country around the mouth of the Rhine; Flanders, Artois, Malines, and Antwerp were now in his possession. His son John the Fearless added further areas by marriage and by conquest, including Hainaut, Holland, and Zealand. In 1430 his successor, Philip the Good, was master of Lorraine, Brabant, and Limburg as well. Philip spent a good deal of his time in the northern part of his divided duchy, for most of his wealth was derived from the great trade routes which passed through his lands there. He kept a monarch's state amid a colourful and cultured assembly, though his court remained thoroughly medieval in character; and in 1430 he founded his chivalric order of the Golden Fleece with the aim of uniting his motley northern nobility – they included Walloons, Picards, and Flemings. He loved music passionately, and his chapel included such important composers as Gilles

Binchois and Antoine Busnois; Dufay was in his service for a time, and Ockeghem and Josquin were born in his northern territories. His son Charles the Rash, who succeeded him in 1467, was an equally distinguished patron of music and himself a composer. He died in a foolhardy attempt to unite the two halves of his dukedom by conquest; when his effects were sold at Basle in 1477, the artistic treasures of Burgundy were scattered over an admiring Europe like seeds from a bursting pod. His French lands – the southern area – reverted to the French crown. The northern territory passed to the Empire a few years later, through the marriage of his daughter Mary.

The rise of Burgundy had been possible because France and the Empire had been hamstrung at the time, France by her defeat at Agincourt, the Empire by rebellions and invasions in eastern Europe. By the end of the century, these two powers had recovered: Francis I and the Emperor Maximilian I, together with our own Henry VIII, presided over brilliant courts, the last in the medieval tradition; and all three made much of their musical retinue.

ITALY

Italy, throughout this period, remained a bundle of states constantly fighting amongst themselves for precedence in arms and the arts. The papacy returned to the peninsula with the ending of the great schism in 1417, though it was some time before the popes resettled in Rome for good. The popes were important patrons of music in the years after their return, drawing most of their singers from the area around Burgundian Cambrai: when Dufay arrived in the papal chapel in 1428, he need hardly have spoken a word of Italian, for the choir-stalls were full of his fellow-countrymen. In the 1470s, feeling safe at last, the popes began to consolidate their establishment, and Rome emerged once more as the leading city in Italy. The rebuilding of St Peter's was set in hand, and in 1473 Sixtus IV founded the Sistine Chapel. The future Capella Giulia was also begun at this time, partly as a training-ground for native Italian singers; it was finished under Julius II in 1512.

The other powers in the peninsula varied widely in character, from the Aragonese kings of Naples, Alfonso V and his son Ferdinand, to the republics of Florence and Venice, which were ruled by great merchants and bankers such as the Medici. Other centres important for their patronage of music and the arts included the Dukedom of Savoy (which extended across the Alps to border on southern Burgundy), and the courts of such upstart princelings as the Sforzas of Milan. The Este family in Ferrara gathered a particularly brilliant society about them, and Hercules I proved an outstanding friend of music in an age remarkable for its patronage. When Isabella d'Este went to Mantua after her marriage, she continued the traditions of her family in her new surroundings.

The lustre of the Italian Renaissance was considerably dimmed for a time by the disastrous invasions of the 'barbarians' from France and the Empire at the end of the fifteenth century. But the institutions which Italian rulers had founded in their first heyday – chapels, choir-schools, and song-schools – survived the depression and eventually helped to train a native company of Italian musicians. It is an odd fact that the first century of the Italian Renaissance produced not one Italian composer of the front rank between Landino and Palestrina, and precious few of the second. As a result, singers and composers from northern Burgundy flocked into Italy to swell the ostentation of the court chapels; and just as every parvenu ruler strove with his neighbours for political power and precedence, so he vied with them for the services of the best artists, scholars, writers, and musicians. Among the leading and secondary composers of Burgundian extraction, only Ockeghem, Binchois, and Busnois appear to have resisted the lure of Italy.

SPAIN AND EASTERN EUROPE

Spain, through most of our period, was gathering its forces to expel the Moors; they were finally driven from Granada in 1492, the year of Columbus's voyage to America. The union of Castile and Aragon under the 'Catholic Sovereigns' Ferdinand

and Isabella provided stable conditions under which music and literature were not slow to flourish. In 1516 their successor Charles V brought his 'Flemish chapel' with him, and northern musicians took root in the Iberian peninsula. Eastern Europe, like Spain, suffered from invasions – the Mongols in the early fifteenth century, the Turks in the early sixteenth. After a promising start, Poland fades from the musical scene until the very end of our period. Under Hussite rule, Bohemia remained largely innocent of sinful polyphony for a century and more. Hungary under King Matthias Corvinus enjoyed a brief period of Italo-Burgundian splendour – he married Beatrice of Aragon, who established her own chapel there. Her singers were greatly admired, and she herself was a good musician, who had learned the art in Naples from the Flemish theorist and composer Johannes Tinctoris.

The political life during this period rarely influenced music directly – though we do find compositions by Dufay, for example, which commemorate such occasions as the signing of a peace treaty between the Swiss cities of Berne and Fribourg in 1438, or the reconciliation of Emperor Sigismund and Pope Eugenius IV in 1433, or even the fall of Byzantium in 1453. What is important is the extraordinary mobility of the early Renaissance musician. The leading composers of the time were nearly all in the employ of powerful princes, and where their masters went, they went too. The travels of Dufay, Isaak, and Josquin alone would make quite an intricate spider's web if they were traced on the map of Europe. Although without the aids of broadcasting and international airlines, the musical world of the early Renaissance was an exceedingly cosmopolitan affair.

THE MUSICIAN'S CAREER

It is time to discuss in more detail the sort of life which a 'serious' musician of our period would have led. The qualification 'serious' is used merely in contrast to the 'light' musician or minstrel, whose circumstances were rather different: he was certainly an important figure, and we shall describe him later on.

One of the surprises which meets us in early Renaissance music is the fact that the great advances of the period were all achieved in the domain of sacred music. In the atmosphere of the fifteenth century in Italy we should have expected much more from secular music. In the fourteenth century, the main stream of musical enterprise had already left the channels of the liturgy, and nowhere more so than in Italy. Why should this reversal have come about?

The later fourteenth century had been a time of disillusionment, even disgrace, for the church. The sight of Pope and Antipope outbidding each other in the hope of being recognized by the kings of Europe was no edifying one for a religious man. Add to this the growing corruption within the religious orders when the crusading spirit of the twelfth and thirteenth centuries had spent itself, and we can no longer wonder that creative talent looked elsewhere for its main outlet. After the crowning scandal of the election of a *third* pope (the first Pope John XXIII, now no longer recognized), reforming spirits such as Jean Gerson finally managed to end the long schism by persuading the Council of Constance (1414–18) to lay all three popes aside in favour of Martin V. The scandal of Western Christendom ended, save for a few minor troubles, men could turn to the church with more respect, and from the 1420s onwards a new spirit of devotion started to spread through Europe. It began with the Brethren of the Common Life, the canons of Windesheim, on Burgundian soil, and its most influential exponent was Thomas à Kempis. His *Imitation of Christ* became one of the most widely read books of its time. Its author was an Augustinian canon, but by this date the monasteries no longer led the field in the production of sacred music. The leadership had passed to institutions such as the papal chapel, the private household chapels of the nobility, and the secular cathedrals and collegiate churches of the north.

From motives of piety (and no doubt ostentation as well), Henry V of England and Philip the Good of Burgundy suddenly changed the character of their court chapels at this time. The princely chapel of the Middle Ages had not been in the first place a collection of specialist musicians. It included the whole administrative staff of the king's household, and travelled with him wherever he went. These trained civil servants were all clerics – hence, no doubt, our word 'clerk', which has now lost all religious significance. There were certainly singers amongst them. Some of the lists of the household personnel of the English kings have survived to the present day, and it is instructive to look through them. Up to the reign of Henry V, no distinction is made in the lists between singers and administrative staff. Then, quite suddenly, we find the musicians of the chapel royal separated out from the secretaries: the former now appear under the title 'Chaplains and clerks of the king's chapel within his household'. And their number has increased considerably. The first wardrobe book of Henry's reign, for the year 1413, records the names of no fewer than twenty-six chaplains and clerks (the latter were only in minor orders), and a list from 1415–16 gives the number of boy singers as nine. This is a choir, not a handful of soloists, even though all the singers may not have been in attendance the whole time.

There are other references in the chronicles of the period to Henry's *ampla cappella*: it was much admired by the Emperor Sigismund and even by the unlucky French – for the chapel accompanied Henry on his Agincourt campaign, of which one of his chaplains has left us an account. The legend of their excellence travelled far. Foreign princes repeatedly sent to England in the course of the fifteenth century for singers: Alfonso V of Portugal in 1438 – to one of whose courtiers we owe a valuable description of the duties and services of the English chapel royal; the Emperor Frederick III in 1442; and Galeazzo Maria Sforza of Milan in 1471. We do not know whether anyone actually went in answer to these particular requests, but we find a couple of English singers at the court of Bavaria as late as 1483: another was active in Bologna in the 1460s, and later in the papal chapel. At least two distinguished musicians from this country spent most of their careers abroad: the widely respected theorist John Hothby taught in Lucca, and the composer Robert Morton was a particular favourite of Charles the Rash, Duke of Burgundy.

CHAPELS AND CHOIR-SCHOOLS

It was no new thing for a prince, a duke, or even an ecclesiastical dignitary, to keep a chapel. The French dukes of
Orleans, Anjou, Bourbon, Bar, and Brittany all had one at
this period. But the scale of Henry V's establishment must
have seemed most impressive to the French and Burgundian
courts, when they met daily with the English in order to
settle and sign the Treaty of Troyes in 1420. The young Duke
Philip the Good had inherited a small chapel from his mur-
dered father, and soon set about improving its constitution
until it rivalled the fame of Henry's. Other princes followed
suit. Few of these newly-founded or newly-expanded chapels
contained as many singers as the chapel of the English kings,
which still numbered thirty under Henry VI in 1451–2,
excluding boys (Edward IV and the early Tudors were content with a smaller choir). The usual number abroad varied
between fifteen and twenty, plus a few boys – though Gilles
de Rais, that stylish Bluebeard, kept between twenty-five and
thirty singers; we have no record of any choirboys in his case.
The papacy employed only nine singers in 1436, though the
number had risen to twenty-four by the end of the century.

Partly taking their lead from their royal masters, the wealthy
burghers of many rich towns started to endow larger musical
establishments in their churches. By the time Ockeghem
entered the choir in the church of Our Lady, Antwerp, in
1443, there were no less than twenty-five singers on the *can-
toris* side, all skilled in performing polyphonic music. The
duties of the twenty-six who sat opposite appear to have been
confined to the performance of plainsong – still one of the main
functions of an early Renaissance choir. The churches of
northern France and the area which was to become northern
Burgundy had already started to increase the strength of their
choirs in the late fourteenth century, although the national
disaster appears to have forced the French to cut down their
expenditure for a time. When the French chapel royal was
dispersed on the death of Charles VI in 1422, it boasted fifteen
chaplains. Chartres possessed thirteen *heuriers* in 1390; Notre

Dame de Paris employed seventeen or eighteen *clercs de matines* in 1398. Cambrai – a diocese which did not form part of France until the time of Louis XIV – enjoyed the services of ten vicars and six boys as early as 1386. Probably less than half of these forces, however, were engaged in singing polyphony at this period.

All of the churches mentioned, together with the churches of Toul, Noyen, and Rouen, also founded choir-schools, where a boy with a good voice could obtain a knowledge of polyphonic notation, and enough Latin to enable him to take minor orders. Such schools were also attached to princely chapels, and even to the smaller collegiate churches, chantries, and hospitals which pious benefactors were endowing in ever-increasing numbers from this date on. Thomas à Kempis apparently obtained his earlier education in one of these humbler institutions in Deventer, where 'the public school was in fact, if not in name, a song-school'. The Sainte-Chapelle of the French kings had included a *maîtrise* from 1299. The song-school of Venice, founded in 1403, appears to have been the centre of a group of northern Italian composers who flourished until about 1420. In this latter year Henry V approved the endowment of such a school in Durham, which was to teach poor persons gratis, receiving money only from those who were able and willing to pay. Philip the Good founded two in 1424–5, in Dijon and Lille, for four children in each case, stipulating that they be 'innocent, of good morals, to serve in the chapel with their master, who shall be a man skilled in his duties and of honest life . . . to teach them the art of music, including chant, counterpoint and descant'. The church of St Donatien in Bruges rapidly imitated his example.

A boy who gained a start in life by entering one of these institutions did not have an easy time. Clement IV had long ago recorded his opinion that choirboys 'should have the Martyr's Office, not the Requiem, said over them when they died'. If a boy stayed the course, however, his 'singer's Latin' would enable him to take minor orders and continue serving as a musician when his voice broke, or to graduate to the priest-hood later on. He could even go to a university: no doubt the great Erasmus of Rotterdam owed his lifelong mistrust of music to his early experiences as a choirboy in Utrecht, apparently under the tuition of the composer Jakob Obrecht. Some of the princely chapels reserved the right to poach their treble singers from other establishments. John Pyamour, the first known master of the children in the English chapel royal, was empowered to do this in 1420. The system was open to abuses, however: later on we find Wells Cathedral paying the King's servants six-and-eightpence *not* to take away three choristers. A well-trained boy who had a good voice and could sing mensural music at sight – especially from the complicated notation of the earlier fifteenth century – was clearly something of a rarity at this date. One such lad was poor '*frater Georgius*', who died in Pisa aged only fourteen: he 'could decipher the most complicated musical texts'. The four boys trained by the composer Nicholas Grenon at Cambrai, who travelled with their teacher to join the papal chapel in 1425, were no doubt similarly gifted. One of them, Bartélémy Poignare, went on to become a composer. Most of the Burgundian masters of the fifteenth century received their early education in this way.

The life of a vicar-choral in one of the lesser secular cathedrals seems to have been rather a humdrum existence. In the provincial towns of England, we learn from the records of bishops' visitations that discipline was often extremely slack. The vicars were frequently hauled over the coals for dicing, swearing, irreverent behaviour, fighting, whoring, and so on. No doubt the same was true of the lay choirs which some of the leading abbeys and monastic cathedrals instituted during the fifteenth century. Duties were heavy, with a long list of chantry-Masses to be said for past benefactors; and the prospects of financial reward were few. The aim of the ambitious singer was to enter the service of a prince or nobleman. Here he could be sure of his keep, his two new robes a year, and a small daily allowance – at the English court the chaplains received sevenpence and the clerks fourpence-halfpenny – and if he pleased his master, he could expect rapid preferment. Edward IV promoted his singers by 'prebends, churches of his patrimony, or by his letters recommendatory, free chapels, corrodies, hospitals or pensions'. In France, Ockeghem ended his career as treasurer of the Abbey of St Martin, Tours – an extremely wealthy house, whose abbot was the King himself. Perhaps Erasmus had this in mind when he commented admiringly on the great composer's 'golden voice'.

Only rarely during the earlier part of our period do we find a serious musician in princely service who was not also a member of the chapel. At the court of Burgundy, the two composers Jacques Vide and Hayne van Ghizeghem held the rank of *valet de chambre*, and their names do not figure in the lists of chapel staff. This was a title also given to painters and sculptors such as Jan van Eyck and Claus Sluter. Later on, 'singers of the chamber' become more common – secular musicians who were not in orders, a class which grew more and more important in the sixteenth century. Vide and Hayne have in fact left us no sacred music, though the same is true, oddly enough, of other masters such as Gilles Joye and the adopted Burgundian Robert Morton, who certainly served in the chapel.

GUILLAUME DUFAY

The career of Guillaume Dufay is one of the few that we can trace in some detail, and it will be instructive to describe it briefly here. He was born, like Binchois, of Walloon stock, and was recruited as a boy by the master of the choristers at Cambrai Cathedral, Nicolas Malin. There he probably came into contact with the composers Nicolas Grenon and François le Bertoul; from 1413 he would have been taught by the new master of the choristers, Richard Loqueville, whom we have already mentioned. He may have heard Henry V's chapel when he passed through Paris in 1420 on his way to Italy. Here he apparently entered the service of the rulers of Pesaro and Rimini, the Malatestas (later notorious for the monstrous behaviour of the *condottiere* Sigismund); his earliest datable works are connected with two weddings within this family, and were written in 1420 and 1423 respectively. He must then have moved north again, for a song dated 1426 regretfully says good-bye to '*ces bons vins de Lannoys*' – the country round Laon, where we know he held two benefices in 1430. In 1427 he obtained leave of absence from his deaconry in Cambrai and moved south once more, this time to join the papal chapel in 1428; he stayed until 1433, which is also the date of a *ballade* dedicated to Nicholas III of Ferrara.

Nicholas was a ferocious husband, having beheaded his adulterous duchess Parisina in 1425, but an amiable music-lover: he enjoyed frequent contacts with French and Burgundian musical life. Dufay then took a post with the House of Savoy, whose present descendants were removed from the throne of Italy after the last war. Amadeus VIII later became the last of the antipopes; both he and his son Louis adored music. In 1434 Amadeus abdicated, and in the same year Louis married Anne of Cyprus, who must have brought in her dowry the famous musical manuscript of the Cypriot school now in Turin. Dufay was in charge of the ducal singers for the wedding. Next year the composer returned to the papal chapel, though not to Rome: thanks to the machinations of Amadeus and others, the newly elected Eugenius IV had fled from Rome to Florence. In 1436 the Pope moved to Bologna with his chapel, and promoted Dufay to several northern canonries, including one at Cambrai. Pluralism and absenteeism were common enough at this date.

Two years later Dufay wrote a motet for two Swiss towns, and after this he becomes hard to trace until 1454. We know, however, that he spent part of this time in the Savoy, and it is piquant to imagine him playing off Pope against Antipope: Amadeus took the name of Felix V in 1439. Dufay also appears with the title 'singer to the illustrious Duke of Burgundy' during this period, though his name does not figure in Philip the Good's surviving archives. Martin le Franc pictures him at the Burgundian court in a poem written *c.* 1435–40. The composer was employed on a diplomatic mission in 1446: as a much-travelled man, his knowledge of the world must have been considered valuable. (Heinrich Isaak also made himself useful to Maximilian I as a political agent – Machiavelli, sent from Florence on a legation to the Emperor, was careful to seek him out on the way; minstrels, too, were often employed as spies or secret messengers.)

As the years progressed, Dufay seems to have spent more and more of his time at Cambrai, taking an active interest in the cathedral's musical life. He was now an honoured figure in the world of international music. He was asked to adjudicate in a musical disputation in Besançon in 1458. A letter from the famous Florentine organist Antonio Squarcialupi, dated 1467, thanks him for sending singers from Cambrai to serve Piero de' Medici; both Piero and his son Lorenzo admired Dufay and his music enormously, and Lorenzo had written a *canzone* which Dufay was requested to set. This composition, if indeed the master complied, does not seem to have come down to us; but Lorenzo's moving sonnet on the death of a famous musician may quite possibly refer to Dufay. The composer died at Cambrai in 1474, and we still possess his will. It lists many valuable tokens of esteem sent to him by European kings and princes with whom he is not known to have had direct contact, bequeathes six books of music to his old pupil Charles of Burgundy, and sets forth in interesting detail the musical arrangements that he desired for his funeral service. He also requested that 'my motet of *Ave regina caelorum*' should be sung during his dying moments, but this proved to be impossible. The motet still survives, troped movingly with the words '*Miserere tui labentis Dufay*': 'Have mercy on your dying Dufay'.

CAREERS OF OTHER COMPOSERS

No other composer of our period could rival Dufay in fame and fortune, except perhaps Josquin des Prés. But several of his fellows travelled equally widely, and were rewarded for their services in much the same way, though not to the same degree. Many masters, on the other hand, seem to have left almost no trace of their passage through the world beyond a name at the head of a piece of music. Of John Dunstable's career we know next to nothing. According to the now vanished epitaphs in St Stephen's, Walbrook, where he was buried, he earned great fame both as a musician and as an astronomer, and died on 24 December 1453; a bishop's register tells us that he was probably a canon of Hereford Cathedral for a time; and a note in an astronomical manuscript which he had once possessed describes him as 'musician to the Duke of Bedford'. His case is typical of many.

Even where we have some biographical details to go on, glimpses of personal character are very rare indeed before the sixteenth century. Occasionally a letter or a will has survived, as with Dufay. A portrait by Jan van Eyck bearing the title of a song by Binchois may perhaps represent the composer's likeness. We know from other sources, however, that Binchois was socially a cut above most of his colleagues: he came of a good family and served honourably as a soldier before turning to music and taking holy orders. If he did indeed become the subject of van Eyck's brush, it was because he was a gentleman and not because he was a musician: the portrait shows a man in ordinary clothes, not clerical robes.

No Vasari arose to record the lives of famous composers. The intense interest which the Italian Renaissance took in the characters of outstanding men of genius largely passed the musicians by. Sometimes a sixteenth-century writer such as Glareanus affords us a few revealing details. It is pleasant to know that Obrecht could write a Mass overnight, whereas Josquin took immense pains, keeping his music by him to correct and polish it for years before he ventured on publication.

This is borne out by another rare piece of evidence, an undated letter to Hercules I of Ferrara, in which a secretary recommended him to engage Isaak in preference to Josquin. Isaak, the Duke learned, 'is able to get on with his colleagues better and composes new pieces more quickly ... It is true that Josquin composes better, but he does it when it suits him and not when one wishes him to.' It was Josquin that Hercules appointed, nevertheless. Josquin, in fact, was the first composer whose posthumous prestige did not become a mere paper legend. His works continued to be printed and performed long after his death. Dunstable, Dufay, and Binchois appear as conventional household gods from the 1470s onwards, when Johannes Tinctoris first linked the three together in a genuine and meaningful tribute to their achievements, but their music did not survive them for long: we can still make out their garbled names in 1613, when Johannes Nucius paid his perfunctory respects to 'Dunxtaple, Dupsay, and Binchoy'. Some of Josquin's music, on the other hand, was still being performed at this date. Though we know infinitely less about him than about Michelangelo, he remains the first 'great man' of modern music.

Josquin certainly deserved his fame. In his works we can recognize the central watershed of the Renaissance. He summed up the main achievements of the previous century – not forgetting many features which had become rather old-fashioned by the time of his death – and passed them on to his successors, indicating many possibilities for future development by the example of his own marvellously flexible treatment of received tradition. We have already noted that in his approach to the words he set, humanist and Reformation ideals seem to have affected him. How far, one wonders, did he know what he was doing? It will be useful, before we leave our consideration of the composer and his place in the society of his time, to pause and examine briefly what the leading musical theorists and other writers had to say about the changing background to composition.

3. The Changing Approach to Music

WHEN Josquin's pupil Adrian Petit Coclico stated in 1552 that his master had left no '*musica*', we blink our eyes in puzzlement before realizing that *musica*, at this date, still meant 'written theory of the art of music'. The *musicus*, in medieval language, was the philosopher of music, a very lofty personage indeed when compared to the mere *cantor*, or practising musician. The former was likened to a theologian, a receiver and interpreter of God-given truths; the latter was only a lesson-reader, who recited the message of his master. By this token, Christ himself was the supreme *musicus*; and this is an opinion which we still find recorded in the pages of Johannes Tinctoris, who wrote the first Renaissance encyclopedia of music in the 1470s. From Boethius onwards, music was considered to be far more than well-ordered sound. It was a *speculum*, a mirror of the divine order. *Musica mundana* was the music of the macrocosm, of the heavenly bodies in their spheres: *musica humana* was the music of the microcosm, of man's mind and of human society. The task of *musica instrumentalis*, the music of human voices and instruments, was to make the all-immanent harmony of the macrocosm and microcosm audible to human ears.

Although some writers of the later Middle Ages had questioned this idea – Tinctoris, a practical man of the new age, rejects it out of hand – it nevertheless retained a strong hold on the Renaissance imagination. The humanist Filelfo found it good that philosophers should approve of music, 'because our mind, the sky, nay the entire universe consists of the proportions of music'. The theorist Gafuri echoed this, and Orlando Gibbons spoke with the same voice in the early seventeenth century. It is an odd fact that Boethius and his ideas should have taken on a new lease of life in the early Renaissance. His works were printed in Venice in 1491, 1492, 1497, and many times more. They formed the staple fare for the new English university degree of bachelor of music: the Oxford B.Mus. was still licensed to teach Boethius in the middle of the nineteenth century! The doctorate of music was the degree for the practising composer; but a mere D.Mus. was frowned upon by the doctors of other disciplines, who did not allow a mere *cantor* to share their jealously-guarded academic privileges.

One suspects that many practising composers were content with their *musica instrumentalis* alone. The scholars' point was that Boethius, who was executed in the year 525, was a classical authority, however late. And, in fact, his *musica humana* lent itself admirably to the Renaissance idea of a musical language symbolizing the human emotions: Erasmus, for example, mentions *musica humana* and the *affectiones* in the same sentence. For the humanists, no less than the medieval schoolmen, were still bound by the idea of authority, and if a classical authority like Boethius had also happened to meet with medieval approval, it did not worry them in the least.

MUSIC AND MATHEMATICS

Medieval musical theorists had also taken over the classical theory of proportions and added it to their armoury. The learned study of music as a member of the *quadrivium* was closely allied to the study of mathematics. Indeed, it was possible to convert a treatise on arithmetical proportions into a treatise on musical proportions merely by changing a word here and there, and one English theorist of the fifteenth century actually does this for us. In Gothic times, perfection of number retained a mystical significance both in the mensuration of music and in its harmony.

We have seen that early Renaissance composers soon abandoned the medieval concept of continually recurring perfect consonances on all strong beats: Tinctoris gives a full definition of the new harmony in his dissertation on counterpoint of 1477. The speculative use of numerical proportions nevertheless continued to fascinate composers up to Josquin's time, and even beyond. Mensuration canons, in which two voices are to be derived in different metres from the same series of notes, were known in the late Middle Ages, and Josquin has also left us some involved examples. The device of writing a piece of polyphony in which each part employs a different time-signature was also practised in the Ars Nova; and then, two or three generations later, just as such mensural sophistications seemed to be dying out with the last vestiges of medieval isorhythm, we suddenly find composers like Ockeghem, Isaak, and Pierre de la Rue reviving the idea, with successively changing proportional signatures of appalling complication. Glareanus, looking back, complained of such habits, and poured scorn on Josquin for 'talking nonsense with his canon . . . For who except Oedipus himself would understand such a riddle of the sphinx?'

In contemporary literature, we can see clearly that similar tricks are merely the last twitchings of medieval formalism in its death-throes: the clever palindromes, puns, acrostics, punctuation-poems which can be read in two opposite senses, verses which praise when read normally and vituperate when read backwards – all make very dull reading today. Yet Thomas Morley still includes a difficult mensuration puzzle in his *Plain and Easy Introduction to Practical Music* as late as 1597.

If we turn to the theory of the fine arts in the fifteenth century, we soon learn why the Renaissance should have remained so interested in numerical relationships. Ancient classical art had evolved a complex system of proportion, not only for architectural purposes, but also in order to superimpose harmonious and stylized composition on the refractory limbs of the human body. Euclid's *Optics* held the key to vanishing-point perspective, and Pythagoras had developed a whole *mystique* of numerology, which he also expressed in musical terms. Here again, there was classical authority close at hand. The architect and polymath Leon Battista Alberti stated that a harmonious ratio in architectural design was one which, when expressed as a musical harmony, yielded a pleasing concord. Leonardo also described his art in terms of music: 'the simultaneous perception of all the component parts [of a painting] creates a concordant harmony which for the eye is a sensation equivalent to that experienced by the ear when listening to music'. It is relevant to note here that Alberti's famous

36

description of beauty applies with striking force to the new imitative polyphony of the early sixteenth century, which had finally fought free of the Gothic methods of additive composition: 'the harmony and concord of all the parts achieved in such a manner that nothing could be added or taken away or altered except for the worse'.

We learn from all this that some of the theories of music which the Middle Ages had derived from the antique – largely through the medium of Boethius – continued to find expression in humanist thought. The old numerological speculations of the Gothic ceased to dominate the new harmony, but still made themselves felt from time to time in complicated proportional puzzles. Many musicians continued to pay at least lip-service to the idea of music as a *speculum*, for neo-Platonism was a vigorous force in Renaissance thought. But here, the strong practical bent of the Renaissance started to assert itself. From the later fourteenth century, we begin to find treatises on discant – simple two-part counterpoint, written or extemporized – and these were compiled by *cantores*, by practical musicians.

Many of them use the vernacular, like the English composer Leonel Power's *Treatise upon the Gam*. Such booklets were intended for practical instruction: without exception, they dispense with the learned speculations of the *musici*. With Tinctoris, these down-to-earth directions begin to enter the more learned books on musical theory, alongside the old traditional matter. Soon, with the rise of instrumental music towards the end of our period, books of practical instructions were written for the leisured middle-class amateurs who now wished to make music for themselves. The first of these simple tutors were in German, beginning with Sebastian Virdung's *Musica getutscht* of 1511, which was soon translated into other languages as well. Music was ceasing to be a mystery reserved for the initiated few. The bourgeois learner merely wished to get enough grammar to be able to play a part from a song on his flute. Thus, highflown speculation and simple pragmatism came to exist side by side in the world of musical theory. The composer-craftsman, the singer, and the instrumental performer begin to count for more than the instructed *musicus*.

THEORISTS AND COMPOSERS

Theorists such as Tinctoris and Gafuri, who were themselves working musicians and composers, managed to reconcile doctrine and practice happily enough. Other learned writers were less pleased with the situation. Erasmus, for example, liked music well enough in the proper place: his friend Glareanus gives us a list of his favourite tunes. Yet it made him uneasy. After listening to a performance of a secular piece, he would throw the sheet of music in the air and exclaim that the music was as light as the paper it was written on. He believed with the ancient Greeks in the ethical power of music. 'What would Plato have said', he wrote in a letter of 1526, 'to the noisiness of modern music?' He goes on to complain of the use of drums and trumpets in church at weddings and on important feast-days, saying that the racket would be more appropriate to a dance or a battle.

Elsewhere Erasmus complained of the excess of music performed by hired choirmen in English churches, where the words were lost in a flood of polyphony. He was continually contrasting the vanity of the music he heard all around him with the marvellous ethical effects of the music of the Greeks, which he had seen described in Plato. The English humanist Richard Pace, writing in 1517, mentioned his own search amongst the ancient codices of the Vatican Library as he attempted to discover for himself what antique music had sounded like. Tinctoris had sensibly observed, forty years before, that there was virtually nothing left of it but theoretical descriptions: he then abandoned the subject. Pace grew annoyed with this lack of interest, which was apparently general amongst practical musicians: 'You can scarcely find a single one who understands what music is,' he wrote, 'and yet they are always singing it.'

In an attempt to master this problem, some theorists began to preoccupy themselves with the ancient Greek modes. Glareanus's impressive *Dodecachordon* of 1547, the first thorough-going treatment of the question, lies outside our period, but draws heavily for its illustrations on the music of Josquin and his contemporaries. The title, printed proudly in Greek characters, means 'twelve strings'; it refers to his new classification of the modes. He proposed to add four more modes to the eight of the medieval church: these were the authentic and plagal forms of our modern major (Ionian) and minor (Aeolian), which composers had been using in practice for some time. Being a musician of some insight and an honest man, he admits that Josquin's music is of the first excellence, even though its unlearned composer commits many sins against the modes.

In effect, however, it proved impossible to reconcile the Greek concept of mode, which was essentially monophonic, with the modern polyphonic style. Further, besides the fact that Glareanus had created two modes which did not exist in Greek theory, he had also failed to observe that medieval theorists had applied the Greek names to the wrong church modes. His book came too late to affect the situation, though his discussion of other topics remains very valuable for us today. If he had lived at the time of Ockeghem, when composers turned unprompted to a more diatonic style, his theories of modal polyphony might have had some effect. Soon after 1547, however, the chromatic experiments of the Italian madrigalists started to dissolve the diatonic structure of Renaissance polyphony.

The only sphere in which the humanists' theorizing bore fruit in practice was that of prosody. Latin was the language of sacred music, and humanists were quick to complain that the composers of their time not only failed to observe the proper stresses of Latin, but obscured the sense of the words with their busy part-writing. The Reformers also urged a simpler treatment of the sacred texts, and in the long run they were undoubtedly more influential in securing it. The humanists' most important experiments concerned the quantitative metres of Latin verse. Just before 1500, the German Conrad Celtes suggested that composers might attempt musical settings which observed the classical Latin quantities; his *Play of Diana*, performed before Maximilian I in Linz, included such an experiment.

In 1507 his pupil, the Tyrolese Petrus Tritonius (Peter Traybenraiff, to give him the name he was born with), published a collection called *Melopoeae* in which he applied his master's ideas to the Odes of Horace. Gafuri included a similar experiment in his *Theoricum Opus*. This stiff and mechanical style, which used only breves and semibreves in four-part homophony, proved surprisingly popular. It was much used for the choruses of the Latin dramas which were a feature in south German schools, and blended with the *Lied* to create the simple note-against-note texture of the early polyphonic chorale. Later on in the sixteenth century, ideas very similar to those of Celtes also led to a quantitative treatment of the French language and to *musique mesurée à l'antique*.

Finally, we should record that the influence of the humanists contributed a good deal towards the final decay of the plainsong tradition. In Tinctoris's time, the chant was sung fairly freely, in uneven notes whose value apparently depended upon the singers themselves. Gafuri (1496), Aron (1516), and Vanneo (1533) observe that the melodies were now sung more mechanically, in notes of equal duration. Blasius Rossetti (1529) wished to apply the rules of prosody to the simpler tunes of the hymns, sequences, and antiphons, but showed some perception in recommending that the ornate chants of the Graduals, Responds, and Introits should be sung in free rhythm. His moderate views, however, did not prevail: the whole repertory was to be 'civilized', its rhythms tidied up. And so the ancient plainsongs of the Western ritual finished their long and distinguished career quite deprived of their traditional dignity, racked and lopped on the Procrustean bed of the disastrous *Editio medicaea* of 1614.

This discussion of the Renaissance musician in a changing world of theory has inevitably taken us beyond our official limits at both ends of the period. We must, however, once more risk prosecution for trespass. The appeal to authority was evidently in many ways as important to the learned minds of the early and middle Renaissance as it had been to the medieval scholiasts; but there also emerged a more practical strain which tended to ignore the higher flights of musical theory.

In Pietro Aron, who wrote in the early years of the sixteenth century, we have the first considerable theorist of the age to throw himself wholeheartedly on to the side of the pragmatists. Four out of his five treatises were written in Italian; he was the first writer to observe that composers had abandoned additive composition; and he was the first to suggest that *all* accidentals should be written out in full, to avoid the uncertainties of *musica ficta* which still plague editors today. He was a real son of the Renaissance, and his attitude seems to represent very closely that of Josquin and his contemporaries.

In 1552, however, a book was published in Nuremberg which purports to retail the actual teaching of Josquin himself: the *Compendium musices*. Its author, the Flemish Adrian Petit Coclico, was a strange figure: he glares out at us from a woodcut on his own title-page, a truculent-looking dwarf, bearded to the knees. He claims to have been a pupil of Josquin, and what he has to say often sounds authentic, though his own compositions are no advertisement for his master's teaching. He starts off by telling us without more ado that 'the ear ... is the master of singing': by 'singing' he means composition, and though his words seem no more than common sense to us today, they must have seemed a daring challenge to authority when they were first published.

Amongst more commonplace matter, Petit Coclico makes two other unusual points which sound like the genuine teaching of his master. The composer, he says, 'must be led to compose by a great desire, and must have a certain natural leaning to prompt him, so that he shall forget food and drink until he has finished his song; for when such a natural impulse urges him, he will do more in one hour than others in a whole month. Composers who lack such inspirations are useless.' This is an almost nineteenth-century approach to 'genius'; but we have already noted that Josquin disliked composing to order, and preferred to wait until it suited him before writing anything new.

Petit Coclico's sixth rule for the composer recommends a careful approach to prosody – usual enough in Josquin's day – and also insists that the composer must not ignore or distort

41

the emotional significance of the words he sets: 'for they err in the dark, worse than the blind, who add sad numbers to words full of joy and consolation, or conversely set happy tunes to sad words'. The idea that music could express *emotions* in this way is a far cry from the medieval and humanist idea of music as an impersonal *ethical* power. Nevertheless, whether or not Josquin himself actually spoke the words which his pupil puts in his mouth, it is a fact that the master's finest music does speak directly to our emotions with an urgency which is often lacking in the more impersonal approach of Obrecht or Isaak, and is hardly present at all in earlier music.

THE REFORMATION

Finally, a word or two about the Reformation attitude to music. The innovations of Luther and Calvin belong more properly in the next chapter, and we shall not discuss them here. Their basic contention, that music must not obscure the revealed Word of God, has something in common, as we have seen, with the humanists' views on the dangers of polyphony. However, we must not suppose that such an idea was confined to the new churches alone: the ideas of the Council of Trent and the Counter-Reformation have a long history within the Roman Catholic Church itself. The death of the polytextual motet of the Middle Ages provides a striking example of this in the domain of music. The words of the upper voices of such a motet were conceived as a kind of multiple trope, an expansion and interpretation of the words of the plainsong in the tenor. As fifteenth-century theology turned away from medieval methods of interpreting the Scriptures by means of three- or even four-fold allegory, the polytextual motet also died a natural death.

We have already mentioned the Hussite heresy. The followers of John Hus, who was burned at the Council of Constance in 1415, destroyed the organs in the churches of Bohemia, banned the use of musical instruments, excommunicated the minstrels in 1435, and permitted only unembellished monophony in their worship; ideas which would have pleased

John Wyclif in fourteenth-century England. From the time of Pope John XXII, more respectable figures also warned musicians to avoid excess. In the fifteenth century, secular music was strongly attacked by Bernardino of Siena, who persuaded the women of Rome to burn their song-books in 1422. Three years later he condemned the use of organs and singing in church, and bade worshippers to beware of improperly enjoying music. Antoninus, Bishop of Florence, who died in 1459, uttered similar imprecations.

Savonarola's notorious bonfire, on the other hand, which consumed musical manuscripts and instruments along with other worldly fripperies including many of Botticelli's secular masterpieces, has earned the friar a perhaps undeserved reputation as a music-hater. In point of fact, he was a musician himself. In 1475, he broke the news to his mother that he was going to leave her by playing to her on his lute. He liked to see the people singing and even dancing at his great public meetings. Choirboys sang 'sweet lays' in Florence Cathedral when he preached there, including a *Lauda* to the crucifix in three parts. What he condemned was excess; if Isaak had to leave Florence at this time, it was probably only because he had served the hated Medici. Erasmus, too, disliked excesses:

Modern church-music is so constructed that the congregation cannot hear one distinct word. The choristers themselves do not understand what they are singing, yet according to the priests and monks it constitutes the whole of religion . . . In college or monastery it is still the same: music, nothing but music. There was no music in St Paul's time. Words were then pronounced plainly. Words nowadays mean nothing . . . If they want music, let them sing psalms like rational beings, and not too many of these.

Such complaints were of course directed against the whole idea of complex polyphony. Few musicians seem to have heeded them before 1520. From the 1450s onward, however, composers had clearly been trying to create a more dignified and monumental style for church music. When sacred music started to reassert itself in the earlier part of our period, it was still largely dominated by techniques adapted from the more progressive world of secular song. Mixed forms such as the song-motet came into being, short sacred works in *chanson* style, which often appear as the first item in an otherwise secular *chansonnier* – a sort of grace before meat, a sacred text over the house-door. The young Dufay took over the graceful dance-rhythms of secular song into his sacred music; his early Masses are written in a contrasting series of well-articulated sections, each of which has the dimensions of a *rondeau* or *ballade*. In his later Masses, though, the sections become longer.

Ockeghem will write for a hundred bars and more without drawing a double-bar or introducing a passage in contrasting metre; even the internal cadences of the music tend to vanish. He abandons the intimate world of song and aims instead at the impressive scale and flowing continuity of monumental architecture; the colourful chromatics of earlier music also give way to an austere diatonic modality. At the same time, secular music begins to adopt a more realistic declamation, and we see the homophonic *frottola* and *villancico* coming to the fore. The two styles cease to resemble each other in scale and texture, even though a Mass could take a secular tune for its model, and a *chanson* could still be written on a plainsong tenor.

By 1520, the foreword to a printed collection of Josquin's motets speaks of his sacred music as very different from that of 'the songs of young ladies and dances'. Composers were trying to write music worthy of the dignity of the divine service. But few of the advocates of reform, whether humanist, Protestant, or Catholic, were prepared to admit that music creates its own laws. Michelangelo could safely scorn the literal-minded realism of the Flemish painters: he himself showed Giuliano de' Medici as clean-shaven on his tomb, though he had worn a beard all his life, saying 'Who, in a thousand years' time, will care what he looked like?' The composer, however, had to stick to his function: a mere *cantor* must not presume to know what his music was about. Only one of the Reformers seems to have had any deep understanding of the growing artistic self-sufficiency of music; and we are fortunate indeed that this exception was Martin Luther.

4. Minstrels and Minstrelsy

THERE is an enormous amount which we shall never know about minstrel music. It is a tantalizing situation: we can study the appointments and movements of minstrels in great detail, using the many surviving account books – we know precisely what their duties were at the Burgundian court, for instance; we can read the numerous contemporary writers who paid tribute to their remarkable virtuosity; we have the texts of some of their songs; we can reconstruct their instruments and assemble them in their proper groupings by examining fifteenth-century paintings which show minstrels performing. But none of their music has survived. Most of them could not read mensural music; they played by ear. We are fortunate to this extent: we do at least possess many of the dance-tunes to which they extemporized their brilliant 'divisions'; and we also have a few polyphonic arrangements of some of these melodies, noted down by more learned musicians – arrangements which were quite possibly modelled on actual minstrel performances. Finally, we cannot doubt that the new instrumental music which begins to appear towards the end of our period borrowed some of its features from the traditions of minstrelsy. For this reason alone, we would not be justified in omitting all discussion of the minstrels from these pages. We must also remember that 'serious' musicians lived in close contact with the minstrels and also played some of the same instruments. Eventually, at the end of the fifteenth century, the rising class of 'chamber musicians', who were properly trained, musically literate singers and instrumentalists, began to take over the functions of the minstrelsy – and therefore some of their musical practices as well.

There were two quite distinct types of minstrel: minstrels of war, and chamber minstrels. The former, apart from their duties on the battlefield, were the overt symbols of a nobleman's state. In war, the function of trumpeters and drummers was obviously to give signals which could be heard from afar.

Thus we learn that at the siege of Calais in 1436, on the Milk Gate tower,

> The Trumpettes lowd did they blow,
> ffor the Duc sholde wel know
> The wacch whan it began.

As one might expect, they were valued for their psychological effect on the enemy, too. The Burgundian chronicler Chastellain relates how Henry V, besieging Melun, had his minstrels of war assemble every evening before his tent, where 'a great quantity of trumpets and clarions played, and the meadows and the woods re-echoed with their sound, so proudly that it seemed as if the whole earth, however great, belonged to him'.

In time of peace, the minstrels of war would go before their master in procession to herald his arrival, sometimes with humbler instrumentalists as well. At the election ceremonies of Pope John XXIII in 1410, Nicholas III of Ferrara was preceded by 'six trumpets and three pairs of minstrels, all playing their instruments'. The use of trumpeters was a coveted privilege, and some of the lesser nobility who enjoyed it apparently made themselves ridiculous by showing their players off on unsuitable occasions. Thus, the Chief Constable of Paris in 1418 – a real Dogberry, it seems – never did the rounds without 'three or four musicians playing brass instruments, which appeared a strange thing to the people, for it seemed to them that he said to malefactors: "Get away, for I am coming."' The Duke of Burgundy kept twelve such trumpeters, and their duties are set out in ritual detail in a description of his court. Whenever he was due to leave a town, they had to play a fanfare beneath his windows to wake him up at the hour appointed; then four of them went off to sound the call to saddle the horses in the four quarters of the town; after breakfast, the chief trumpeter attended the Duke, waiting for the signal to mount; when all was ready, the call to horse was sounded, and the different estates of the household assembled under their leaders; at the next signal, everyone gathered before the Duke's lodging; the trumpets then blew a final call as the Duke himself mounted – 'and all the trumpets must play at all entries and departures'.

On unusually important occasions, huge numbers of trumpeters would foregather to welcome some exalted personage, no doubt in hopes of princely largesse. They flocked (with other instruments as well) to Henry V's wedding, to play before the bride's chariot: 'and you should know that many a player appeared there that day because it had been ordered that each of them should receive a gold coin for the day, which King Henry had recently begun to mint.' When Philip the Good's third wife, Isabella of Portugal, arrived in Bruges in 1429, there were more trumpets and minstrels waiting to herald her arrival than had ever been known, with 'at least 120 silver trumpets' in the procession, and seventy-six more by the Duke's gate. They 'made such a noise that the whole town resounded with it'. The terrific din was much valued – even the relatively quieter instruments of the early fifteenth century made much more noise than their Renaissance successors.

DOMESTIC MUSIC

Household minstrels were employed in great numbers by the princes of the time; ecclesiastics kept them too, and so did towns; even ships took a band with them. They played either *hauts instruments* or *bas*, and sang as well. The louder winds and the *trompette de ménestrels* belonged to the former family (the minstrel trumpeter played the more agile slide-trumpet or sackbut, not the straight instrument of the trumpeter of war); stringed and keyboard instruments, and the gentler winds, comprised the latter group. Wind instruments were much more common than any other: when he died, Henry VIII owned no fewer than seventy-seven recorders.

Minstrels were free to go away on their own from time to time, and formed a very mobile international confraternity. They set up something very like a trades union in England in 1469, to regulate the apprenticement of the craft and to ensure that cheapjack impostors did not pass themselves off as liveried servants of a nobleman and thus claim hospitality from the towns that they visited. Since they were forbidden to exercise their profession during Lent, under pain of excommunication, this became the season for the great international gatherings of minstrels, to which they came from far and wide to compare notes and exchange the latest new songs. A likely new boy (even, on occasion, an ex-choirboy whose voice had broken) would be properly apprenticed to an established expert, to learn the mysteries of the craft. Thus the organist of Maximilian I, one Bredemers, was told to teach 'a young son', drummerboy to the archduchesses, to play 'flutes, clavichord, organ and other instruments'. (A choirboy normally had to study keyboard instruments as part of his training as well.) Very few minstrels indeed knew how to compose; an exception seems to have been Jean de Villeroye, alias Briquet, who served in the Court of Love founded by Charles VI: he has left us a song which shows some learning.

The singers must have enjoyed fantastic memories, though some roughly scribbled texts of their songs have come down to us. They either repeated verse after verse ballad-fashion to the same tune; or else, like the instrumentalists, they extemporized over one of the basses that became popular in art-music later on in the sixteenth century. One of the two poems of Sir Thomas Wyatt to survive with music has just such a succession of chords for a lute, and uses just such a bass: there is no 'tune'. The poet Giustiniani, who wrote *O rosa bella*, a *ballata* which was set by both Ciconia and Dunstable, used to extemporize verses to his own accompaniment; he died in 1446. He was of course no minstrel, though he appears to have used minstrel techniques. The same would have been true of other learned *improvvisatori* of Renaissance Italy.

These included Leonardo da Vinci himself, who apparently went to Milan in the first place as an improviser, not as an artist. The poet Serafino dall'Aquila was another. Benedetto Chariteo intoned Virgil to his lute. At the court of Pope Leo X, who learned to admire the improvisers from his father, Lorenzo the Magnificent, they performed extraordinary feats. Panfilo Sassi extemporized verses in Latin; Andrea Marone, from one report, seems to have been quite a nineteenth-century virtuoso figure, for 'the singer's eyes stare and shine, sweat trickles down, the veins of his forehead swell'. Leo would applaud their efforts and then proceed to cap their verses himself.

The court minstrels provided music for all occasions. They played in processions and during dinner; they supplied a musical background for the play of courtly love, at Mayings, at Christmas, in the New Year, at jousts and tourneys, pageants, mummings, disguisings, and dances. In 1414, Duke Louis of Guienne entertained Nicholas III of Ferrara at dinner with *bas instruments*: harp, viol, lutes, and gittern. The remarkable magnificence of the musical arrangements at Philip the Good's famous crusading banquet of 1454 have been well described elsewhere: the minstrels and trumpets of war played in alternation with the trained musicians of the ducal chapel. For the courtly play of love, 'serious' musicians also composed their *rondeaux, ballades*, and *virelais*: Dufay has left us many examples. At the jousts organized in 1444 by the Duke of Cleves and Jacques de Lalain, 'the trumpets blew so loudly that you could not have heard God thundering'.

DANCE MUSIC

Dances were an important field for the minstrel to display his skill in. The fifteenth century was a great age of the dance. The *basse dance* reached the French and Burgundian courts from Spain some time before 1445. It was second in favour only to the morris, which had the added attraction of fancy dress. Dances proved an agreeable ending to a festal evening, but they were also a symbolic act in the ritual of courtly love. The band would consist of a small group of minstrels, normally sitting in a gallery or on a raised dais. *Al fresco* occasions and more formal gatherings would normally require *hauts instruments*; more intimate surroundings would have suggested *bas*. When these dances became popular in Italian circles, they changed their character completely. Domenico da Piacenza seems to have been the father of the Italian *bassadanza* and *ballo*. He worked at the Este court in Ferrara, and most of the succeeding generation of Italian dancing-masters learned their art from him. The Burgundian *basse dance* consisted of a fixed series of rigidly prescribed steps, whatever the tune. Each Italian *bassadanza*, however, was a particular balletic creation of an individual master, a spatial exercise in the true Renaissance manner.

The music of these dances has left some traces for us to study. There are many dance-manuals from Italy and elsewhere, and we have the magnificently illuminated manuscript collection of tunes which may have belonged to Margaret of Austria, Regent of the Netherlands. The *basse dance* tunes consist of a string of 'coloured' breves, and it is clear from one or two polyphonic arrangements of these melodies how they were performed: while the sackbut played the recorded tune in equal notes as a bass, one, two, or even three shawms would extemporize running counterpoints above. This arrangement is also described in instrumental treatises of the next century, and Tinctoris tells us that a family group of shawms makes an agreeable noise, particularly with a sackbut taking the bass.

The music of the *bassadanza* was very like that of the *basse dance*. In both steps and music, however, the *ballo* was much more freely constructed. It consisted of a chain of sections which could frequently change measure. The tunes for the *balli* were not tenors in equal notes, like those for the *basse dance*, but treble melodies with a rhythmic life of their own. Each genre took at least some of its tunes from polyphonic art-song, including several examples by known masters such as Binchois or Pierre Fontaines. For the *basse dance*, the tenor parts were extracted from the *chanson* and then ironed out into notes of equal value. The *balli* took the treble over whole, in the original rhythm. It was obviously quite easy to sing a *ballo*, though we also have some references to singing in connexion with *basses dances* too. One could even dance to one's own singing. Giovanni Ambrogio of Pesaro, the famous dancing-master, accompanied Ippolita Sforza of Milan to Naples in 1465. He wrote back to her mother to say that his pupil had composed two new *balli* to tunes which she had taken from French songs. Her father-in-law King Ferdinand 'has no other pleasure and knows no other paradise than when he sees her dancing and also singing'. The manuals also offer us three *balli* which Lorenzo the Magnificent composed as a young man.

The bourgeoisie enjoyed dancing too. A picture of a wedding on a Florentine dower-chest of *c.* 1450 shows us five couples dancing a *chiarenza* or wedding-dance under a canvas awning set up before the Baptistery. The musicians, on a shallow, raised platform at one side, consist of three shawms and a sackbut. We can see from the bannerets attached to their instruments that they are the town waits of Florence, hired by the Adimari family for the occasion. The English woolmerchant George Cely has left us a list of his personal expenses during a stay in Calais from 1473 to 1475. He employed a professional harper, Thomas Rede, to teach him twenty-six dances on the harp, and fifteen more, including a hornpipe, on the lute. Cely also studied the 'footing' of several dances, including some *basses dances*. Rede further taught him to play some songs, amongst whose titles we find Dunstable's *O rosa bella* and the lovely *Go heart, hurt with adversity*, which still survive.

All sorts of characteristic and national dances became the rage towards the end of the fifteenth century; the *tedesca*, the *branle*, the *schiavo*, round dances, the *zingaresca*, Spanish, Polish, Turkish, and Neapolitan dances, and latterly the *pavane* are amongst those recorded. Preachers and moralists tended to object to this new craze, and no wonder: Leo von Rozmital relates how he attended a magnificent ball in a convent near Neuss in 1466; in Venice, some young scamps of noblemen celebrated the election of the Abbess of Zelestria in 1509 by dancing all night with the nuns, *con trombe e pifari*. The minstrels were certainly kept busy.

A minstrel could not hope to rival the success of a Dufay or a Josquin, but he could save his rewards and invest in property for his retirement. Some became internationally famous, like Pietro Bono, lutenist at the court of Ferrara, who is singled out for mention by the admiring Tinctoris; he travelled as far as Budapest. Giovanni Arnolfini, whose portrait by Jan van Eyck will be familiar to many, made his fortune selling silks to Philip the Good: he had come as a young man from Lucca to the Low Countries as a *pauvre compagnon chanteur*, 'a poor minstrel singer'.

MINSTRELS AND SERIOUS MUSIC

We ought not to leave the subject of the minstrels without considering one or two points where they come into contact with 'serious' musicians at one end of the scale, and the traditions of popular and folk-music at the other.

We find references to folk-tunes, though very rarely the tunes themselves, in all classes of society and therefore in all classes of music. Dufay appears to have been the first to incorporate them in church music. Amongst other examples, we find what is obviously a folk-song used with the text of a Latin trope as an insertion in the 'Amen' of an early *Credo* and *Gloria* of his. He gives the full words of the little song: *La villanella non è bella, senon la domenica* – 'the *villanella* is at its loveliest on a Sunday', we may translate it. It is clearly a folk-song, with its syllabic style ($\frac{6}{8}$) and major tonality, though only a tiny scrap. Why Dufay should have associated this reference to stolen fruit with a Marian text at this point, must remain a mystery. We also find him using a folk-song as the tenor of a *chanson*: *La belle se sied au pied de la tour.* Later on, folk-songs were occasionally used as *cantus firmi* for the tenor-Mass: one anonymous example uses an otherwise unknown song called *Herdo, herdo.* More often however, we have to be content with a mere title, without any music. In the well-known *London Lickpenny*, a satirical poem of the mid fifteenth century, the hero goes to Eastcheap, where 'there was harpe, pype and mynstrelsye . . . Some songe of "Ienken and Iulyan" for there mede'; here we find minstrels directly associated with what appears to have been an early version of *Jack and Jill*. Many English folk-songs which survive from a later period, such as *Greensleeves* and *The Oak and the Ash*, can easily be fitted to one or other of the popular extemporizers' basses which we have already referred to: such tunes may have started life as minstrelsy, or music which was popular by destination, rather than in its origin.

The relationship between minstrels, 'serious' performers, and skilled amateurs, would make an interesting study in itself. Once or twice we come across suggestions that learned musicians helped minstrels to learn new songs – perhaps in order to play written polyphony. In 1511, an observer proudly recorded the fact that Louis XII's shawms played '*chose faicte*' before the Duke of Lorraine: it was clearly unusual, even at this late date, for minstrels to play a prepared piece of music. In 1479 a trained singer of King René – himself famed in song – was instructed to 'show' (*montrer*) some songs to a minstrel.

Noble amateurs are comparatively rare as composers in the earlier part of the fifteenth century, but become more numerous as time goes on and musical notation grows simpler. Henry V, we now know, was the 'Roy Henry' or 'Le roy' who left a total of four pieces of sacred music (one of them fragmentary); an *Alleluia* has just turned up which bears the unequivocal ascription '*Henrici Quinti*'. Charles the Rash, as we have noted, learned his skill from the admired Dufay. In 1460 he 'made a motet and all the music, which was sung in his presence after Mass was said, in the venerable church of Cambrai, by the master and the children'; a secular piece survives from his pen. Isaak, then organist of the Baptistery in Florence, taught music to Lorenzo de' Medici's sons. The younger, Leo X, whose accession to the papal throne Isaak celebrated in the fine six-part motet *Optime pastor*, has left us amongst other pieces a respectable canon. Henry VIII also composed, though he was decidedly more of a dilettante than the distinguished figures already mentioned.

Noble amateurs were more common as performers than as composers. A Florentine lady's letter tells us that Benedetto degli Strozzi, who was born in 1387, was extremely skilled in all music, and played the organ, clavichord, flute, and lute with equal proficiency. Charles, Duke of Orleans, one of the most outstanding French (and English!) poets of his time, played the harp and organ – as did his mother, Valentina de' Visconti – and the psaltery as well. At the age of nineteen, before his long captivity in England, he had a gown made with the song *Madame, je suis plus joyeulx* embroidered on the sleeves, words and music: the notes were represented by 568 pearls. The harp was the usual instrument for the noble amateur at the beginning of our period, the lute at the end. In 1410 Richard Loqueville was teaching the harp to the son of his master, Robert, Duke of Bar. Philip the Good and his son Charles played it, and Henry V: so did the luckless Parisina, Nicholas III's 'last Duchess'.

The lute came into its own – it was more suitable for polyphony and chromatics – with later figures such as James IV of Scotland and Henry VIII. Henry was a skilled all-round performer: he also played various keyboard instruments, the cornett, the recorder, and the strangely named *lira de' flauti*, whatever that may have been. We even learn of Sir Edward Stanley singing a *ballade* to the 'clarycorde' in the same period; this suggests that 'clavichord' was a general term not confined to its modern meaning, since one has only to breathe heavily for a clavichord proper to become inaudible.

The ladies also played, sang, and danced, for these skills enabled them to show off a shapely neck, a trim waist, a fine pair of shoulders, a lovely arm or mouth: and musical performance, we should remember, was also one of the 'communings' of courtly love-play. In his *canzonetta* to the ladies of Florence, Angelo Poliziano includes musical skills amongst card-games, dicing, and chess as accomplishments which 'will reap you a good harvest of songs, verses and fame. I have seen certain she-devils who do very well out of their singing; I have also seen women whom everyone loves for their dancing. It is well known that to play some instrument of music can enhance beauty itself.' He adds, a little tartly, 'but you should start to play without excuses as soon as you are asked – it's more polite.'

Towards the latter part of the fifteenth century, the distinction between minstrels and learned performers becomes rather blurred. Throughout our period, of course, 'serious' composers were also skilled keyboard players. A well-known miniature in a manuscript of Martin le Franc's poem *Le Champion des dames* shows Dufay and Binchois together:

Dufay is playing a portative organ and Binchois a harp, symbols respectively of sacred and secular music. A contemporary poem describes a famous occasion when Hayne van Ghizeghem and Robert Morton played together on *bas instruments*. We have noted that the chapel singers also composed and performed a vast amount of secular love-song, which has come down to us as the minstrels' music has not. The secular art was taught to choirboys too: at Cambrai in 1449, 'two altar-boys sang a little song, one of Duke Philip's gentlemen taking the tenor.'

When music adopted duple time as its maid-of-all-work metre in the latter half of the fifteenth century, notation became much simpler and started to drop such arcane tricks as ligatures, coloration, and (in secular music) proportions. Music suddenly became much more accessible, for duple metre did not exact a knowledge of the complicated rules of perfection and alteration: *all* lute music, in fact, was written in duple metre – even when the effect is triple in terms of actual sound. During the same period, ensemble music for instruments began to take after the character of vocal music. The medieval love of noise – which could make a chronicler note, in all seriousness, that 'then sounded guns and other instruments' – and also the older groupings of contrasting tone-colours, started to give way to the quieter Renaissance medium of a blending family of equal voices.

We have noticed the use of a group of shawms in connexion with dance music. As early as 1414, the English bishops were welcomed to Constance by sackbuts playing together 'in three parts, as people usually sing'. A quartet of flute-playing wolves featured in the positively zoological concert at the marriage of Charles the Rash and Margaret of York in 1468; such a quartet also performed at the Banquet of the Pheasant in 1454. At Lucretia Borgia's wedding in 1502, the entertainments included a consort of six viols; we come across a group of eight large lutes in the Ferrara carnival of 1506. Such 'choral' families could and did play transcriptions of vocal polyphony, and the German instrumental manuals of the early sixteenth century give copious directions for transferring vocal music on to flutes, viols, and so forth.

The distinction between minstrel and 'serious' musician therefore became blurred: the former learned to read art-music, and the latter turned his earnest attention to instrumental writing. Francis of Bosnia, for example, knew enough about 'serious' music to be able to arrange *frottole* and *recercari* for two of the publisher Petrucci's lute collections in 1509–11: he was presumably descended from the famous minstrel lutenists who served at the court of the Bosnian kings during the fifteenth century.

The organ was an instrument shared from the first between minstrels (who played the little portative) and learned musicians. It is not therefore surprising that the first serious attempts to create a substantial written repertory of instrumental music should have come from the organists. Through the example of the famous German masters Conrad Paumann (*c.* 1410–73) and Paul Hofhaimer (1459–1537), the organ developed an ornamental style of its own, which players of other instruments were recommended to imitate in the early sixteenth century. Hitherto, the role of the organ in sacred music had not apparently called for any such virtuoso treatment. In the Middle Ages, the huge organs that we read of were never used to accompany the singers, but always in alternation with them: they were only played as a spectacular effect at major feasts, when they 'shook the church to its foundations'. The increasing use of smaller positive organs which we observe in the churches of the later fourteenth century quite probably reflects their growing employment in secular music at this time: the great Landino, master of *trecento* song, for example, was a most distinguished organist. In the larger churches and chapels royal of the early fifteenth century, there was no provision for a special organist: the clerks and chaplains took it in turn to play for the service 'if they were able', and any contrapuntal additions to the chant in *alternatim* passages would no doubt have been kept fairly simple.

THE RENAISSANCE VIRTUOSO

The emergence of organ-playing virtuosi, such as Paumann and Hofhaimer, poses an interesting problem of social and musical classification. Paumann, for example, was not called a 'chaplain' or a 'clerk', though he undoubtedly played sacred music on occasion: his famous *Fundamentum organisandi* is a detailed manual on the ornamental treatment of a *cantus firmus*. Nor was he called a minstrel, although he was also a virtuoso performer on the *bas instruments*: his tombstone in the Frauenkirche in Munich shows him playing a little portative organ, with his other instruments all around him – lute, harp, theorbo, and flute. He was almost certainly the 'blind man, playing several instruments', who performed before Philip the Good in 1454. Yet the document does not refer to him as minstrel, chaplain, or clerk: he is noncommittally called a '*servant* of the two young dukes, sons of Duke Albert of Bavaria'. His official post was that of 'court organist'. Hofhaimer, too, was successively court organist to the Archbishop of Innsbruck and to Maximilian I, though he became cathedral organist of Salzburg towards the end of his life in 1528. With men like these, we see a new specialist class of musician emerging: the learned instrumental performer, who was at once virtuoso and composer.

We find others at the court of Henry VIII. The friar Dionisio Memmo arrived there from St Mark's, Venice, in 1516. He took the precaution of bringing his own instrument with him. In July 1517, 'after dinner, his Majesty took this ambassador into the Queen's chamber ... giving him amusements of every description, the chief of which ... was the instrumental music of the reverend Dionisio Memmo, his chaplain, which lasted four consecutive hours': quite a test of endurance for organist and ambassador alike. Though Memmo is here called Henry's 'chaplain', he took no part in the services of the chapel royal. Nor apparently did Benedictus de Opitiis, another skilled organist who had arrived from Antwerp in 1516, though unlike Memmo he has left us some sacred vocal music.

Another virtuoso, Zuan da Leze – this time a harpsichordist – failed to impress the King: he was so upset by his cool reception that he went away and hanged himself, like the wretched cook mentioned by Mme de Sévigné. The Venetian envoy, Sagudino, to whom we owe many a lively description of

Henry's musical propensities, was himself an organist, and was quick to blame the two English professionals who played an organ duet during the Maying festivities of 1515, 'but very ill forsooth: they kept bad time, and their touch was feeble, neither was their execution good, so that my performance was deemed not much worse than theirs.' 'Their touch was feeble . . .' – were the actions of Renaissance organs so heavy that players still had to *pulsare in organis* – to 'strike the organs', in the medieval phraseology?

MUSIC AND DRAMA

Another sphere in which minstrel and 'serious' musician met was that of the drama. The fifteenth century was the great age of the medieval mystery or miracle-play in the vernacular. Musical references in our own famous cycles make it clear that both minstrelsy and art-music existed side by side. The French cycles of plays equalled ours in length and magnificence of presentation. The playwright Arnoul Greban was also organist and director of the choir-school of Notre Dame de Paris in the middle years of the century, so it is not surprising that a good deal of sacred music is required in his dramas. The *Mystery of St Louis*, which was one of Greban's more economical efforts, taking a mere three days to perform, is full of musical passages; they include examples of plainsong, *chansons*, minstrelsy for dinner and dance, and at least two motets. One of these, *Sanctorum meritis*, is sung by angels as they carry heavenward the souls of some knights who have been killed in battle – a sort of medieval *Walkürenritt*. The other, merely called *ung beau motet*, was to be played on wind instruments: an early example of music being transferred from one medium to another – though we should perhaps recall that 'motet' could also mean a secular piece at this date (*c.* 1450). There are also instrumental episodes called '*silete*' or '*pose*', apparently used to draw attention to the entrance or speech of some important character.

The Italian *sacre rappresentazioni* were of a similar character and also made use of minstrelsy; they call for lutes, viols, and even dances, including the morris and perhaps the *bassadanza* too. The Spanish musician and playwright Juan del Encina has left us some *villancicos* and occasional compositions; his plays, published in 1496, include eclogues and pastorals which begin and end with a short motet.

The Renaissance revival of classical drama in Italy was ultimately to become far more important for the development of music than the medieval mysteries had ever been. Pomponius Laetus staged antique plays in his Roman academy as early as the 1470s, though we know little about the details of his productions. Poliziano's miniature *Orfeo* was the first vernacular play on a classical subject. It was probably written for Mantua in 1480. The savage final chorus, sung by the Bacchantes as they tear Orfeo to pieces for blaspheming against love, is entitled '*canzone a ballo*'; though no music for it survives, it has the popular beat (though not the charming obscenity) of a Florentine carnival song.

At this time too, Hercules I, Duke of Ferrara, was staging Plautus's comedies in Italian, as an entertainment on a lavish scale. He introduced *intermedii* from the first – interludes of music, dance, and mime between the acts of the main play. These additions originally had some symbolic connexion with the rest of the drama, or at least with the court event, often a royal marriage, which had given rise to the festive occasion. They soon grew more independent, though, and developed a life of their own; in the end, they turned into opera. As early as 1502, Isabella d'Este found the play presented at Lucrezia Borgia's wedding a very dull affair, saying that she could only sit it through for the sake of the *intermedii*. We know very little about the musical side of these entertainments at this date, but it is worth recalling that the mythological allegory of the first court operas has its origins in our period. The Florentine *camerata* was inspired by precisely the same ambition to revive both the techniques and the ethos of the ancients, which fired the scene designers of our period and sent them ferreting through Vitruvius for details of classical staging. Raphael himself was one of them.

5. The Raw Materials of Music

VOICES AND INSTRUMENTS

OUR earlier discussions have inevitably covered much of the ground already, but some details remain to be filled in. First, what *sound* did voices make during this period? We moderns can only hear the music of the Renaissance sung by voices whose training has been influenced by conditions unknown at that time – the need for one solo voice to carry over the sound of a large orchestra, for example, in theatre or concert-hall. Is there any evidence of the *colour* which vocalists used in the fifteenth century? There are a few scraps. It is clear that the change to choral polyphony brought about a new ideal of tone-production. Fifteenth-century painting and sculpture, which were concerned from the first with minute realism of detail, help us a good deal. Paintings from the earlier part of the century, such as Hubert and Jan van Eyck's famous Ghent altar-piece, the *Adoration of the Lamb* (painted 1420), invariably show singers with strained faces and furrowed brows. We sometimes see such contorted features on our concert platforms today, and they are associated with a strident, tightly-produced, nasal tone-colour. This appears to have been the noisy, penetrating sound which the Middle Ages enjoyed. If soloists were to be heard in the huge cathedrals of the Gothic era, there would certainly have been a tendency to strain. Later on, however, the faces become relaxed, as we can see from Luca della Robbia's *pulpitum* for Florence Cathedral, or a triptych by Hans Memling of 1480. This suggests the modern approach of relaxed muscles and open throat. Vibrato, however, is condemned.

Boys were used more and more in the course of the years. At the same time, vocal range began to expand downwards. From the three tightly interlocking parts which were normal in medieval times, the texture alters into a wide-ranged, carefully-spaced series of layered strata, in which all the voices – four of them now – have room to move. Later still, composers experimented with combinations of up to twelve voices. In the standard four-voiced texture, the old contra or contratenor has split into two separate halves. The contra was disentangled from its traditional involvement with the tenor – both parts often had the same clef – and divided into contra altus, or high contra (whence 'alto'), which kept above the tenor, and contra bassus, which kept below; composers were puzzled as to what they should call this new bass part at first, and we have a fine selection of odd names in the manuscripts – baritonans, baricanor, baripsaltes, basis, basistenor, theumatenor, and subcontra are some examples.

CHOIRS

Choirs were not large. We have discussed their numbers earlier on. A familiar sight in fifteenth-century art is the small choral group standing round a lectern, all singing from the same copy. The copy was admittedly pretty big, for huge folio choirbooks developed very soon after the establishment of the chorus. The largest distance usually represented between the farthest singer and the book seems to be about ten feet; the number of singers in most cases averages ten. A larger choir would have sung from part-books, which come into use from about 1460: each voice is copied into a separate volume, like the parts of a string quartet today.

Instruments continued to be used to support vocal polyphony, or to play an independent part; *a cappella* singing was however known. The pictorial evidence is fairly equally divided on this point during our period. We should remember, too, that Zarlino speaks in 1588 of '*un harmonia et un concerto de voci*', which he values more highly than instrumental combinations. Other instruments than the organ became more and more popular in church as the fifteenth century progressed, though not until later in England; cornetts (wooden trumpets), sackbuts, and shawms were all favoured. From the last third of the fifteenth century, sets of two large choirbooks begin to appear, which suggest that *both* sides of the choir now performed part-music; we have already seen that the *decani* singers of St Donatien, Bruges, were reserved for plainchant as late as 1443.

There is evidence that the whole choir of Cambrai Cathedral took part in polyphony from a much earlier date than was normal elsewhere: the earliest surviving folio books were copied for Cambrai, and though they are not identical twins, a high proportion of compositions are common to both (eighteen out of thirty). Certain payments are also recorded there for copying music in an unusually large script in a folio choir-book – the lines of the stave stood over an inch high, and the noteheads were magnified accordingly. We even learn of the existence of huge tomes in *double* folio there. The beautifully illuminated choirbook now in the possession of Gonville and Caius College, Cambridge, measures a good yard from top to bottom; to turn its stiff parchment pages in the cloistered quietness of a reading-room is an alarming experience, both for the student and for those working at other tables.

We learn from Adrian Petit Coclico that Josquin taught his pupils to ornament the music which they sang, though there would obviously have to be some prior agreement if a whole choir were to attempt such practices. He gives several examples, first plain, and then 'elegantly, seasoned with salt and mustard'; he adds that the Burgundians were particularly good at such 'divisions'. They were renowned, too, for their cavernous bass voices, 'like a huge organ-pipe': Ockeghem possessed such a voice.

A valuable book by Blasius Rossetti (1529) sets out the duties of the church organist, who, he says, was originally admitted into the church with his instrument 'to relieve the singers and give them a rest'. He now had three tasks: (1) 'to provide a contrapuntal accompaniment for the plainsong in hymns, proses and sequences' – certainly in alternation with the choir; (2) 'to play blameless preambles, or improvise elegantly on parts of the Mass' – again in alternation; and (3) 'to play buoyantly the mensural music which is added on feast days, blending with the choir and keeping in good time with them'. Surviving manuscripts of organ-music for (1) and

(2) give only the alternate verses; the choral arrangements supply the rest.

INSTRUMENTS

Although instruments were still used in church, the new colour of choral polyphony deeply impressed the Renaissance mind. Raphael, in his famous *St Cecilia* at Bologna (*c*. 1515), shows the saint turning in ecstasy from her secular instruments as four angels summon her to higher things: they are singing *a cappella*. Although such an idea was probably far from the painter's mind, he could not in fact have symbolized more tellingly the importance of this one great innovation of the musical Renaissance. The neglected 'worldly' instruments at her feet, all broken, include no complete consort: tamburine, viol, triangle, flutes, kettledrum, and nakers. From her hands there slips a portative organ, its pipes falling loose; the organ reminds us that the concern of the 'grand manner' for an effective composition should make us mistrust its handling of detail, for Raphael has painted it back to front. We have to be careful, even with such conscientious realists as the Flemish painters. They can be trusted to portray every detail of an instrument perfectly – we can count the strings on a harp, the pipes of a positive, and we can note with respect the presence or absence of a quill plectrum between a lutenist's fingers. But in grouping musical instruments together, they follow medieval habits. The well-known miniature in René II of Lorraine's psalter, for example, is not a literal representation of a contemporary orchestra, but an allegorical assembly of the whole world of music.

Similarly, the medieval love of exhaustive cataloguing leads Molinet, in his poem *Le naufrage de la pucelle*, to compile an immensely long list which includes every instrument known to him. When a Renaissance poet uses a musical image, on the other hand, one can normally deduce that his readers would have grasped his point immediately. Even if we had no other information, we could be quite certain that pedal-boards were used in Italian organs of the early sixteenth century, when we read in Folengo's mock-epic *Orlandino* that the amorous ladies and gentlemen, touching foot with foot beneath the banqueting table, were playing '*organetti coi pedali*'. The account-books of the time, of course, are also first-rate sources concerning the actual numbers of performers: where money changed hands, the medieval bursar forgot the allegorical tendencies of his age.

Accounts, however, tell us little about how instruments played, or how they were made. Here we are fortunate in the instrumental tutors which began to appear in the early sixteenth century. Sebastian Virdung and his successors are worth the world to us. His *Musica getutscht* of 1511 has been mentioned already. 'Music put into German' is an admirably clear illustrated guide for the musical man-in-the-street, the first of its kind and highly original in its method. Virdung divides the instruments of his time into clear categories: strings, wind, and percussion receive lucidly ordered descriptions made clearer still by a lavish supply of woodcuts. He goes on to give concise directions on the construction, tuning, and playing of the clavichord, lute, and recorder. We learn that a chest of recorders consisted by this date of two discants, two tenors, and two basses. He explains the tablatures for the three instruments, and gives examples of how to arrange a part-song for instrumental performance. It comes as a shock to realize that *Musica getutscht* is the first complete book about musical instruments in history.

MANUSCRIPT AND PRINTED MUSIC

One can tell a lot about music from the way in which it has been preserved. An immense amount of manuscript and even printed music has vanished irretrievably. Something like half the surviving repertory of music up to the year 1600 exists in one copy only. Music went out of date quickly as fashions changed. Since the collapse of patronage and the invention of that in some ways very regrettable institution, the public concert, Western music has posed the composer with a problem: he now has to compete for programme-space with the best music of all ages. Before Beethoven's day, one heard *only* modern music. So there was no point in holding on to a manuscript if the music it contained had ceased to be performed. It took up valuable space in your library, when its parchment pages could be put to good use to line the cover of another, more serviceable book. The surprising thing is that so much material *has* been preserved.

The visual appearance of a musical manuscript mattered considerably to its medieval owner. In the Renaissance, it came to matter less. Though there are still many most sumptuously illuminated presentation copies, many of the sources are homely, practical affairs, dog-eared and tallow-stained from everyday use. We have commented above on the folio choirbook and the partbook. In notation and format, they reflect their employment very clearly. So does the little pocket music-book of the German doctor Hartmann Schedel, who took it with him to Italy as a student and filled its pages with an extraordinarily varied collection of musical serendipity. Nothing gives one the 'feel' of a period more directly than the handling of such a book. In many ways the scribes of the early Renaissance were infuriatingly inconsiderate, from the point of view of the modern scholar. They muddle or mis-spell or omit the names of composers. They copy the music wrongly and leave it uncorrected, although they must surely have sorted the mistakes out in performance. They garble the language of the words: some very odd French must have been sung in fifteenth-century Italy.

Nevertheless, the books take us close to their time. When choral performance became the accepted norm of sacred music, for example, the change was reflected almost immediately in the underlay of the words. While polyphony was the preserve of soloists, there was no need to be at all precise in placing the syllables of text under the notes: the singer would work it out for himself, and in any case his audience would not worry over discrepancies. In fact the words were often copied into the book before the music. In the 1470s, though, a Burgundian choirbook now in Brussels set a new standard for practical manuscripts. The handwriting of the musical notes is in itself outstandingly beautiful – it is the sort of script which Petrucci used as a model for his music-type. More important still, the words are much more scrupulously underlaid: several singers would have taken each part, and it was important to obtain unanimity.

Sometimes we can trace the survival of antiquated musical ideas because they preserve the form of notation appropriate to them when it has fallen out of general use. English sources of the fifteenth century, for example, are almost alone in preserving the old form of notation in score for their more functional music, an arrangement which vanished from continental manuscripts during the fourteenth century. Yet it was precisely this freak of conservatism which led the English composers of Dunstable's generation along the road to euphonious harmony and smooth texture: there can be no doubt that the *sight* of three voices aligned one above the other as they would be today, helped the English to consider their harmony as a whole, and not as two separate parts which were calculated independently of each other, against a third. As early as the fourteenth century, the score arrangement tempted the English into allowing the plainchant to wander easily from one voice to another. This type of 'migrant' *cantus firmus* remained unknown on the Continent for a long time.

Notation can be a good friend to the composer; it can also stand in his way. Our present notation, for example, is appallingly difficult for a child learning the pianoforte (or indeed any other instrument). Tablatures have been devised – visual representations of what the fingers actually do – which would make the piano-teacher's life much easier. Yet, merely because we have all had to learn it, we stick to a notation which is only really suited to vocal music. Atonal music, too, needs a new, non-diatonic form of notation. Renaissance musicians were far more practical than we are: the new instrumental tablatures which they invented were triumphs of rational simplicity. The one exception which proves the rule is German lute tablature, which is said to have been invented by a blind man – and looks it every bit.

Vocal notation underwent an odd change, starting in the

1420s: hollow noteheads replaced the black ones of medieval tradition. The results must have seemed very strange to a contemporary musician: if you substitute negatives for all the photographs in your family album, you will feel as he must have felt. Various reasons have been suggested for this change. One scholar connects it with a change in metrical fashion – which took place, alas, some years later. The commonest answer seeks the reason in the simultaneous adoption of cheap paper instead of the traditional parchment: in some cases where the old black noteheads were used on paper, the acid in the ink has eaten its way right through, often severely damaging the manuscript. But this chemical action clearly took a long time to produce its effect: why else should Michelangelo, decades later, have chosen the harmful gall ink for almost all of his pen drawings? He would surely have used the less destructive bistre ink – made from soot – if he had known. The change must have come about because paper was *rougher* than parchment or vellum: the quill nibs could no longer splay out easily to produce the typical black lozenge. They spluttered. It proved much quicker to leave the note-head empty. One has only to copy out some piece of music in black and then in void notation, using a fairly thick nib, to discover the difference. Here, perhaps, scholars have failed to follow the example of the Renaissance and seek the quickest route.

An incidental result of this change was that music became easier to read. In the old 'full' notation, semiminims (our crotchets) were distinguished from black minims by a tail, and at this date it was not customary to join the tails of successive notes together in a single line as we do today. When minims became void, however, the semiminim remained black, so that the tail was no longer needed – in short, it now looked like the modern crotchet. The performer could distinguish between minim and semiminim by looking at the head of the note alone, which made for easier reading. *Fusae* (our quavers) remained rather a rarity for some decades. The fashion for void notation seems to have started simultaneously in England and Italy, though it did not become general in this country until the sixteenth century. Needless to say, the new way of writing had no effect on the sound of music: it was a purely visual change, introduced for the convenience of copyists.

We can certainly trace the more practical and business-like attitude of the Renaissance in the change to void notation, and also in the large number of unadorned, workaday manuscripts of sacred music, which were not intended for the eye of some princely patron. The most famous illuminated manuscripts of the time are undoubtedly the sumptuous volumes destined for the private devotions of art-loving magnates, such as the Books of Hours of the Duke of Berry and John of Bedford, or the Antiphoner of King Matthaeus Corvinus of Hungary. Less well-known are the many beautifully decorated secular *chansonniers*, often commissioned as precious gifts fit for a king. The loveliest of these is the 'Chansonnier Cordiforme' now in the Bibliothèque Nationale of Paris: it is pear-shaped when closed (which might have pleased Erik Satie), and opens out to form a heart. The vellum pages are so richly worked that a single song takes up considerably more space than the two or four sides usual in a less lavish book. Once copied, however, such a volume probably never entered the hands of a musician again.

Few of the hundred-odd surviving *chansonniers* of our period, however, are as precious as this. Most of them are small, plainly written pocket-books intended for practical use. The type came into existence in the 1430s, precisely when the first folio choir-books appeared. This was no coincidence. The typical musical manuscript of the first third of the fifteenth century was a quarto volume, in which sacred and secular compositions were copied side by side: both classes of music were meant for solo performance. When the chorus established itself as the medium of sacred music, however, secular music had to find a home of its own, for it was still performed by soloists and could have no place in a volume of choral works. Nearly all of the new *chansonniers*, in fact, are so small that only three or four soloists could have performed from them: and secular music, as the manuscripts suggest, retained many of its medieval characteristics for several decades. Towards the end of the fifteenth century, however, partbooks made their appearance in the domain of the *chanson*. This would have allowed two or three singers or instrumentalists to a part, and it was surely no accident that from this time the character of secular music began to change. With Josquin's generation, the old fixed forms of the *chanson* melted away, and their place was taken by the more plastic techniques of choral polyphony. Solo performance did indeed remain the rule, but the soloists were now a blending group of singers; though instruments could participate in the Italian madrigal of the 1530s, all parts were now provided with words, and the hopping, un-vocal contratenor of the fifteenth century was a thing of the past.

We have to exercise some care over the matter of words in secular music. It is a surprising fact that the majority of the songbooks of the fifteenth century do not provide anything more than the first few words of the text of a *chanson*. Even the editor of the *Odhecaton*, the Spaniard Petrus Castellanus, provided full texts only for the few Latin pieces he included, although Petrucci's book was the first printed collection of polyphony and must have been intended for a sizeable market. We have to supply the words from the few *chansonniers* which do preserve them complete, or else from purely literary sources such as the *Jardin de plaisance* (published 1502) and the Cardinal de Rohan's manuscript in Berlin. Although we know that instruments played the lower parts of many a *chanson*, and often performed the whole piece without the help of a singer, we cannot say that the absence of words in a musical source positively indicates instrumental performance: no doubt the singers knew the repertory well, and would have supplied the text from memory. The words of many *chansons* were certainly very popular, for poets such as Jean Molinet delighted in weaving whole poems out of *chanson*-titles. This sort of literary *quodlibet*, futile juggling though it was, would have had no point at all if the readers had not been able to recognize the well-known words. Here, as in the minstrel tradition, memory must have played a large part.

Even where a musical manuscript of the fifteenth century does give us the whole text of a song, there is not one example where all the words are fitted to the appropriate music. Only enough words are underlaid to take the singer through the music once. The additional verses are invariably written out on their own at the foot of the page, and repetitions of the refrain sections are there indicated by the first few words only. Since the music rarely provides any satisfactory cadences except at the end of each of the two obligatory sections, we assume that the traditional methods of the thirteenth-century *rondeau*, for example, still hold good for the *rondeaux* of Dufay or Busnois. Poets such as Villon, however, often did not repeat the whole refrain in the longer *rondeau* of the fifteenth century; and one cannot help wondering whether musicians sometimes shortened their repeats in the same way. A long *rondeau* with a refrain of six or even seven lines can become very tedious to listen to, unless the inevitable repetitions are ornamented or differently scored each time they come round.

It has been reliably estimated that only about a tenth of the music composed prior to 1600 has come down to us today. When we consider the great number of poems in the fixed forms of the fifteenth century which have survived without any musical setting, we cannot help asking ourselves how many of them may once have attracted the attention of some composer. The surviving literary manuscripts, however, outnumber the musical *chansonniers* quite overwhelmingly, and we are probably justified in thinking that the relationship between the two was about the same in the fifteenth century as it is today: the ravages of time have probably attacked each class in equal proportion. A musical setting was clearly a rare privilege, and at this date a poet did not normally write words on purpose for a composer to put them to music. We have several examples of new words being written to old music, on the other hand. In the fourteenth century, Chaucer wrote a roundel of which 'the note, I trowe, maked was in France'; and we have many similar examples from our own later period. An Italian or German poet, for instance, would not bother to *translate* a French song for his fellow-countrymen: he would provide an independent text in his own language. He would probably keep to the poetic form of the original, and he would still use the international jargon of courtly love, but it was the music that concerned him, not the meaning of the French text. Since polyphony was so precious a commodity, we even find a great number of '*contrafacta*' ('counterfeits') which transform a secular song into a little sacred motet with Latin words, disregarding even the poetic form of the original. One exceptional case of a secular contrafactum which tries to keep something of its model is a French *ballade*, *Soyez apprentis en amours* ('Apprentice yourselves to love'): the music is that of a song by the English composer Walter Frye, who flourished from about 1450 to 1480. The anonymous French poet has tried to keep the sound of the first few words of the English version, though not their meaning: 'So is emprinted in my remembrance.'

On the whole, then, the manuscript evidence does not suggest that poets expected their verses to be set; and the impersonal approach of the earlier fifteenth-century composer, who was not normally concerned either with the emotional expression of the words, or with the naturalistic reproduction of human speech, made it possible for the same music to serve for quite different texts. Even where composers wrote their own words, like Busnois, there is no close union of words-and-music such as we find in Thomas Campion's songs a century and a half later. We know that a patron would sometimes commission a composer to set some verses which pleased him: when the Duke of Suffolk was laid up in Paris after falling from his horse in 1424, he asked Gilles Binchois to set the *rondeau*, *Ainsi que à la fois*, and rewarded him well for his services. The music has not survived. Several poems by Suffolk's friend Charles of Orleans have come down to us in musical settings, and since he was himself an amateur musician of some accomplishment, he may well have commissioned them on his own account. At least one is by Binchois. It is also interesting to note that an important manuscript of Charles's poems, now in the British Museum, has the verses written 'on the lower part of the page, a blank space being left for the insertion of the music later on'. The Duke of Orleans, however, was clearly an exceptional case, and the general weight of the evidence points in the other direction. Only one of Villon's poems, for example, has a contemporary musical setting, however attractive they may have been to Debussy: the moving *rondeau, Mort, j'appelle de ta rigueur*. The anonymous composer has provided some agreeable music, but could not at that date match Villon's impassioned language with an equally noble setting.

The name of the Venetian music-publisher Ottaviano de' Petrucci has already cropped up several times in the course of this chapter. It is time to consider his achievement in a little more detail. His *Harmonice musices odhecaton A* of 1501 was, as we have already said, the first printed collection of part-music, containing all the best Franco-Flemish *chansons* of the past forty years. Publishers were slow to recognize the possibilities and advantages of printing mensural music. Between the Gutenberg trial in 1439 and the end of the fifteenth century, some nine million ordinary books had been printed. German printers had started to migrate all over Europe from the 1460s, taking light equipment with them so that they could cast new founts of type in the countries where they settled: they reached Italy in 1465, France in 1475, England two years later. Yet, in spite of several isolated experiments, nobody thought of printing music on the same scale as ordinary books until Petrucci petitioned the Signoria of Venice for a twenty-year privilege on 25 May 1498. The earlier experiments were confined to the notes of the chant in liturgical books. As early as 1457, two of Gutenberg's associates in Mainz provided music in a psalter by printing staff-lines and filling in the notes by hand – a tedious process which, however, had the advantage of allowing local variants in the music of the ritual to be copied into the books without re-setting the blocks of type. In 1473, an Esslingen edition of Gerson's *Collectorium super Magnificat* prints the notes of a musical example from separate dies, but reverses the methods of the Mainz printers by omitting the staff-lines. The pitch of the notes is shown by an F-clef only – an odd throw-back to the days of staffless neumes. Movable type makes its appearance for the first time in a Roman missal published in Parma three years later; lozenge-

shaped notes are used for the chant, but the music is not continued throughout. Six months after this, another missal
appeared in Rome which employed the double-impression
printing exploited by Petrucci: the staff-lines were first run
off (in this case in red), and the notes were added (in black) by
sending the sheets of paper through the press a second time.
The liturgical *incunabula* published by Scotto in Venice from
the 1480s onwards also include examples of double-impression
printing. Even the old-fashioned Gothic 'choral-notation'
appeared in a Würzburg missal of 1481.

The first attempts at printing mensural music, as opposed to
plainsong, are to be found in theoretical works. A Venetian
grammar of 1480, printed by a German, uses musical notes for
an illustration of the quantities of Latin verse; the notes are
printed from type, or possibly from an inserted metal block,
but since they form an example of rhythm there was no need
to show their pitch, and the staff-lines are therefore omitted.
The first known printed part-music occurs in the theorist
Nicolo Burzio's *Musices opusculum*, published in Bologna in
1487. It is an arrangement of Guido d'Arezzo's famous hymn
to St John, the *Ut queant laxis*, which gave the solmization-
syllables of the hexachord their names. In 1493, a political
composition was printed in Rome, a *frottola* on the conquest of
Granada. There are a couple of pages of mensural music in a
dancing-manual by Michel de Toulouze published between
1488 and 1496. The first Spanish music-printing appeared in
Seville in 1493, from the press of four German craftsmen.

Petrucci, then, was not the first publisher to print part-
music; nor was he the first to use double-impression printing.
But he chose his moment well. As we have seen, music was
losing its medieval mystery at the close of our period. Petrucci
had the wit to see that there was a growing middle-class demand for domestic music; and, just as the German publishers
of the later fifteenth century suddenly found a market for
woodcuts in the popular demand for devotional books, so
Petrucci saw his chance to cater for the music-hungry amateur.
His great scheme for a series of fifty-odd publications must
have been planned from the start, at least in outline. He

cornered the market not only for voices, but for lute and organ too – the favourite instruments of the amateur, as we have already noted. The 'A' in the Odhecaton's title contains the promise of the *Canti B* and *Canti C* which followed in 1502 and 1504 respectively. In this latter year, Petrucci published the first of his eleven books of *frottole*, a strictly Italian form for which a sudden demand had recently grown. His sacred collections were issued in partbooks. In 1510, conditions in Venice were threatened by the invasion of the French. Petrucci withdrew to continue his activities in Fossombrone, and some slight signs of carelessness appear in the hitherto immaculate format of his music-books. Even so, a Petrucci print remains a most beautiful object to look at: there was nothing amateurish or experimental about these first printed collections of polyphony.

In 1510 too, Petrucci's collaborator Andrea Antico left Venice and set up on his own account as a music publisher in Rome; he returned to Venice when Petrucci's sole patent expired shortly before 1520 and set up a rival press in partnership with Scotto, taking care to protect himself through various papal privileges. Henceforward, music-printing spread rapidly into France and Germany, though there seems to have been little market for it in England until the very end of the sixteenth century. Single-impression printing, in which each musical symbol is set on its own little section of staff, rapidly became the norm: its history belongs in the next chapter, like the first attempts at music-engraving. There were also a few experiments in printing music from woodcuts in Germany and Holland, but they bore no fruit.

The immediate effects of music-printing were less dynamic than one might imagine. The number of copies in a single printing was small, and they cost as much as or more than a modern limited edition. At this early date, a manuscript copy was undoubtedly cheaper. Surviving inventories from private or church libraries never list more than one exemplar of a printed choirbook or set of partbooks, and it is clear that such a publication was often used, like certain manuscripts, as a precious 'reservoir' of music, from which performing parts would have been made for each composition. Nevertheless, printing must have disseminated music more widely and more rapidly than hand-copying could ever have done; and as the market grew during the sixteenth century, prices fell to a mere fifth of what Petrucci had charged. Eventually, the royalties from the sale of published works became an important factor in giving a successful composer an independent income and freeing him from the demands of patronage. If it had not been for Petrucci and the early music-printers of the Renaissance, Beethoven could never have hawked his *Mass in D* around the publishers of Europe as he did, living comfortably off the advances which each paid him for the sole rights.

THE DEVELOPING LANGUAGE OF MUSIC

We have now spent a good deal of space in talking about the materials, functions, and philosophy of music in early Renaissance society: too much space, some will perhaps say. But misconceptions about the *purpose* of early composers have often hindered performer and listener alike from regarding early music as anything but an appealing or even a rather precious curiosity. A Mass by Dunstable or Dufay needs its background of associations just as much as an opera or a symphony from an age nearer to our own. An old painting looks at its best in its contemporary frame, and in the architectural surroundings for which it was designed; a beautifully cut gem, for all its intrinsic worth, shines at its loveliest in the setting which was originally made for it. The 'aesthetic' enjoyment of fine art has led us to assemble huge collections of old paintings and sculptures inside buildings which are often totally unsuitable for them; old music, which needs the interpretative skills of singer and instrumentalist, also suffers when it is torn from its surroundings and fed into a microphone, or displayed on the concert platform, in white tie and tails instead of surplice or gown. The best of it is certainly worth this kind of translation and nobody would bother to play it if it were not. We cannot, of course, ask the Church of England to return to the Latin ritual of pre-Reformation Salisbury in order to hear, say, the

Holy Week music of the Egerton manuscript in its original setting: institutions and audiences have changed far too much, and such an attempt would be wrong-headed aestheticism of another kind. We should have got out of one ditch only to fall into another, on the opposite side of the road. Nevertheless, I hope that the above pages have provided some sort of background for the imaginative listener to bear in mind when he hears a *chanson* by Busnois or a motet by Josquin.

The other difficulty which prevents the wider enjoyment of early Renaissance music is more easily overcome. The master-pieces of the generations preceding Josquin normally charm the ear on first acquaintance; but many listeners find it hard to follow the logic of musical style, to see why a composer should have preferred one note to another. And it is the simple, everyday turns of phrase which puzzle people the most, not the forbidding technicalities of the isorhythmic motet or the tenor-Mass. These last pages will therefore be devoted to a dozen short extracts from the works of early Renaissance masters, arranged more or less in chronological sequence. Space forbids us to quote more than ten or fifteen bars in each case, but the examples will serve as talking-points for a more general discussion. The reader who wishes to hear some complete works, or better still, to play them over for himself, will probably be able to get hold of the *Historical Anthology of Music*, or some of the other publications and recordings which are listed at the end of this book. Here, we shall confine ourselves for the most part to minute particulars. It is attention to detail which makes the master. Most students of composition can plan a large symphonic movement very well in prose: far fewer know how to devise an interesting texture, or even to modulate firmly and convincingly from tonic to dominant. For the moment then, we shall prefer the parts to the whole.

Example 1 is the beginning of a *ballade* by the little-known minor composer François Le Bertoul. All we can say about him is that he sang in the choir of Cambrai cathedral in 1409–10, when Dufay had just joined as a young treble. We have chosen a fairly simple piece of late Gothic music, for some of the more complicated specimens are almost impossible to play on the piano, with their fidgety cross-rhythms and congested part-writing. Even this *ballade* becomes decidedly tricky to manage later on.

Au pain — fai - tich ne me ——— veul plus te- nir

Le Bertoul's *ballade* was probably written before our period had begun, but its harmony already makes much use of the 'imperfect' intervals of third and sixth – no doubt in tribute to the suavity of the Italian *trecento*. Its structure is thoroughly medieval, nevertheless. The *ballade* form, a great favourite in the fourteenth century, was soon to fall out of favour. True to type, Le Bertoul writes a short prelude (and later, interludes) for instruments alone: there is no text, and the joining of many successive notes in ligature suggests instrumental performance. Ligatures – shown here by square slurs – remained one of the arcane 'mysteries' of music until the middle of the fifteenth century; partly in answer to popular demand, they then fell out of use as the decades progressed. The rhythm of *Au pain faitich* may well prove a stumbling-block, even for those who can play their '*48*'. The transcription has assembled the separate parts in a modern score, imposing bar-lines which of course were not in the original, and dividing the composer's note-values by eight (later examples only quarter them): the modern scholar aims to present old music in a modern format. Le Bertoul's original was in fact more complicated than our score suggests. We have been content to show his cross-rhythm as $\frac{3}{4}$ inside the prevailing $\frac{6}{8}$; he himself, though, gave these '$\frac{3}{4}$' passages a time-signature of $\frac{2}{4}$, which would require a barline after every *two* undotted crotchets. This was pure wilfulness on his part, like some of the more 'advanced' notation of modern composers.

If we disregard such paper difficulties, however, we are left with a fairly simple little piece. You will probably find it rather dissonant: play through the top two parts alone, and then the bottom two, and you will discover that most of the dissonances have vanished. This is because the song is an example of additive composition. Le Bertoul first wrote the treble or the tenor (the middle part, here); he then completed the top pair by writing the other voice. The bottom part in our score was then composed against the tenor, independently of the treble: it makes smooth harmony with the former, but jolts uncomfortably against the treble in several places (the top C and bottom D in bar 3, for example). For the same reason, Le Bertoul was not able to fit the contratenor into the imitative pattern which he sets up between treble and tenor in bars 7–11, where the singer begins. The contratenor part is altogether bumpier in melody and rhythm than the other two, hopping about above and below the tenor and fitting its notes in where it can. It is a makeweight, filling in the harmony and adding rhythmic life to the ensemble. Notice how it completely alters the cadences in bars 6–7 and 10–11. This sort of contratenor did not die out in three-part writing until the end of the fifteenth century, though it became smoother and more singable as time went on. Note that the piece consists essentially of treble and tenor – the contratenor can easily be omitted altogether, or a second one added to make a four-part piece; or a quite different contratenor might be substituted or even improvised by some other composer or performer. Like a Gothic building, such a composition is never 'complete' in the classical definition of the Renaissance.

The reader will have noticed that the treble has only one flat in its key-signature, while the lower parts enjoy two. This is a frequent phenomenon throughout the fifteenth century, and other combinations than this are also to be found. The explanation for these 'partial' key-signatures is twofold. First, although composers of Dufay's generation liked colourful accidentals and even the thrust of dominant key-relationships, their music was still largely governed by modal scales: in Example 1, for instance, the lower parts employ the first mode, transposed from D to C. The A of this scale is not flattened; and whenever the treble has an E, the presence of an A-natural in the lower parts forbids us to flatten the upper note, in case augmented intervals or tritones should result. Second, the contratenor normally cadenced above the tenor at this date; Example 1 is rather an exception in this respect. The tenor would fall a tone to the cadential note, while the upper two parts paralleled each other, moving upwards in perfect fourths – there are three such cadences in Example 4. The treble cadence must normally be sharpened in accordance with the laws of *musica ficta*, to produce a major sixth before the final octave. In the earlier part of the fifteenth century, it was common practice to sharpen the inner part also: the contratenor would therefore employ sharp 'Lydian' subdominants a lot of the time, to produce the necessary leading-note to the dominant. Furthermore the treble would also have to sharpen the fourth degree of the scale whenever the tenor cadenced on the dominant, which was fairly often. It was thus a perfectly logical practice *not* to inflect the subdominant in the key-signature of the upper parts at this date, but to insert the flat only when it was specially needed: the note would thus remain sharp for the frequent cadences in the course of a piece. For the same sort of reason, composers of Purcell's time did not bother to flatten the sixth degree of the minor mode in their key-signatures. Purcell's G Minor has only one flat. Bach's 'Dorian' toccata is another case: the only thing about it that is Dorian is the lack of a B-flat in the key-signature. There can be no doubt, too, that the early fifteenth-century composers liked the Lydian fourth, and the constant ambiguities which partial key-signatures produced. By Josquin's time, however, they had come to think otherwise. Franchino Gafuri noted in 1498 that the Lydian mode had virtually ceased to exist: by constantly flattening its fourth degree, composers had created the Ionian, our modern major, long before Glareanus came along to make an honest woman of the new mode on C.

Au pain faitich is music for soloists, presumably three *bas instruments* and voice, not forgetting the addition of drones and percussion. Very probably, the performers would have ornamented their lines, at least on the repeat of the opening section. This applies to all the examples we shall present. In this early period, we have no instrumental tutors to tell us how this was done. We can make some deductions, however, from a few ornamental keyboard transcriptions of sacred and secular music; and sometimes we find a piece like a *Credo* by Zacharias which appears in two different sources, in Modena and Bologna. In contrast with the simplicity of the Bologna copy the scribe of the Modena manuscript has introduced liberal embellishments into the upper part.

Le Bertoul's song is a fairly representative example of the simpler style of the years *c.* 1400–20, though the treble of this opening section is not set off from the lower parts by a more florid treatment. His structure depends on *ballade* form rather than unity of musical style. His treatment of the words – almost a note to a syllable – is rather modern for its time, and looks forward to the early *chansons* of Dufay. The other types of texture current in his day were *ballata* style, with tenor and treble both conceived for voices and provided with text; the style of the polytextual motet, where the two upper parts bounce and clash over a less animated tenor (and sometimes a fourth supporting voice of the same pitch), and discant or 'conductus' style, a simple, functional harmonization of a plainsong in three parts, all of which move in more or less the same rhythm.

It was the latter type of texture which lay behind the harmonic innovations of the English school. English sources from the later fourteenth century onwards contain a large number of these old-fashioned, unpretentious little movements, always employing sacred texts and usually a ritual plainsong too, and invariably written down in out-of-date score notation, with all three voices neatly aligned one above the other. The text was copied beneath the lowest part, though the official chant lay, more often than not, in the middle voice. Since there are no records of any musical instruments except organs in English churches of this date, and since organs were only used in *alternation* with voices, we must assume that these pieces were sung by three blending soloists. In the reign of Henry V, as we have seen, the English Chapel Royal grew into a choir; and the Old Hall manuscript, copied for Henry's chapel, was one of the first practical sources which were big enough for a small choral group to read from in comfort. Much of the music in this volume still requires solo performance, but the mass-movements and antiphons in discant style clearly call for blending voices. When the manuscript was copied, John Dunstable was still unknown or unrecognized, for the only contribution from his pen is a work which was added to the collection much later on. He appears to have started composing in the 1420s, and rapidly became one of the few British composers who have enjoyed fame and influence abroad. Most of his sixty-odd works, indeed, survive only in continental sources. In his hands, discant style flowered into music such as that of Example 2.

This is taken from a setting of the antiphon *Ave regina caelórum*, which has come down to us in manuscripts now in Modena, Trent, and Florence. Dunstable has placed the Marian plainsong in the treble, adding thirteen notes of his own to the fifteen of the chant (marked with crosses above), and rounding off the section with a short coda. He has endowed the antiphon with a rhythmic and melodic life so perfectly poised that one would hardly suspect the presence of a borrowed tune. No longer does the chant stump along in the tenor, the stern voice of authority which governed the medieval motet. Dunstable prefers to place it in the treble, fashioning it into the plastic, convoluted line which so attracted his contemporaries Binchois and Dufay. Tinctoris hailed him in the 1470s as the leading composer of the earlier English school, saying that the new age in music began with his compositions. Writing in about 1440, the poet and amateur musician Martin le Franc also noted how the Burgundians had 'taken after

the English guise and followed Dunstable in *musica ficta*, pause, mutation, and sprightly consonance'. The first three terms refer to melodic features. Example 2 is a good specimen of what he meant by 'sprightly consonance', a trait which Tinctoris also singled out for special mention: 'in the old music [i.e. before *c.* 1435], there were more dissonances than consonances'. In Example 2, Dunstable allows himself only seven dissonances: three of them are tiny ornamental features, like the F in bar 2, or the treble G in bar 11; the remainder are prepared and resolved in the classical manner of the sixteenth century, like the seventh and the fourth in the final cadence: a far-reaching innovation. Apart from the close, the whole little coda from bar 12 onwards, for all its lively rhythm, contains not one dissonance. This rapid patterning of pure euphony was no doubt one aspect of the 'sprightly consonance' which surprised the early Burgundians. It was particularly common in two-part writing, and stemmed from the highly-developed techniques of extemporized discant of which the English were masters.

One of these techniques explains much of Dunstable's harmony in Example 2: the practice of 'faburden'. This was closely related to the continental device known as '*fauxbourdon*', though musical scholars are still arguing inexhaustibly about which came first. You will find a short example of early *fauxbourdon* in Example 4: the small notes towards the end of the excerpt do not appear in the manuscript, but have to be supplied in parallel perfect fourths beneath the treble. The early English technique of faburden, on the other hand, was not normally written out in full: all that was needed was a plainsong, and three singers. One singer sang a metrical version of the chant as it stood in the book; a second singer sang exactly the same notes a fourth higher; and a third sang the faburden proper, which consisted of thirds, with occasional fifths, beneath the chant. The result, in terms of figured bass, was a series of $\frac{6}{3}$ and occasional $\frac{5}{3}$ chords, with a few suspensions at cadences. This sort of harmonization underlies the first eleven bars of Example 2, but not the little coda, which is free of chant. The notes of the plainsong can be traced in the middle part as well as the treble, although the rest of the composition makes it clear that the treble is the structural voice. Except for three bars, the main harmonies are all $\frac{6}{3}$ and $\frac{8}{5}$ chords, if we disregard the ornamental insertions. This sort of writing can be traced back into English music of the fourteenth century, though it rarely has the variety and grace so characteristic of Dunstable. Discant and faburden played a most important part in evolving the careful control of dissonance which proved so essential for the new style of choral polyphony.

Dunstable's rhythms call for a word or two here. In Example 2, the rhythmic texture of the whole is remarkably homogeneous, compared with Example 1: apart from a few ornamental notes in the treble, all the parts move in the same note values, and each voice is interesting and singable, though the music still makes sense without the contratenor (here the middle part). The flowing, unitary metre of 'perfect time' has replaced Le Bertoul's finicky cross-rhythms. We are also a very long way from the texture of the medieval motet, though Dunstable has left some unusually fine examples of isorhythmic structure in other works. Notice the subtlety of his figuration here: apart from four repetitions of the hovering, dance-like ligature in bar three, no two bars of the treble are exactly alike. And how delicately the composer balances phrases of $\frac{6}{8}$, $\frac{5}{8}$, and $\frac{2}{4}$ against the prevailing $\frac{3}{4}$ of the last five bars. Bar 14 also contains a tiny five-note imitation in all three voices, with a different rhythm each time, though it is so subtle that one would hardly notice it in performance. All these features were admired and imitated by Dufay and Binchois.

One of the most striking trends in fifteenth-century music, as we have observed, was the way in which composers once again came to reserve their finest music for the service of the church. The 'new English guise' developed almost entirely within the domain of sacred music: until Tudor times, we have only one short song for every ten or more extended liturgical works (we except the carol from this reckoning, for it stands half-way between sacred and secular). Dunstable has left us only two secular pieces; Leonel Power, his older contemporary who died in 1445, none at all. Their music was almost entirely concerned with the ritual of the church. The Old Hall manuscript is largely devoted to settings of the Ordinary of the Mass – a field which had virtually lain fallow since the earliest polyphonic experiments of the Winchester Tropers. Dunstable and his English contemporaries, as we shall see, were among the first to create a distinctive style for Mass-music: composers of the French *ars nova* and the Italian *trecento*, when they had set parts of the Ordinary, had sought their models in secular music and in the motet.

The motet, too, returned to its sacred functions with the new English school. In spite of its liturgical *cantus firmus*, the typical French motet of the fourteenth century had a secular text: some of the 'political' examples, indeed, with their references to topical events, must have seemed almost like highly sophisticated revue turns. The English motets of Dunstable's generation, however, are without exception intended for church use: not one of them employs a set of verses limited to one particular occasion, like the political motets of Dufay or the Venetian school. Dufay and Dunstable were the last great masters of the isorhythmic motet, into which they poured a richness of sonority and a delicacy of melodic filigree unknown to the late Middle Ages. But medieval isorhythm, that triumph of rational speculation, proved unsuitable for choral performance; after the death of Dufay, composers turned away from its iron logic and developed less rigid methods of musical construction.

One of the strongest forces which assisted the general return to church music was the rising tide of Marianism. Many of the new institutions founded to perpetuate the memory of some pious benefactor were dedicated to the Blessed Virgin; and when the institution included a choral foundation, like Henry VI's colleges at Eton and Cambridge, it was the practice for the choir to perform an antiphon to Our Lady every evening. The Eton manuscript, which has recently been published entire, contains a repertory of part-music suitable for such an occasion, drawn from the latter half of the fifteenth century. These antiphons were sung on their own, without the usual psalm. Since they were now divorced from their proper liturgical surroundings, composers felt free to depart from tradition in setting the texts to music. The majority of Dunstable's polyphonic antiphons and sequences, for example, dispense entirely with the appropriate chants. Most of these free compositions are quite indistinguishable in style from those which are based on plainsong: we find the same kind of subtle, finely wrought tracery in the upper voice, the same discreet harmonic support from the two blending lower parts. The art of paraphrasing the chant had developed melodic resource to such a degree that Dunstable and his fellows were now able to write music without the traditional Gregorian 'voice of authority'. These works depend on purely musical logic for their construction: the upper voice dominates the ensemble, which is varied by duet sections and contrasts of metre. In a sense, 'abstract' music was born in the early Renaissance.

Nevertheless, we should not forget that one of the most striking features of Dunstable's style owes its origin to the chant: its melismatic flow. Not all the plainsongs which he set have the exceptionally long phrases of the final 'alleluia' of *Regina celi letare*, or the opening word of *Alma redemptoris mater*; but most of them employ two, three, or four notes for many of their syllables. When Dunstable's paraphrasing added even more notes between those of the original chant, the old pointed declamation of the traditional motet vanished from his music. In place of a syllabic prosody we find an endless flux: the consonants are almost forgotten in the long phrases which Dunstable sets to each vowel.

In striking contrast to these *vocalises* are one or two of Dunstable's shorter movements, where he exploits, not the flow of discanted plainsong, but its homophony. Here he makes a feature of simultaneous declamation, more or less a note to a syllable, in all parts. The little motet *Quam pulcra es*, the hymn *Ave maris stella* and the *Magnificat* represent this manner. The former, which alone of the three does not use plainsong, was one of his most popular pieces during his lifetime and is frequently revived today. In a way this is a pity: for all its appealing simplicity, *Quam pulcra es* is one of Dunstable's humblest and least characteristic compositions. All the same, it remains one of the very earliest examples of a purely choral style in the history of polyphonic music.

Example 3 is the first section of a *rondeau* by Gilles Binchois (*c.* 1400–60). Binchois, as we have already observed, was in English employment in 1424, and seems to have been strongly affected by the 'new English guise'. Although the lower voices of *Plains de plours* have no text and were presumably intended for instruments, their rhythms are all of a piece with the upper voice: indeed, the middle part, is later on rather livelier than the singer's line. The textless interludes in the top part, too, probably imply the presence of an instrument. Note also the un-vocal leaps of the contratenor, which involve the unusual interval of an augmented fourth in the final cadence (not shown in this excerpt). The last chord in this cadence is actually a full triad with major third, unthinkable before the English had legitimized the 'imperfect' intervals of the third and sixth. The musical declamation is rather less pointed than Le Bertoul's, but since the piece is a secular song we cannot expect the long winding phrases of a Dunstable.

Plains — de plours — et — ge-mi-se-mens

Like Dunstable, however, Binchois and Dufay were masters of contrapuntal rhythm, though they cadence more frequently and prefer more regular phrase-lengths: all three try to keep the music moving along over the internal cadences. In bar 5 of the example, for instance, the rhythm is not allowed to pull up: Binchois is careful to overlap his phrasing. The harmony is beautifully clear, though Binchois enjoys anticipating the movement of the tenor with a fleeting quaver dissonance in the upper voice, as in bars 4–5. He varies his cadences with great subtlety: the traditional tenor cadence, with its step down to the key-note, twice finds its way into the treble, in later bars. The first of these two cadences produces a positively medieval inversion of the parts, with the treble taking the bottom line. Dunstable's favourite $\frac{3}{4}$ measure had by this date been widely adopted on the continent, the natural rhythm of dancing and breathing, of the heat's systole and diastole. (Many Continental composers, Dufay amongst them, preferred to use $\frac{6}{4}$, a quicker, 'diminished' version of the same metre; since the

English enjoyed less regular phrase-lengths, they normally kept to simple $\frac{3}{4}$ at this date.)

Plains de plours is a *rondeau*: with the contemporaries of Binchois, this ancient form suddenly returned to lead the field. In the Venetian manuscript from which Example 3 is taken, there are three *rondeaux* for each *ballade*. Note that Binchois depends entirely on the poetic form for his unity. He makes no attempt here to link the parts through imitative writing, though he does in other songs. The old medieval verse-forms survived until the end of the fifteenth century and even beyond. Poets extended their scale in an attempt to keep them alive, and musicians followed suit; but as soon as the imitative style was able to stand on its own feet, the old moulds were broken and cast aside in favour of less rigid patterns. The French language, too, which had been the undisputed *lingua franca* of courtly love-song since the time of Binchois, was also dethroned: the nations of Europe began to use their own vernaculars more and more, and of course developed individual musical traditions to go with them.

Example 4 is from a motet by Dufay, *Supremum est mortalibus bonum*. It was written for the reconciliation of Pope Eugenius IV and the Emperor Sigismund, which took place in the spring of 1433. Our excerpt shows that *fauxbourdon* was as important to Dufay as faburden was to Dunstable. Compare the harmony of the opening section with the strict *fauxbourdon* of the last three bars: the schematic parallel sixths of the latter have lent their sweetness to the cadences of the former. Even in bars 7–9, where all three voices unite to acclaim the newly allied potentates, sixths are plentiful; only two of the long-held chords lack their mediant.

Dufay was reared, of course, in the tradition of the French Gothic, and spent some of his most impressionable years in Italy, where he must also have learned to admire the complexities of late *trecento* music. He seems to have had much less direct contact with the English than Binchois. In any case, the latter started his career as an amateur composer; he would probably have been much more amenable to new influences than Dufay, who matured early and received a proper professional training. Dufay's music was slow to lose the jerky rhythms and irrational dissonances which his masters had admired. Although *Supremum est mortalibus bonum* is almost certainly a later work than Binchois' *Plains de plours*, Dufay has kept to the rather bumpy $\frac{6}{8}$ metre so common in late Gothic song. His early *fauxbourdons*, too, are far removed from the singing suavity of English faburden. He introduces a good

many 'perfect' $\frac{8}{5}$ chords in order to break up the sequence of 'imperfect' $\frac{6}{3}$s; and spiky little passing dissonances such as the second semiquaver of bar 11 are extremely common.

Nevertheless, Example 4 contains one striking feature which could easily pass unnoticed. In bars 7–9, the contratenor crosses beneath the tenor and stays there: it is a true bass line, with its sturdy, 'table-leg' fourths. In this brief passage of pure choral euphony, Dufay allots to each voice its own territory. The three parts never cross: each has room to move and make itself heard. No doubt this may owe something to the 'layered' style of *fauxbourdon*; but the step of placing a harmonic bass under the authoritarian tenor, as Dufay does in this simple little passage, was essential to the evolution of choral part-writing for four balanced voices. Notice that the tenor keeps its traditional motettish function in the first six bars: it moves in slower values than the upper parts, and almost always takes the bottom note of the texture. This is partly because it quotes a Gregorian *cantus firmus*. (The second section is freely composed.) The text of the ritual melody is *Isti sunt due olive* ('These men are two olive-trees'), an aptly chosen comment on the new Concordat between pope and emperor. We should note, however, that in other parts of this isorhythmic motet Dufay writes a low-lying second tenor underneath the first, which bears an unidentified plainsong. Ten or fifteen years later he was regularly using such a bass-line, and a four-voiced texture had become the rule.

Example 5 is taken from Dufay's Mary-Mass *Ecce ancilla Domini*, and well illustrates the master's later style. All four voices play an essential part in the structure, and the interlocking, densely woven part-writing of the Middle Ages has become a thing of the past. Dufay has achieved a fully choral style. The bass line which supports the tenor *cantus firmus* underpins the harmony of the whole passage, and cannot be omitted without leaving several forbidden fourths groping in mid-air. The composer has reached a new stage in the art of composition. First of all he tailored the tenor from the notes of the Marian antiphon which gives the Mass its title – and in requiring the tenor to use the original liturgical text, he remains to some extent old-fashioned. His next task was to compose the bass, which here keeps to the lower fifth of the gamut. It never crosses above the tenor. The two lower voices unite to form a strong, simple harmonic structure, upon which the upper pair trace their decorative lines in notes of slightly shorter value. In the opening section, for four voices, Dufay does not make a point of using imitation. He liked, however, to link the voices together by repeating little fragments of melody throughout the texture: notice how the alto of bar 1 is repeated in the bass of bar 3, and how in bars 3–4 the G F D E of the tenor is echoed in the F E C D of the treble. In just this way, a painter will work delicate touches of the same colour into the surface of his picture at many different points. Such tonal resonance was first exploited on a large scale by Raphael and his contemporaries of the Grand Manner; at exactly the same period, composers were producing a strikingly similar effect into their music by throwing the same thematic material systematically from voice to voice in the imitative style.

At the time of Dunstable and Dufay, though, these tiny repetitions are not a fully-fledged technique of construction; even the more conscious imitations at the end of Example 5 do not deserve that title. Like the new awareness of controlled dissonance, or the growing interest in the subtleties of spacing, they reflect the desire of early fifteenth-century composers to give their music depth and perspective: the same desire which led the painters of the day to abandon the flat golden background of Gothic art, and to tackle the problem of representing three dimensions on a two-dimensional surface. Just as artists now tried to lead the beholder's eye into their paintings, so composers now adopted a more logical ordering of sound, so that the listener's ear could sense more easily the relationship between melody and countermelody. The 'tenor-directed' music of the late Gothic, in which the separate parts made sense only in relation to the authority of the chosen chant, went the way of the old 'altar-directed' church, which focused the worshipper's attention, as soon as he entered, on the central authority of his faith. The great nave of the Gothic cathedral was either forgotten in the new basilicas of Renaissance architects such as Brunelleschi, or else reduced to human scale, broken up into a series of more intimate and accommodating segments. The altar was dislodged from its central position: in its place stood the spectator, whose eye had now become the main axis of the building. Early Renaissance music, too, demoted the tenor, the 'keeper' of the chant, until it became merely one voice among equals; the new polyphony was composed very much with the ear of the listener as its central judge.

At this time, too, the Mass displaced the motet as the chief vehicle for religious music. Originally, composers had been content to apply the techniques of secular music to the prose texts of the Ordinary. Or they used the appropriate Gregorian melodies as tenors in discant style, or in the manner of the motet. In the middle of the fourteenth century, one or two composers such as Machaut had started to follow the example of certain chant-books by grouping all five sections of the Ordinary together in one setting. These early cycles have little musical unity about them. Around 1430, indeed, we find Italian copyists grouping separately composed settings of the *Kyrie eleison*, *Gloria*, *Credo*, *Sanctus*, and *Agnus Dei* into 'pseudo-cycles'; they would also combine a disparate *Gloria* and *Credo* into a pairing never intended by the composers; the shorter *Sanctus* and *Agnus Dei* were similarly treated. Clearly, the idea of a unified, cyclic Ordinary was in the air.

Dufay's Mass on *Ecce ancilla Domini* is just such a cycle. The master had taken the concept of a 'tenor-Mass' from the English composers Power, Dunstable, and Benet, who had produced the first examples around 1420–30. The notion of using the same ritual melody as the tenor of all the successive parts of the Ordinary must have derived from the isorhythmic motet (contrary to received opinion, the English *did* include the *Kyrie* in their mass-cycles). Two forms of tenor-Mass came into existence at about the same time. In one, the tenor was treated in strict isorhythm: it kept exactly the same rhythm in all movements. In the other, the tenor was treated 'isomelically': though the tune remained essentially the same for each movement, it was subjected to different rhythmic patterns for every fresh appearance. Dufay took over both types, strict and free; he also added a unifying device of his own, the 'motto' – a short phrase for two or more voices which recurs at the beginning of each section of the Ordinary, and even of sub-sections within the main divisions. As a further refinement, we find masses like *Ecce ancilla Domini* which employ not one but two such mottos; this work is also exceptional in drawing on two separate antiphons for its *cantus firmi. Beata es, Maria* appears alongside the antiphon of the title. Still other cycles are based on secular tunes, like Dufay's famous Mass on the tenor of his own song *Se la face ay pale.* In the cyclic Mass, the early Renaissance produced a form comparable in length and musical weight with the Viennese symphony, or with an act of an opera.

Example 6 is taken from the Mass *Caput*, by Johannes

Ockeghem (*c.* 1420–*c.* 1495). Born in Burgundian Hainaut, Ockeghem spent most of his mature life in the service of the Kings of France. Molinet mourned him as '*sol lucens super omnes*', a phrase which had more truth in it than many an obituary, for he not only 'shone like a sun' on all musicians, but taught most of the next generation of composers himself, like William Byrd in late sixteenth-century England. Like Byrd, too, he never allowed his astonishing mastery of technique to tempt him into easy paths. He delighted in the unexpected, and neither Dufay nor Josquin – who both enjoyed a positively Mozartean capacity for putting other men's ideas to their own use – could rival his bewildering and unpredictable variety of style. In his Mass *Caput* he directly imitates Dufay's cycle on the same tune, the final melisma of an English antiphon for the ceremonies of Maundy Thursday. He keeps intact the rhythmic pattern which Dufay had imposed on the chant, and writes the whole tenor out at Dufay's pitch; but by means of a verbal canon he tells the singer to transpose the notes down a whole octave, so that a part which Dufay had placed inside the ensemble now becomes the bass line. The tune hinges round a constantly repeated B; but since Ockeghem resolutely refuses to sharpen more than one or two of the Fs in the upper parts, or to flatten any of the Bs in the bass, the harmony constantly tacks and veers in the most surprising manner. Bars 2–3 of the above excerpt – the first entry of the *cantus firmus* in the *Credo*, after the customary opening duet – show one of these characteristic side-slips; bar 5 contains an unavoidable diminished fifth. The constant doubling of the mediant is also an unexpected trait, after the luminous spacing of Dufay.

The cosmopolitan Dufay was by far the most Italianate composer of his time – not only did the musical art of the *trecento* communicate its elegance to him, but his music also seems to share the rational proportions and grace of line which informed the Italian painting and sculpture which he must have admired during his visits to the peninsula. Ockeghem never seems to have crossed the Alps, and his sacred compositions return to the brooding mysticism of the north. At first glance, the few bars quoted above seem to surge on with a strangely featureless energy. Except for the fact that all the parts move in much the same note-values and hardly ever tangle with each other, we seem to be in a very different atmosphere from the humane clarity of Dufay. There seems to be no rational organization, no regular cadencing, no attempt to pair the parts off or to link them with imitation – nothing but an apparently purposeless striving in the void. Yet most of the passage is constructed almost 'serially', out of two little melodic figures of three notes, with their inverted and retrograde forms, and an occasional note repeated or inserted. One of these germs is taken from the first three notes of the *Caput* tune (which immediately pivots back on itself, be it noted); the other by the first three notes of the tenor, a rising semitone (or later a tone) followed by a rising third. Addicts of serialism may care to prove the 'internal unity' of Ockeghem's style by going through the passage with a pencil: in Example 6 and the next few bars (here omitted), only 29 notes out of 107 cannot be accounted for in this way. Of course, this may prove nothing more than the fact that Ockeghem prefers conjunct motion with few skips greater than a third.

Only the upper voices of Example 6 are underlaid with text in the manuscript – and even so the source gives only short tags: the words printed in italics have been supplied by the editor. It should not escape notice that the phrases of the Creed have been divided up between the two parts. As a result, we hear two different texts being declaimed at the same time, a medieval proceeding which did not survive Ockeghem for long. Its use in the Ordinary of the Mass seems to have begun with Dunstable and his English contemporaries, who also shortened the words of the Creed by considerable omissions. One *Gloria* by Dunstable divides the text between all three voices, so that he manages to fit his whole setting on to a single page; no doubt this work was designed for a simple ferial occasion, on the analogy of the Elizabethan 'Short Service'. In isorhythmic tenor-Masses, of course, where the metrical structure of the *cantus firmus* dictated the proportions of the movements, composers were bound to make some such adjustment in order to accommodate the differing lengths of the Ordinary texts. The shorter *Kyrie, Sanctus*, and *Agnus Dei* needed long melismas to husband out their few syllables. The much longer *Gloria* and *Credo* called for a declamatory *parlando*; another method of fitting more words into the latter movements was to provide much longer duets for the upper voices between the appearances of the tenor *cantus firmus*.

Example 7 is an extract from *Quant ce vendra*, a *rondeau* by Antoine Busnois, who flourished from about 1460 to 1492, the year of his death. He worked at the court of Burgundy. It has become the fashion to call the thirty years 1460–90 the 'age of Busnois and Ockeghem'; but we should remember that Busnois, for all his charm, was quite a minor figure beside the Protean mastery of Ockeghem. He excelled chiefly in secular music, in which his ear for graceful detail made him justly famous. In his love of the old fixed forms, and in his preference for triple metre, he remains rather old-fashioned: the charming song-composer Hayne van Ghizeghem (d. 1472), for example, never once used triple metre throughout his small but distinguished output. Duple measure was establishing itself as the 'common time' of music even before the death of Dufay in 1474. Composers were gradually coming to rely on the power of 'suspended' dissonance to drive their music forward, and turned as a result to the more mechanical move-

1. The Emperor Maximilian among his musicians

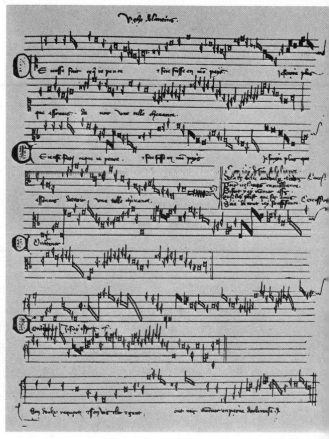

2. *Ce ieusse fait* (Hugo de Lantins). Oxford *chansonnier*,
fifteenth century

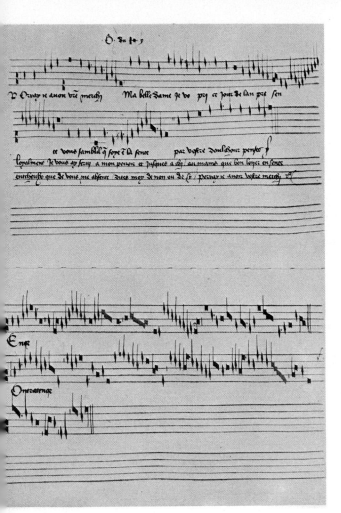

3. *Pouray ie avoir vostre merchi* (Dufay). Escorial *chansonnier*, fifteenth century

4. Musicians and dancers

5. Basic materials for musicians and dancers
(Michel de Toulouze)

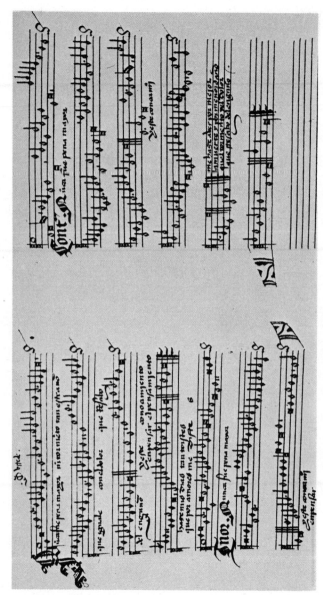

6 *Numca fue pena mayor* (Urrede), Cancionero de Palacio, Madrid

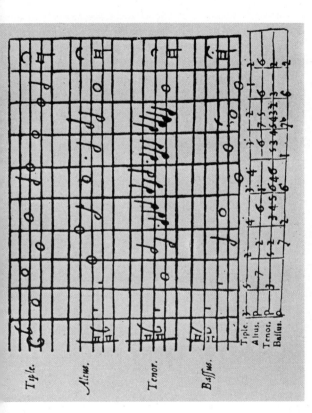

7. Spanish tablature set out beneath score (Henestrosa)

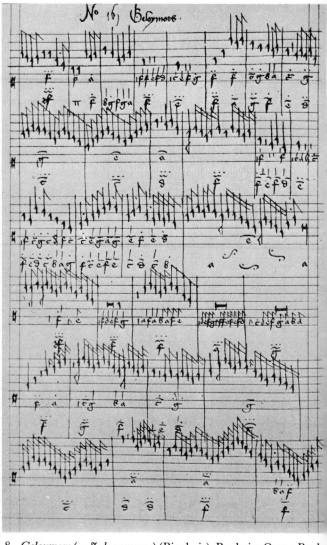

8. *Geloymors* (= *Je loe amours*) (Binchois). Buxheim Organ Book

9. Lady playing a portative organ

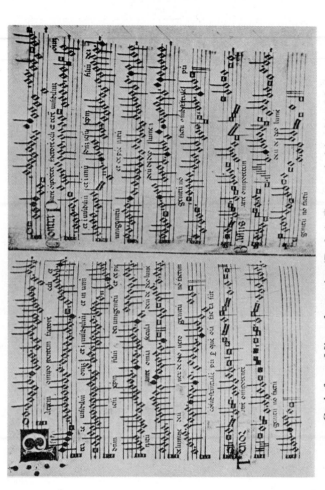

10. *Credo* from *Missa Ave regina* (Dufay). From a choirbook at Modena

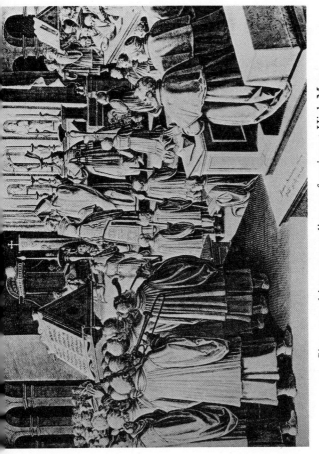

11. Singers and instrumentalists performing at High Mass

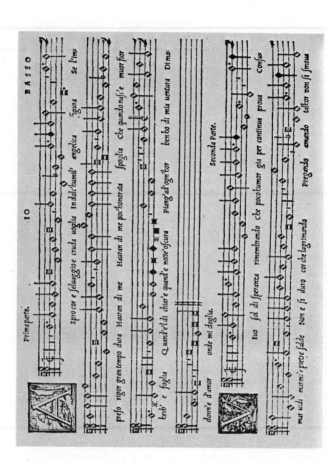

12. *Aspro cor e selvaggio* (Giaches de Wert). Sixteenth century

13. Italian outdoor concert. Sixteenth century

14. *Grene growith the holy* (Henry VIII)

15. Lassus and some of the Duke of Bavaria's private musicians

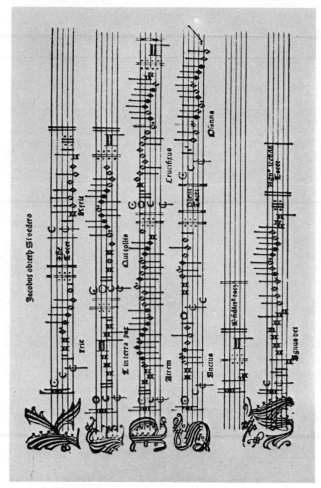

16. *Missa Si dedero* (Obrecht). Printed by Petrucci

ment of $\frac{2}{4}$. There are *two* weak beats in a $\frac{3}{4}$ bar, so that a dissonance would normally have to be prepared on the last crotchet, held over on to the first beat of the next bar, and resolved on the second crotchet. Though frequent cross-rhythms in $\frac{3}{2}$ ('hemiola') could help to break up this uniform, wave-like motion, $\frac{2}{4}$ metre offered the advantage that the resolution of one dissonance could elide with the preparation of the next.

Example 7 shows us a texture typical of Busnois: the voices are spaced well apart, a whole octave between each pair. In this section, all three begin together in the medieval manner; but later on they imitate each other – first, treble and tenor (the middle part), and then all three. The interval of imitation is the octave. Busnois was also fond of imitating at the unison: the classical alternation of plagal and authentic in imitation at the fourth or fifth had not yet established itself. Notice how Busnois binds the voices together in the opening bars by prefiguring the treble of bar 2, in diminution, in the lower parts in bar 1. Notice, too, the decidedly instrumental character of the bass, with its constant leaps from tonic to dominant and back. This strongly tonal kind of bass line vanished when the next generation turned to a more thoroughly imitative texture. One last feature of the harmony calls for comment: there are no structural fourths between any two voices. The flowing $\frac{6}{3}$s of *fauxbourdon*, with their constant parallel fourths, have been banished from the music. This 'non-quartal' harmony is a characteristic of Busnois and his contemporaries. It ensures that *any* two parts make sense on their own, and perhaps reflects the growing interest in double counterpoint which was bound to arise with the growth of the imitative style.

Example 8 is taken from the *Missa Carminum* of Heinrich Isaak (*c.* 1450–1517), one of the greatest of Josquin's peers. He was a widely-travelled Fleming, whose work for Maximilian I did much to set the new school of German-speaking composers on a firm footing. He also spent a great deal of time in Florence and shorter periods in Switzerland. He set out to compose a complete cycle of pieces for the Proper of the Mass, based on the chants of the Constance ritual, providing polyphony for each Sunday of the church year and certain Saints' Days as well. He threw in some settings of the Ordinary for good measure. Isaak's great work, planned on the scale of Byrd's *Gradualia*, or Bach's cantatas, was completed on his death by his friend and pupil Ludwig Senfl, who saw it through the press under the title *Choralis Constantinus* as late as 1550–5.

This renewal of interest in the polyphonic treatment of the Proper is paralleled by the emergence of other parts of the liturgy in musical settings at the same period: *Magnificat*, hymn, *Requiem*, Passion, and psalm gradually claimed more and more of the composer's attention. No doubt the task of setting the words of the Ordinary over and over again began to pall after a time, in an age which became more and more preoccupied with the meaning and expression of words.

Example 8 may well strike some readers as familiar. The second and third voices present a canon at the unison, based very closely on Isaak's *Innsbruck ich muss dich lassen*, a moving farewell to Innsbruck in the form of a German *Lied*. The Mass does not employ the better-known of Isaak's two arrangements of this tune: we have here the second version, probably written for instruments alone. In short, our example is a *contrafactum*, a work transferred from one medium to another. Isaak, like all his Flemish contemporaries, was a master of canon; but it is interesting to see that he does not scruple to change a note here and there when it suits his purpose. Like Bach, he was not prepared to sacrifice his sensibility to pursue the intellectual 'logic' of a formal device. Notice, too, how subtly he glides back into a repeat of the opening phrase in bar 5, and how tellingly the E flat of the treble moves against the E natural of the lower voices in bar 3.

Isaak's *Missa Carminum* is based, not on one song alone, but on a whole host of popular tunes, many of which still await identification. It is a gigantic *quodlibet*, which the Spanish would have called an *ensalada*, or salad. Innumerable masses of the late fifteenth and early sixteenth centuries, of course, employed secular tunes taken from famous *chansons* for their *cantus firmi*. Normally, the composers would be content to choose the tenor or the treble of their model, and to treat this one voice as they would have treated a melody of more exalted origin. Towards the end of the fifteenth century, however, it became the fashion to take over all voices of the original, and re-work them *in extenso* to form the entire texture of the new mass. This technique of 'parody', as it later came to be called, had in fact been employed in the fourteenth century and early fifteenth. But it lay forgotten until Obrecht's Mass on Caron's *Rosa playsant* finally set the stamp on the technique for his successors.

The very idea of plagiarism used to raise pious protests in the romantic nineteenth century. Even today, our journalist music-critics are on the whole far more concerned with novelty than with quality. If a composer writes a new work, it is supposed to be as different as possible, not only from the styles of other composers, but from everything that he himself has written to date. Earlier ages were wiser. It was not merely that 'a good idea belongs to him who knows how to use it'. In the fifteenth century, to work anew an older piece of music was at once a compliment to the original composer, and an opportunity to demonstrate one's technical skill. In contemporary literature and fine art, parody was recognized as a valuable means of grafting new ideas on to old stock. We of the present day have lost much in our restless quest for innovation.

Example 9, from Obrecht's motet *Si sumpsero*, shows the composer at his best. Jakob Obrecht was born, a Dutchman, in 1450, and died at Ferrara in 1505. He was a strange mixture of medieval formalism and modern suavity. In the *Credo* of his Mass on Hayne's famous *De tous biens plaine*, for example, he subjects his *cantus firmus* to the most abstruse manipulations. First he extracts all the longs from the tune, and strings them together in succession; then he does the same with the breves, and finally with the semibreves. He then reverses this procedure, starting with the shorter values first. In his Mass on Busnois's *Fortuna desperata* he adopts a device favoured by the dodecaphonists of the present century. In the *Gloria* he presents the first half of his *cantus firmus* backwards, follows up with the second half in its proper order, and then repeats the whole. The *Credo* starts off with the second half of the tune in reverse, followed by the first half the right way round; again, the whole is then re-stated. Yet, hearing these two works, the casual listener would probably notice nothing of Obrecht's complexities. They were a private means of construction important to the composer alone. Unlike canon, this purely intellectual treatment of a *cantus firmus* gives no audible *musical* unity to the structure. This is provided by Obrecht's strongly personal style, his handling of detail from bar to bar; and in this, his outlook was totally modern.

Obrecht does not employ much dissonance in the example given. It is the subtlety of his rhythmic counterpoint which proclaims him a master. He prefers to write in the $\frac{2}{4}$ metre which had come to dominate music during his youth, and it is easy to see why. (It is customary to run two $\frac{2}{4}$ bars into one of common time, in transcribing this music: it avoids our having to peer at the notes through a forbidding fence of barlines.) Duple metre allows the composer to counterpoint a great variety of different rhythms against the prevailing pattern of alternate strong and weak beats. In a similar way, Keats was able to achieve marvels of phrasing by counterpointing different rhythms against the outline of the iambic pentameter: a line like 'Young companies nimbly began dancing' makes its extraordinary effect because we *expect* a series of iambic stresses. Obrecht, too, was a master of this kind of movement. Example 9 starts off regularly enough, with its imitations at the unison and octave. In bar 3, the composer begins to interlock and dovetail the voices, balancing phrase against phrase in a manner rare for his time. In bar 6, he suddenly contrasts this with a simpler motion in thirds; the way in which he leaves the G of the middle voice echoing in the upper air, while the treble moves down beneath to join with the bass, vouches for the growing delight which composers now took in 'orchestrating' for different vocal groupings. Obrecht, like John Bull, has often been reproached for his facility, that 'copiousness of invention' which Glareanus remarked upon. Yet his music grew quite naturally out of the human voice, just as Bull's seems to have been gathered straight from his virtuoso finger-tips. In performance, one forgets these paper judgements, sharing again in the composers' true feeling for sheer sonority. Haydn is another master whose music still suffers from the eccentric modern belief that it is as easy to read a score as it is to read a book. Spacings which on paper look simple to the point of dullness often come alive in the most remarkable way, once the actual sounds of the music vibrate in the air.

The composer of Example 10, the Picard Pierre de la Rue (fl. 1477?–1518), has remained less well-known than his music deserves. The above excerpt is taken from the second *Kyrie* of his Mass on *L'Homme armé*. This old folk tune seems to owe its first polyphonic arrangement to the Englishman Robert Morton. For some reason, it became popular amongst the composers of Mass-cycles. Ockeghem wrote the first known tenor-Mass on the melody, using a slightly obscure form of notation which he owed to the English. During the next two centuries over thirty other such Masses were written, including a set of six, all composed by the same anonymous master, in a Neapolitan manuscript; two each by La Rue, Josquin, Morales, and Palestrina; an example from Scotland by Robert Carver; and even an unusually late setting by Carissimi in the seventeenth century. A Mass on *L'Homme armé* was apparently expected of any ambitious young composer, and we could almost write a history of the tenor-Mass using the settings of *L'Homme armé* alone. Why this particular tune should have become such a popular *cantus firmus* remains a mystery. One would like to think that the 'man armed with an iron hauberk', of whom 'one should beware', was identified with St Michael the Archangel, who was of course commander-in-chief of the heavenly host. The Mass on *L'Homme armé* by Joannes Regis (*c.* 1430–85), who was for a time Dufay's secretary, associates the words of the antiphon *Dum sacrum mysterium* with the old tune, and draws on other chants too: nearly all of this additional material is taken from the ritual of the Feast of St Michael. Similarly, it would be interesting to find out whether the Masses on *Caput* by Dufay, Ockeghem, and Obrecht were connected with the Maundy ceremonies which the Queen still celebrates today. Obrecht's master, Hercules I of Ferrara, for example, instituted such ceremonies as soon as he inherited his dukedom, entertaining over a hundred paupers to a meal and actually washing their feet himself as 'his chapel sang the *Mandatum*'. The antiphon *Mandatum* (whence 'Maundy') was one of a number associated with the feast. Another, the *Venit ad Petrum*, ends with the word *caput*, from which the famous *cantus firmus* was derived: 'Not my feet only, but also my hands and my *head*', in the words of St Peter.

Example 10 illustrates the Netherlandish love of achieving a simple texture by the most complex means. The lower two voices present *L'Homme armé* as a mensuration canon. La Rue has changed the rhythm of the tune to suit his own purposes; he then copied it out only once, but with two different time-signatures, leaving the singers to puzzle out how the two versions fitted together. The bass enunciates the melody in triple metre, so that most of the crotchets have to be subtracted from the value of the previous dotted ('perfect') minims and semibreves. The tenor (the upper part of the lowest pair), which sets off at the same moment as the bass, has to be sung in duple measure, where the rules of 'imperfection' do not apply – ideally, we should have given it an independent time-signature of $\frac{2}{4}$, each minim corresponding to a dotted minim of the other voices. As a result of this proceeding, the bass gradually draws away from the tenor, and the canon becomes progressively easier to handle. The third *Agnus Dei* of this Mass is even more complicated: La Rue there derives all four parts from a single line in the same sort of way. Yet the music sounds perfectly natural and convincing. We should not forget that these intricate devices of early composers, from the isorhythmic motet down to the invertible counterpoint of Bach, all had to satisfy the demands of standard harmony and counterpoint within which they were employed. They never became the sole *raison d'être* of the music. The upper parts of La Rue's *Kyrie* hold another surprise in store for us. The composer has already accomplished a difficult feat in the mensuration canon of the lower voices. One would have expected him to rest upon his well-earned laurels, to content himself with two free voices when he came to complete the ensemble. The alto is indeed a completely independent part. But the treble contains yet another version of *L'Homme armé*: the notes which we have marked with crosses are all derived from the tune. Three voices out of four are constructed from pre-existent material. In short, composers now wished to spread the notes of their *cantus firmi* throughout the whole texture of their music. They were no longer content to place the chosen melody in one voice alone, sealing it off from its fellows in a watertight compartment. By a gradual osmosis, elements of the *cantus firmus* now began to leak out into the other parts. Slowly, the imitative style came into being.

Example 11 gives the opening bars of Josquin's *Missa de Beata Virgine*, which was printed in 1514. Here, the new style reaches its full maturity. All four voices share the same thematic material and move in the same rhythms: only the few ornamental semiquavers of bar 5 recall the highly figured treble of the earlier fifteenth century. The authoritarian dictatorship of the *cantus firmus* has been overthrown, and in its place we have a democratic discussion between four equal partners. The imitative 'point' which passes fugally from voice to voice is derived from the opening phrase of the present *Kyrie IX* in the

Roman liturgy; again, we have marked the notes of the chant with a cross, on their first appearance in the treble.

Josquin has constructed his little exposition with a logical economy which Obrecht rarely attained. First, the tenor imitates the treble at the octave, after an interval of three minims. After a further three minims, the alto and bass sing

exactly the same notes, starting a fourth lower. Each voice lies a fourth or a fifth beneath the one above: we have arrived at the modern categories of Soprano, Alto, Tenor, and Bass, which have governed choral writing for four and a half centuries since the time of Josquin. The strained tone and narrow compass of the Gothic have given way to a relaxed style of singing, which permitted the 'natural' registers to develop in answer to the needs of imitative composition. The new style of 'pervasive imitation' was still one of many different techniques in Josquin's time. Its growing importance had earlier been noted by the theorist Ramos de Pareia, who called it '*fuga*': even today, many people who ought to know better forget that 'fugue' is not a form, but a kind of texture.

Notice how Josquin carefully avoids stopping at any cadence. As one voice drops out to take a breath, the others intervene and keep the music moving. Suspensions have become more common, and most of them here are of a cadential nature.

This preoccupation with the dissonant cadence, and its invariable suspension of the keynote, is demonstrated in a curiously negative manner by Jean Mouton: self-conscious in matters of style, like nearly all French composers, he once wrote a Mass *sine cadentia*, with the aim of avoiding cadences wherever he could.

It is interesting to find that Josquin was regarded as a dangerously impulsive composer for some years after his death. Glareanus wrote of him in 1547:

If this man, besides that native bent and strength of character by which he was distinguished, had had an understanding of the twelve modes and of the truth of musical theory, nature could have brought forth nothing more majestic and magnificent in this art; so versatile was his temperament in this respect, so armed with natural acumen and force, that there is nothing he could not have done in this profession. But moderation was wanting for the most part and, with learning, judgement; thus in certain places in his compositions he did not, as he should have, soberly repress the violent impulses of his unbridled temperament.

Exactly the same sort of complaints were made about Mozart's music, which now seems to us – like Josquin's – a model of effortless grace. Glareanus, of course, was an academic theorist who wished all music to conform to his own artificial and *a priori* patterns. It was probably Josquin's motets and psalms which surprised their hearers so much, rather than his more restrained Mass-music. In another passage, Glareanus reproves Josquin for mixing his modes in the *Planxit autem David*, a deeply-felt setting of David's lament for Saul and Jonathan. He then, to his credit, goes on to defend Josquin's naturalistic treatment of his passionate text:

Throughout the motet, there is preserved what befits the mourner, who is wont at first to cry out frequently, then to murmur to himself, turning little by little to sorrowful complaints, thereupon to subside or sometimes, when passion breaks out anew, to raise his voice again, shouting out a cry. All these things we see most beautifully observed . . .

Composers were now turning more and more to the scriptures, rather than the liturgy, for words which would allow them to exercise their imaginations more tellingly than could the texts of the Mass and the everyday ritual. Antoine Brumel seems to have been the first to take verses from a psalm and clothe them in polyphonic garb. Josquin took up the idea in his *Motetti de la corona*, printed by Petrucci in 1514. The moving *Miserere* of 1519, a setting of the Latin Psalm 51, is probably his most famous example. Some of his psalms seem to be based on the liturgical tones, but most of them are free compositions.

Example 12 shows what Josquin could do with an old tune. *Adieu mes amours* made its first appearance in recorded history as monophonic *bergerette*, or one-stanza *virelai*, in the Bayeux manuscript. Like *L'Homme armé*, the melody was frequently re-worked in one form or another by Josquin's contemporaries, Obrecht and Mouton amongst them. Josquin's own arrangement appeared in the *Odhecaton* of 1501. It takes the form of a gentle reminder to his royal master, Louis XII of France, that his servant's salary was overdue, like Chaucer's 'Complaint to his purse'. 'Farewell my loves … unless the king's money comes more often', runs Josquin's text. Josquin seems often to have felt himself undervalued, for several of his works apparently take an obscure revenge on some thoughtless patron.

His early employer Cardinal Ascanio Sforza, for example, had the reputation of being extremely tight-fisted towards his household retinue, though he was quite prepared to pay an enormous sum for a parrot which could recite the Apostles' Creed. We know that Josquin complained to the poet-composer Serafino dall' Aquila about him. It was probably this prelate whom Glareanus had in mind, when he wrote that Josquin's mass on the solmization-syllables *La Sol Fa Re Mi* (A G D F E) enshrines the phrase '*Lascia fare mi*' – 'Leave it to me' – with which some unnamed princeling was wont to send petitioners empty away. The charming little *frottola*, *El grillo*, which tells how the cricket, that excellent singer, can exist on a diet of dew alone, also evokes satirical overtones. Louis XII, however, seems to have satisfied Josquin's demands, for the composer later wrote a charming piece in which one voice is entitled '*Vox regis*' – 'the king's part'. Louis was notoriously tone-deaf when it came to singing, and the '*Vox regis*' consists of one note, constantly repeated. Alongside the new emotional power of Josquin's finest motets, it is pleasing to find these touches of recognizably modern humour in his slighter works.

The *bergerette* form of *Adieu mes amours* is both embroidered and foreshortened in Josquin's setting. Originally, the tune consisted of two sections of music, repeated with fresh verses (except for the final recapitulation of the opening refrain) in the pattern $A'b'b''a''A'$. Not only does Josquin omit the final repeat of the refrain A', but he writes out the music of the other verses in full, making slight alterations each time. He has abandoned the strictness of the old fixed form, and now uses its conventional repetitions for his own purposes. Just as the self-sufficient logic of musical art had supplanted the symbolic use of *cantus firmi* in sacred music, so it now freed secular song from the artificial verse-forms of previous centuries.

Josquin's experiments with the French *chanson* often make use of techniques more commonly associated with sacred music. A number of his secular works are written for as many as six voices, moving in a suave counterpoint which is thoroughly motettish in texture, and very different from the *chansons* of his French contemporaries. *Adieu mes amours* requires only four voices, but its structure is noteworthy. The lower two voices are in free canon at the lower fourth; the bass moves into the lead in the second phrase. It is not a complicated mensuration canon like La Rue's, though Josquin too could pen a pretty puzzle when it suited him; like La Rue, however, Josquin also allots an ornamented version of the opening bars of his model to the treble singer. The rhythms of his upper voices are far more perky, indeed far more instrumental, than those of his sacred music. One could go so far as to say that imitative rhythm itself is beginning to assume equal rights with strict melodic imitation, as a unifying agent in the texture. Notice how important the little running figure of a dotted quaver and three semiquavers becomes; the combination $\frac{3}{8} + \frac{2}{8} + \frac{3}{8}$ also occurs no less than five times in these ten bars – a syncopated rhythm which remained a favourite trick of Renaissance composers even as late as the English madrigalists of the early seventeenth century.

Here our brief survey of the developing language of early Renaissance music must end. We have omitted an enormous amount of material from this discussion. Our examples include no Italian *frottola*, no Spanish *villancico*, no German *Lied*, no English carol; we have not discussed in any detail the rising school of German organ music, and we have barely mentioned the amazingly rich texture of non-imitative counterpoint which English composers developed in the later fifteenth century. We have merely dipped into the main stream of music at all too rare intervals over the period, in the hope of providing a few selected samples which will help the interested listener to get his bearings. In dealing with an age so rich in innovation, so crowded with major and minor masters, hardly any other course was possible in this short chapter. But if a few small choirs have been tempted into exploring the early years of choral music, or if one or two chamber-music groups decide to ask a singer to join them in order to perform some fifteenth-century *chansons*, then the music of the early Renaissance may one day become popular enough to earn a whole volume to itself. It certainly does not deserve its present neglect.

NOTE

The author of the foregoing chapter owes much to the following books and authors, and strongly recommends them for further reading on the period in question.

Stevens, John, *Music and Poetry in the Early Tudor Court*, London, 1961. Often ranges far beyond the scope of its title and is well worth the layman's attention. Particularly excellent on the relation between words and music, Courtly Love, and the immediate significance of the Renaissance to those who lived through it.

Dart, Thurston, *The Interpretation of Music*, London, 1954. A valuable guide to the performance of early music. It contains an account of Philip the Good's banquet mentioned on p. 49 above.

Brown, Howard Mayer, *Music in the French Secular Theater*, Cambridge, Massachusetts, 1963. A valuable appraisal of 'popular' music in the fifteenth and early sixteenth centuries. (It appeared too late to be used in writing this chapter.)

Van den Borren, Charles, *Études sur le XVᵉ siècle musical*, Antwerp, 1941. Still valuable for its musical insights, and most beautifully written. Owing to the outbreak of the Second World War, this and the next two items remain untranslated and little known in this country.

Pirro, André, *Histoire de la musique de la fin du XIVᵉ siècle à la fin du XVIᵉ*, Paris, 1940. Condenses an astonishing amount of valuable material into the most elegant prose; much used in writing this chapter.

Marix, Jeanne, *Histoire de la musique et des musiciens de la cour de Bourgogne sous le règne de Phillippe le Bon*, Strasbourg, 1939. An object lesson in the use of historical records to illuminate a whole social and musical *milieu* – in this case the court of fifteenth-century Burgundy.

II · THE LATE RENAISSANCE

Anthony Milner

1. Music and Society

IN the sixteenth century, as in the fifteenth, music was considered an indispensable part of the life of a well-educated man. Baldassare Castiglione, in his *Book of the Courtier* (1528), one of the most famous and influential works of its time, puts this very forcibly:

You must think I am not pleased with the Courtier if he be not also a musician, and besides his understanding and cunning upon the book, have skill in like manner on sundry instruments. For if we weigh it well, there is no ease of the labours and medicines of feeble minds to be found more honest and more praiseworthy in time of leisure than it. And principally in courts, where (beside the refreshing of vexations that music bringeth unto each man) many things are taken in hand to please women withal, whose tender and soft breasts are soon pierced with melody and filled with sweetness. Therefore no marvel that in the old days and nowadays they have always been inclined to musicians, and counted this a most acceptable food of the mind.

In consequence of this attitude, princes, prelates, and noblemen not only strove to be accomplished amateur musicians but vied with one another in the splendour of their musical establishments. The almost bewildering variety of forms and styles brought into being by the enlightened patronage of the secular and ecclesiastical courts and aristocratic circles is best introduced by examples of the ways in which music was employed and of the occasions for which it was written. This fundamental orientation of music towards social function is unknown to the present age save in music for worship, theatre, cinema, and dancing, and there exhibited all too often in works of which the self-appointed arbiters of fashion disapprove.

SECULAR CEREMONIAL

The display of wealth and grandeur by Renaissance princes was not merely the result of their love for ostentation: magnificence was considered a necessary princely virtue even by theologians. Moreover, as Macchiavelli cynically insisted, 'men judge generally more by the eye than by the hand, because it belongs to everybody to see you, to few to come in touch with you.'

Innumerable contemporary descriptions testify to the important share allotted to music in exhibitions of princely pomp. Florence under the Medicis set fashions that were copied by many other states. At the wedding of Duke Cosimo I to Eleonora of Toledo in 1539, the new Duchess was welcomed at the entrance to the city by a Latin motet in eight-part counterpoint beginning with the words 'Enter thy town with the happiest omens', 'sung over the archway of the great door of the Portal al Prato with 24 voices on one side and on the other 24 trombones and 4 *cornetti*'. Music for voices and instruments also figured largely at the wedding ceremony and subsequent Pontifical High Mass in the church of San Lorenzo. The state banquet was eaten to the accompaniment of background music; this was a normal practice at meals in princely houses, but on an occasion of this sort especially brilliant and colourful sounds would be required. In the evening after supper a comedy was performed with musical interludes of madrigals, the singers being doubled or accompanied by instruments. The play ended with a ballet danced by four satyrs and four bacchantes 'with various instruments all at once'.

At Venice religious and civil ceremony were combined. Holy days and saints' festivals were marked by state processions to the church of St Mark for Mass, wherein the Venetian love of colour and brilliant costumes was eagerly indulged. A city that admired the paintings of Titian, Tintoretto, and Veronese expected equally colourful music. The following description by Francesco Sansovino, though dating from the middle of the seventeenth century, holds true for the sixteenth also:

Elegantly dressed as at the coronation, the body which goes with the Doge as its head consists of many ranks of personages and the civil authorities. And they come in a fixed order as follows, beginning with the eight standards which were presented by the Pope. Next follow the silver trumpets, held up in front on the shoulders of several youths. And two by two the heralds, these clothed always in turquoise blue which is peculiar to their costume, with long cloaks, wearing on their heads the red beretta with a small gold medallion bearing on one side the impression of St Mark. Behind them come the players with trombones, clad in red, playing harmoniously all the way. These are followed by the Squires of the Doge, two by two, dressed in black velvet. Then six canons wearing priest's vestments, because it has always been our custom to accompany the temporal with the religious. Near them walk the Stewards of the Doge, then the Secretaries of the College, the Senate, and the Council of Ten; and then come those two chancellors of the Doge called *inferiori* and *ducali* according to the greatness of their service to the Republic. And behind these comes the Grand Chancellor; and all these are dressed in purple with closed sleeves with the exception of the Grand Chancellor who is dressed as a Senator. Immediately behind is the chaplain of the Prince with the bearer of the Ducal Cap who carries a candle, with the Doge's page. Next come the ceremonial Chair and Cushion, the one to the left, the other to the right with the umbrella. And nearby comes the Doge in person, with the ambassadors of foreign princes around him. And in triumph, he always wears the ermine cape. After these come the Councillors and Procurators of St Mark's, two by two, the judges, the Council of Ten, the army council, and the other senators and civil authorities, hand in hand after the law, all clad in crimson silk with the sleeves *alla ducale* giving a magnificence and splendour which could never be surpassed.

Italy was richer in musical activity than many other parts of Europe, since each of its numerous small states acted in some degree as a musical centre, but similar examples of the ceremonial employment of music in public functions could be quoted from most countries of western and central Europe.

LITURGICAL RITUAL

The Papal Chapel (= choir) and the chapels of the kings and princes were the centres where a new 'secularized' style of church music developed under the influence of the humanistic thought of the Renaissance. This 'secularization' was further fostered by superficial but extensive additions to liturgical ritual. These were not merely due to the fact that if a High Mass was celebrated in the presence of a monarch or ruler it inevitably gained additional ceremonial grandeur. From the fourteenth century onwards, religious ritual tended to absorb more and more details of royal ceremonial. Nearly all bishops, for example, owned large estates, and were thereby temporal lords, and it may be readily understood how the marks of etiquette due to a man as a civil potentate were incorporated in the ritual of honour paid to his priestly office. This process is most obvious in the development of the ritual of a Papal High Mass, but it can be observed operating in greater or less degree in the ritual surrounding all ranks of the ecclesiastical hierarchy. Hence throughout the Renaissance the parade of pomp and colour was equally evident in the music for Catholic worship and secular ceremonial. The chief methods by which the Mass and Office were enriched with polyphony followed the basic principles established by the practice of previous centuries: either embellishing the plainsong, or replacing it with new music. But as a consequence of such techniques the details of the rites tended to be obscured by the wealth of musical sound. Men went to church more often for musical pleasure than prayer. This naturally aroused opposition in the more serious-minded clergy, who renewed the complaints about polyphony that had been voiced at intervals throughout the Middle Ages. A passage from Erasmus (which incidentally affords a description of contemporary customs) is typical of these:

We have introduced a laborious and theatrical kind of music into our sacred edifices, a tumultuous bawl of diverse voices, such as I do not believe was ever heard in the theatres of the Greeks or the Romans. They clash out everything with trumpets, clarions, reeds, and lutes, and human voices vie with these instruments. There are heard vile love ditties, to which harlots and mimes dance. People flock to the sacred edifice as to a theatre to have their ears charmed. And for this purpose artisans of the organ are maintained at high salaries, and troops of boys all of whose time is consumed in learning these things, and who study nothing good in the meantime.

In spite of the changes brought about by the influence of the Reformation and Counter-Reformation movements (which will be discussed later) the pomp and colour of Catholic church music was in no way diminished during the later years of the century; quite the contrary. Under the influence of the new attitudes towards liturgy and ritual, music became even more elaborate and gorgeous than before.

THE VOGUE FOR INTIMATE SOCIAL MUSIC

In an essay on the later Venetian painters of the Renaissance, Berenson shows that 'painting had reached the point where it was no longer dependent upon the Church, nor even expected to be decorative ... but was used purely for pleasure'.[1] An analogous process may be observed in the appreciation of music. Music-lovers ceased to be satisfied merely with hearing music at church or as an accompaniment to processions: 'they attended musical performances organized for the sole purpose of enjoying music, and often joined the ranks of the performers.'[2] Groups of poets, musicians, artists, and amateurs formed societies called Academies which held regular meetings to discuss artistic and intellectual topics, to arrange musical performances and to criticize the verse and music of the members. One of the first to be firmly established was the Accademia Filarmonica of Verona, founded in 1543 primarily for musical purposes. Many other Italian towns, large and small, followed Verona's lead. Not a few such societies were instituted by the local princes. For example, Duke Alfonso II of Ferrara and his two sisters (who, like nearly all the d'Este family, were passionately fond of music) founded an Accademia dei Concordi to foster musical intercourse between the town and the court. The thirty-two musicians of his household joined forces with the amateurs among the townspeople, who often rivalled the professional musicians. Concerts were held almost every evening whose standards of performance greatly

1. Berenson, *The Italian Painters of the Renaissance* (Phaidon, 1956), p. 31.
2. P. H. Lang, *Music in Western Civilization* (Dent, 1942), p. 700.

impressed visitors to the d'Este court. A description survives of 'an ensemble of ladies playing wind and stringed instruments. After the performers had silently assembled at a long table, the *maestra del concerto* entered and, with a long polished stick, gave the signal to begin, whereupon the group played with marvellous unanimity.'[1] Other forms of ensemble mingled lutes, viols, lyres, and harpsichord. The Duke's sisters and other noble ladies sang in vocal ensembles. Every year the Ferrara Accademia would meet a similar group from Mantua in friendly contest. The poet Vincenzo Giustiniani has left an account of the performances of the rival choirs, praising especially their control of *crescendo* and *decrescendo*, their execution of soft passages 'interrupted by *esclamazioni*' (broken sighs), their appropriate facial expression and control of bodily gestures.

The cultivation of music spread from the nobility to the gentry and bourgeoisie. Vocal and instrumental works were equally popular. Dancing was a universal pastime of the period, and the dances were performed in various arrangements as ensemble music in addition to their normal use. The madrigal composers relied as much on the support of the middle classes as on that of the aristocracy. Choral music was 'arranged' for performance by groups of instruments or for solo instruments such as the lute and harpsichord. Certain snobbish distinctions were drawn: instruments were grouped into 'noble' and 'plebeian' classes. Bagpipes, trumpets, and harsh-sounding instruments were considered unsuitable for educated people. Noble amateurs were expected to perform only upon the more delicately-sounding lute, viol, and harpsichord. So much did amateur music-making become a feature of social life that writers of manuals on etiquette felt compelled to offer advice concerning it. Thus Della Casa writes in his *Galateo* (1558): 'You should take care not to sing, especially solo, if your voice is discordant and tuneless. Many people are thoughtless about this and, in fact, the most frequent offenders seem to be those who have the least gift for singing.'[2]

1. Gustave Reese, *Music in the Renaissance* (Dent, 1959), p. 546.
2. Translated by R. S. Pine-Coffin (Penguin Books, 1958), p. 25.

MUNICIPAL AND CIVIC MUSIC

Throughout the Renaissance, the corporations of all large towns and cities maintained groups of instrumental musicians to provide entertainment at civic functions and *al fresco* music during the summer evenings. In Italy these city bands were generally composed of wind instruments: *pifare* (a generic term for pastoral instruments such as the shawm, fife, and bagpipes), trumpets, and trombones. Each player was required to be master of at least two instruments, and also to be able to sing pleasantly. The standards of performance exhibited by these bands were so high that they were frequently hired out by the civic authorities to local noblemen, and thus gained not only greater reputation but also considerable additions to their pay. Benvenuto Cellini's father played *pifara* in a Florentine town band, and taught his son to play so skilfully on the flute and cornet that, at the early age of thirteen, he too became a member of the band.

In Germany the town musicians were called *Stadtpfeiffer* (town pipers), even though they frequently included string players. For example, a series of woodcuts depicting a triumphal procession of the Emperor Maximilian I show, in addition to the Emperor's musicians, several wagons packed with band players from towns and cities. One of these contains five performers on various stringed instruments plus three on wind instruments of whom one carries a tabor (light drum).

The English town musicians were called waits, having originated in the bands of medieval watchmen who blew a species of horn as an alarm or signal. From the middle of the fifteenth century onwards their musical functions were officially recognized as pre-eminent. The London waits were professional musicians of high standards, regularly including performers on both wind and stringed instruments. In the annual ceremonies for the inauguration of the Lord Mayor the waits always formed the principal band of musicians. Their duties required them to perform in front of the houses of the mayor and sheriff on all great feast days and public holidays.

In addition they had to hold themselves in readiness to supply any special requests for music by the aldermen. Sometimes their services were lent to noblemen whom the aldermen wished to compliment. In 1587 the aldermen hired a wagon to take them to the country to play before Queen Elizabeth. Commencing in 1571 they were ordered to 'play upon their instruments upon the turret at the Royal Exchange every Sunday and holiday towards the evening' during the period from Lady Day to Michaelmas (25 March to 29 September). The pleasure afforded to Londoners may be judged from a passage in *The French Schoolemaister*, published in 1573:

Have you not heard the minstrels and players of instruments, which did play so sweetly before the city's storehouse, from midnight even unto the breaking of the day? I would you had for your sake: for it would seem unto you to be ravished in an earthly paradise.

MUSIC IN THE COUNTRYSIDE

The evidence of numerous contemporary paintings, etchings, and woodcuts reveals that music played as large a share in the life of countryfolk as it did in that of town-dwellers. The countryside had its own music, the traditional repertoire of folk-song and folk-dance, which serious composers used as material for polyphonic vocal and instrumental music. Examples of this are legion, ranging from the incorporation of folk-tunes in *chansons* and madrigals to the elaborate sets of keyboard variations on popular tunes. Certain traditional bass patterns used as a foundation for the extemporized chanting of popular verse were developed by composers into the ground-bass patterns of the seventeenth century. Such practices reveal that folk-music was enjoyed and valued by sophisticated music-lovers; there seems to have been little or none of the superior attitude to it evidenced by later periods, while the unhappy division between 'art-music' and 'popular music' which bedevils the appreciation of music in the twentieth century was unknown. Folk-music was allowed a place in public celebrations, as, for example, in the midsummer watch processions of London which, though headed by the waits, included a large body of morris-dancers and musicians at the rear. The text of one of Morley's madrigals published in 1594 gives a lively picture of a group of morris-men, the music vividly depicting the excitement of the spectators:

Ho! who comes here all along
With bagpiping and drumming?
O the Morris 'tis I see,
'Tis the Morris dance a-coming.
Come, come, ladies, out come quickly
And see about how trim they dance and trickly.
Hey! there again, hey ho, there again,
Hey ho! how the bells they shake it!
Now for our town, hey ho!
Now for our town there and take it!
Soft awhile! Not away so fast, they melt them.
Piper! What Piper ho! (Who calls?)
Be hanged awhile, knave. Look, the dancers swelt them.
Out there, out awhile. Stand out. You come too far, I say, in.
There, give the hobby horse more room to play in.

Some of the sophisticated art of the courts and the *Accademie* of Italy was also known to the peasants. Montaigne records how in Tuscany he saw the 'peasants with lute in hand and even the pastoral poems of Ariosto on their lips, but this you may see throughout Italy'.[1] Similarly the gondoliers of Venice made songs by fitting the verse of Tasso and Ariosto to popular tunes. The boatmen of either end sang alternate verses as they guided the gondola forward, often being answered from other boats in the distance.

1. *Diary of a Journey to Italy in 1580 and 1581*, translated by E. J. Trechmann (Hogarth Press, 1929), p. 24.

2. The Composer and His Art

THE choirs of the cathedrals and larger churches were the training grounds of composers: nearly every composer began his musical life as a choirboy. Singing was regarded as the foundation of all practical music. If a boy showed promise, then the choirmaster (generally himself a composer) would arrange for him to be taught various instruments, probably commencing with the lute, viol, and organ. A competent musician was expected to have practical knowledge of most instruments; even if he showed special aptitude for one he still had to learn to play as many as he could. Composition was only taught to those who were already well-trained singers and proficient on at least two or three instruments. Adrian Coclico, who claimed to have been taught by Josquin, described some of his master's methods in his *Musical Compendium* (1552):

> He was able in a short time to form complete musicians, because he taught his pupils the rules in a few words, through practical application in the art of singing. And as soon as he saw that his pupils were well-grounded in singing, that they knew how to embellish melodies and how to fit the text to the music, then he taught them the intervals and the different methods of inventing counterpoints against plainsong. If he discovered, however, pupils with an ingenious mind and promising disposition, then he would teach them in a few words the rules of three-part, and later of four-, five-, six-part, etc., writing, always providing them with examples to imitate. Josquin did not, however, consider all suited to learn composition; he judged that only those should be taught who were drawn to this delightful art by a special natural impulse.[1]

In the second part of his *Plain and Easy Introduction to Practical Music* (1597) Thomas Morley assumes that the same method is to be used, and though (being in a book) his examples are printed, the pupil is continually making remarks such as 'Now

1. Quoted by Reese, op. cit., p. 230.

122

I pray you set me a plainsong and I will try how I can sing upon it.'[1]

As a consequence of such training, a composer was a complete master of his art in both its theoretical and practical aspects. Sometimes, however, his training was interrupted. While still a choirboy, Lassus was kidnapped three times on account of the beauty of his voice; the last of these abductions resulted in his entering (at the age of thirteen) the choir of Ferdinand Gonzaga, Viceroy of Sicily. It is to be hoped that few choristers shared the experiences of the boy kidnapped by John Shepherd from Malmesbury, who was tied up and dragged all the way to Oxford.

Choirboys also received general education in the humanities. Those who were 'apprentice' composers were given opportunities to take their studies further. Consequently most of the leading musicians were good Latinists, not a few knew Greek, and many were skilled linguists.

POSTS AND PREFERMENT

Composers hoped to obtain their first salaried posts as singers in one of the chapels of the nobility or hierarchy, rather than in a cathedral or church choir where opportunities of taking part in music other than ecclesiastical were limited, if not non-existent. Even a junior post in a chapel involved many duties; in addition to singing at religious services, the members were expected to share in performances of chamber music, to teach noble amateurs singing and playing, and to provide a little music when required. A composer's future career would in all probability depend very largely on the manner in which he fulfilled the duties of his first post. If he pleased his employers, he might either be promoted to a larger share in musical activities, or be recommended for another post. The nobility competed with one another for the services of first-class men, tempting them with offers of high salaries. Many composers took advantage of this state of affairs to change employment

1. Modern edition by R. A. Harman (Dent, 1952).

fairly frequently and thus move around Europe, gaining varied experience.

The Diary of the Sistine choir, which provided the music for the daily services in the Pope's private chapel, records the election of new singers from 1535 onwards (all earlier entries have not survived); the names include many of the famous composers of the age. Some stayed in the choir permanently; others absented themselves for longer or shorter periods, and, though they were supposed to be fined for non-attendance, quite frequently had their pay continued without any cut; many would move on to another post after two or three years. The Diary contains details of fines for unpunctuality, of special celebrations, of presents made by the Pope to members on great feast-days, the date of each singer's death or resignation, and the name of his successor. The choir was required to sing during the papal meals on all important occasions. Pope Paul III (1534–49) increased the number of singers from twenty-two to thirty, and engaged a band of instrumentalists to join with the choir for his private entertainments. Both choir and band naturally accompanied the Pope whenever he went out of Rome; thus it is recorded that the musicians were given money to buy horses for the visit of the Pope to Nice in 1538 for the peace treaty between the Emperor Charles V and Francis I of France. Motets by members of the choir were sung to mark the occasion; one of these was composed by the Spaniard, Morales.

The Papal Chapel was naturally the most splendid, though the Imperial Chapel was almost its equal. But the deeds and duties of its members are typical of those of all the chapels and musical establishments of the age although not necessarily involving the top ranks of the ecclesiastical and political scene.

The constant competition for the services of composers ensured a high level in incomes. The Duke of Mantua, Guglielmo Gonzaga, paid Jachet de Wert a hundred gold crowns a year, allowed him free residence, 'board expenses for two persons, and medicines as required'. This was considered a very lucrative post. Most composers settled down in middle life as *maestro di cappella* of a church or a nobleman's establishment. A constant production of works was expected of them as part of their duties. Church posts involved harder and much more regular duties than those of a princely house; court composers managed to obtain prolonged leave of absence fairly frequently, but this was not often possible for the directors of church choirs who were bound by the daily requirements of the liturgy.

Lodovico Zacconi, who sang in some of the most famous choirs of Europe, wrote in his *Practical Music* (1592) that 'the singer lives surrounded by great admiration and esteem and is everywhere received with open arms. He is always considered a gentleman and is favoured and honoured by everyone.'[1] The same held true for composers. Some achieved high social rank: Lassus, for example, was knighted by the Emperor Maximilian II. Others, however, found that their participation in the life of the nobility had definitely marked limits: the composer Wert mentioned above fell in love with Tarquinia Molza, a famous poetess and one of the chief ladies at the court of the Duchess of Ferrara, but her family forbade the marriage. In addition, the lady, despite her considerable musical gifts, was dismissed from all her court appointments and banished by the Duchess to Modena. Wert was required to return quickly to his work at Mantua.

An interesting correspondence has survived which illustrates the relations between composer and patron. Guglielmo Gonzaga commissioned Palestrina in 1578 to write a set of Masses for the private use of the choir at St Barbara's, Mantua. The terms of the commission stated that the Masses were to be based on plainsong melodies selected and revised by the Duke. In the first of the letters, dated 18 October 1578, the Duke's agent informs his master that Palestrina has begun work on the first Mass and has played the opening movements to him on the lute; this Mass was sent to the duke on 1 November. After some discussion of the plainsong melodies and the Duke's revisions, Palestrina sent a second Mass on 15 November, a third on 10 December, and the last three on 21 March 1579, with a receipt for the payment received: one hundred gold

1. Lang, op. cit., p. 303.

scudi, a sum equal to almost half Palestrina's regular annual income at that time.

THE PERFORMANCE OF MUSIC

The sixteenth century has been called the age of *a cappella* music (i.e. unaccompanied choral singing) for so long that the musical man-in-the-street thinks of this method of perform-ance as typical of the period. The quotations in the previous chapter reveal the inaccuracy of this description. Plates 11 and 15 are typical of hundreds of prints and pictures illustrating the normal practice in church and chamber music. (Admittedly there were exceptions: for example, at Rome the Sistine Choir always sang liturgical music unaccompanied, and other church choirs did the same during the penitential seasons of the ecclesiastical year, Lent and Holy Week.) The term *a cappella* did not acquire its present meaning till the beginning of the seventeenth century when it was used as the opposite of the new term '*concertato*' which described the styles of Monte-verdi and his contemporaries. 'Whenever we refer to the renaissance as "the *a cappella* period" we unwittingly apply a Baroque term with questionable implications.'[1]

Title-pages of printed music often display woodcuts of the composer directing his *cappella*. Thus, one of Lassus's Masses shows him seated at the organ surrounded by singers and instrumentalists. Music printed towards the end of the century refers to alternative methods of performance in lengthy titles, which leave absolutely no doubt about the general use of such methods. Here are a few:

Adriano Willaert: *Ricercars suitable for singing and playing on any instrument* (1559)

Andrea Gabrieli: *Motets most suitable to be performed some-times by the living voice sometimes by all kinds of instruments* (1565)

Giovanni Bassano: *Fantasias for 3 voices for singing and playing on every kind of instrument* (1585)

1. Manfred Bukofzer, *Music in the Baroque Era* (Dent, 1947), p. 70.

John Wilbye: *The Second Set of Madrigals . . . apt both for
viols and voices* (1609)
Robert Jones: *The first set of madrigals for viols and voices,
or for voices alone, or as you please* (1607).

Note that instrumental music could be performed by voices
and vice versa. As far as ensemble performance was concerned
'instruments could be used more or less at the discretion of the
musical director of any particular performance; they might
replace the voices or they might double them.'[1] The universal
practice of interchanging musical media is further demonstrated by the great number of arrangements that survive:
madrigals arranged as pieces for wind instruments; part-songs
as lute, organ, and harpsichord music; dance-tunes converted
into solo songs, and so forth. The list could be extended considerably. Much music was also written and published in the
idiosyncratic styles of various instruments, but even this more

often than not was derived from vocal models. Example 13
shows three versions of the first bars of a three-part song by
Anerio, published in 1589. The music is printed on opposite
pages: the vocal setting on the left, the instrumental versions
on the right. Several other versions are made possible by

1. Thurston Dart, *The Interpretation of Music* (Hutchinson's University Library), p. 137. Chapter 7 of this book is a succinct discussion of the problems of Renaissance performance.

various combinations: e.g. of the soprano with the lute part to make an accompanied solo song.[1]

The written or printed appearance of the music does not necessarily give a true notion of its sound in performance, for the extemporized ornamentation of a written polyphonic part was an accepted feature of all performances. Numerous printed treatises set forth the principles and methods by which ornaments were to be applied. This practice, in which all professional singers and instrumentalists were trained, was termed *diminutio* (in English, 'division') since it involved the replacing ot longer notes by shorter. Example 14 shows the opening of the soprano part of Arcadelt's madrigal *O felici occhi mei* as it stands in the original, and as ornamented by Diego Ortiz in a treatise published at Rome in 1553.

Ornaments could be applied by one, several, or all parts, either as arranged in previous rehearsal, or introduced freely by performers. (An analogous practice can be seen today in the 'breaks' of jazz soloists.) In solo performance, or in the upper parts of ensemble performance, ornamentation was frequently a vehicle of virtuoso display. Example 15 is a portion of the vocal line of an accompanied solo madrigal by Luzzaschi, in which the composer adopted the unusual method of printing all the embellishments in full.

Allied to this technique was the very popular procedure of improvising one or more parts over a plainsong. In the Constitutions of the Papal Chapel drawn up in 1545 under Pope Paul III, the singers are required to have skill in 'inventing extempore additions over the tenor part', thus introducing

1. All music referred to in detail in this chapter is available either in *Historical Anthology of Music* or in vol. 4 of *History of Music in Sound*.

what John Dowland, in a charming translation of an early-sixteenth-century treatise, called 'sudden and unexpected music'. For a skilled musician educated in the manner previously discussed, such additions were not quite as difficult as the twentieth-century performer would think. Morley, in the work already quoted, takes the connexion between composition

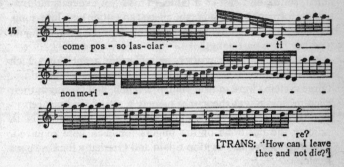

15

come pos - so las-ciar — — — -ti e____

non mo-ri — — — — — —

- — — — — — - re?

[TRANS: 'How can I leave thee and not die?']

and extemporization for granted. 'When one talks of a Descanter it must be understood of one that can, extempore, sing upon a plainsong.'

MANUSCRIPT AND PRINTED MUSIC

Two practical factors determined the written and printed appearance of sixteenth-century music: the cost of materials and production, and the method of performance. At the beginning of the century there were two methods for ensemble music, whether vocal or instrumental: the choirbook, and part-books. In the choirbook, all the parts of a polyphonic piece were set out separately on the left- and right-hand pages of an open book. The part-books were similar to those of modern orchestral and chamber music. As the century developed the part-book method became general, though the choirbook layout was still used, modified in details. Jacques Moderne of Lyons was perhaps the first printer to put two voice-parts in opposite directions on each page so that singers sitting on either side of a table could sing from the same volume.

Dowland's *Third Book of Airs* published in 1603 shows a further modification of choirbook layout: the soprano part with the lute accompaniment set directly underneath as in a modern accompanied song is placed on the left-hand page; the parts for the three lower voices are disposed on the right-hand page in such a way that they can be read by three singers seated north, south, and east of a table. (This layout reveals alternative performance methods: the piece can either be a lute-song, the singer accompanying himself, or four singers can join together for a part-song.)

Music for lute was written in *tablature*: a notation which showed the player where to place his fingers on the strings. Three systems were in use: Italian, French, and German; their basic principle was the same, namely a set of six lines representing the strings of the lute with letters or numbers to indicate the positions of the fingers for each note required. Tablatures were also used in Spain and Germany for keyboard music.

Italian keyboard music was usually written in a manner closely resembling that of present-day piano scores; the earliest printed examples were published in 1523. Towards the end of the century an alternative method was used called *partitura* in which a separate staff was used for each contrapuntal line of the composition. The first examples of *partitura* are arrangements of ensemble music, such as Cipriano de Rore's publication of 1577, *All the madrigals for four parts set out and arranged for playing on every sort of harmonic instrument* ('harmonic' implying organ and harpsichord, as opposed to 'melodic' instruments such as viols and wind).

Full scores were almost unknown in the sixteenth century.

Most composers made use of what were called *cartelle*: blank sheets of parchment or paper, incised with a dozen or more sets of stave-lines. A polyphonic composition would be drafted on these in pencil or ink; a set of parts could then be prepared from this score; and finally the original text could be erased with a single sweep of a wet rag or sponge, leaving the sheets clean and ready for future use.[1]

1. Dart, op cit., p. 134.

Occasionally a score was published for purposes of instruction and study. Paper, ink, and printing were all expensive, and thus copies of music were very costly, though manuscript copies were generally cheaper than printed publications.

Undoubtedly music-printing assisted the popularity and dissemination of music, but it should be remembered that the number of copies of a work printed in one edition was small by modern standards. From the contracts that have survived it appears that an average edition amounted to about 1,500 copies with a possible difference of 500 each way. On the other hand, a large number of compositions was published. The great houses of Petrucci in Venice, Attaingnant, Haultin, and Ballard in Paris, and many others, kept up a steady flow of publications which were sold throughout Europe. Naturally, printed music would have had a wider circulation than MSS.

Petrucci, though he was not by any means the first to print music, has been compared to Gutenberg; both were the first in their respective fields to accomplish printing in an important way. Petrucci's method employed double-printing: staves and notes were printed separately from metal type. In 1525, Pierre Haultin of Paris introduced musical type in which small fragments of staff were joined with the notes and thus achieved single-printing. His type was copied by Attaingnant and Ballard. Étienne Briard of Avignon (c. 1530) designed type with oval note-heads instead of the square and lozenge shapes of the earlier printers. The printers of the smaller publishing houses continued throughout the century to use engraved plates and even woodcut blocks as alternative processes to type-printing.

3. General Features of Sixteenth-Century Musical Development

THE amount of music that has survived from this period in prints and MSS. is enormous: a list of the several hundred composers alone would take many pages. What is more important is the general high artistic level maintained in the great majority of compositions. In this survey only the greatest names can be mentioned, and those but briefly, as the outstanding masters of what has long been called 'the Golden Age of music'.

THE INTERNATIONAL 'LANGUAGE' OF IMITATIVE COUNTERPOINTS

The achievements of Josquin and his French, Flemish, and Dutch contemporaries formed the stylistic basis for the main musical development of the rest of the century. Their pupils disseminated an international 'Flemish' style throughout Europe whose principles were followed by all composers. This style was grounded in an integrated method of composition by which all aspects of a work were considered in relation to the whole. The theorist Pietro Aron summarized this in his treatise *Il Toscanello in musica* (1523) when he wrote that 'the music of the moderns is better than that of the older composers because they consider all parts together and do not compose their voice-parts one after another'. The chief characteristics of the new style may be summarized thus: (1) a homogenous contrapuntal texture produced by maintaining the imitation of short motifs, each motif being discussed in a quasi-'fugal' passage; (2) an increased feeling for the expressive qualities of harmonies, not only in the succession of chords but also in the spacing of the parts and the planning of chordal sonorities; (3) the gradual abandonment of the older fixed forms such as the *cantus firmus* Mass, and the development of freer methods of construction involving varied repetition.

Considerations of texture are fundamental in any discussions of sixteenth-century music. The technique of imitative counter-points produced a polyphonic web of sound in which every note was supplied by the melodic design of each part, all being logically ordered by the interchange of motifs. Josquin's successors tended to avoid strict (canonic) imitation and to repeat a motif several times in each part before proceeding to the next. The resulting plasticity of treatment became the basis of a virtuoso contrapuntal style whose capacities for producing varied beauty of expressive sound have probably never been surpassed. Nevertheless, the modern listener should bear in mind that this music can only be appreciated in one of two ways which are mutually exclusive: he can share in the performance, relishing the beauty of his part and its relation to the whole; or he can remain outside the performance, enjoying the total sound, but inevitably missing much of the melodic and rhythmic detail. This ambivalent approach reflects the social orientation of Renaissance music-making: music was not merely something to be listened to but an activity to be shared; hence it was more important for the composer to please the performers than to gratify the passive listener.

Example 16 shows the first fourteen measures of Palestrina's motet *Sicut cervus*. If the reader plays (or, preferably, sings) each vocal line, he will have analysed a typical treatment of 'a point of imitation' in detail. The first six bars of the tenor form a motif which is taken up by the other voices. The last ten beats of this become a subsidiary pattern which is expanded by the alto in bars 8–9 and by the soprano in bars 9–13. Since modern bar lines tend to give a false impression, the first ten measures are printed here with score lines *between* the staves only: each part is thus written in a manner which closely approximates to that of the original part-book. These measures may be compared with bars 11–14 representing the usual practice of modern editions. At first sight the $\frac{4}{4}$ time signature appears meaningless, since the metre of the individual parts is obviously variable. (The notes that receive accentual stress in performance are marked > ; for the most part they coincide with those set to the stressed syllables of the text: *Sícut cérvus desíderat ad fóntes aquárum.*) The alto part, for instance, if barred according to modern principles of notation, has the shifts of metre illustrated in Example 17. Time signatures in the music of this period have practically nothing to do with the metrical structure of the melodic lines. They indicate a fundamental grouping of 'strong' and 'weak' beats, whose relation

[TRANS: 'As the hart panteth after the waterbrooks']

134

to the musical rhythm is analogous to that between the metre of a poem and the rhythm of its verse, and which provides an essential framework for the organization of the harmony. Palestrina's style represents the final systematization of this treatment of dissonance, being the culmination of a development that begins with Josquin. All cadences have their final chord on a 'strong' beat (e.g. bar 13); 'prepared dissonances' (or 'suspensions') are consonant notes held over from a weak beat to make a dissonant interval on the succeeding strong beat, moving by step to another consonance on the next weak beat. Thus in Example 16 the minim F in the twelfth bar of the soprano makes a third with the tenor D on the second beat, but becomes a fourth with the C on the 'strong' third beat; this latter interval is a dissonance, so the soprano moves down to E on the fourth beat to make another third with the tenor.

Since each individual line is free in rhythm and arises normally out of the natural stress of a verbal text, or at least from the implications of a vocal mode of thought, and since the lines habitually overlap, any vertical cross-section taken at a given moment must reveal a combination of stresses of different intensities ... The metrical beat is rendered plastic and fluid and deprived of obviousness by the interwoven rhythms, and these are deprived of aggressiveness by the balance and proportion of the collective rhythm.[1]

THE MODES, AND CHANGING NOTIONS OF HARMONY

Since the main impulse of musical composition was still primarily melodic, most problems of technique tended to be discussed from a melodic or linear standpoint. The theorists, whose opinions for the most part lagged considerably behind the practice of the composers, clung to the language of traditional description and attempted to define the new musical idiom in terms of the older modal theory. Although the major and minor scales had been more or less in use from the middle

1. Wilfrid Mellers, *Music and Society* (Dobson, 1946), pp. 48–9 (1st edition).

of the fifteenth century they were not included in the 'official' list of modes till a hundred years later. In his *Dodecachordon* (1547) Glareanus advocates a system of twelve modes, authentic and plagal forms of the major (Ionian) and minor (Aeolian) modes being added to the previously acknowledged eight. When, however, he comes to analyse Josquin's works, his terminology is manifestly incapable of providing a useful description of the composer's tonal organization. Previous theorists had agreed for convenience to regard the mode of a bass-part of a composition as the mode of the entire work. But Glareanus not only has to admit the simultaneous use of authentic and plagal forms of a mode in different voices as a habitual feature of Josquin's procedure, but is forced to talk of combinations of different modes and of single parts changing from one mode to another. The modal terminology survived to the end of the century, though it bore less and less relevance to the facts of musical development. By 1600 the major scale had virtually absorbed the Lydian and Mixolydian modes, while Dorian and Phrygian merged into the minor scales.

It is still sometimes asserted that sixteenth-century music is 'built on modal harmony'. This is false. As the preceding paragraph has shown, musicians considered modes to be melodic phenomena and nothing else. Harmony was chiefly thought of as a combination of concordant intervals. From the beginning of the century the theorists compiled tables of suitable mixtures of intervals which produced what would now be called triads in root position and first inversion. These chords, however, were not organized by the functional methods of later centuries: the notion of a succession of chords either implying a key, or the movements of whose notes were rigorously controlled by established rules, was unknown. Only at cadences was there a feeling for harmonic progression which revealed itself in prescribed patterns; every theorist writing in the second half of the century gave stock formulas for cadences in various groupings of parts. The apparent strangeness of much of the harmony of this period to the untutored ear is solely due to the absence of the functional and tonal patterns that dominate music from Bach to Wagner. On the other hand, the later composers of the century exhibit a preference for chords whose order and progressions at times approximate very closely to later notions of major-scale and minor-scale harmonic tonality.

The treatment of dissonance previously mentioned, which is one of the chief differences between the harmonic technique of the fifteenth century and that of the sixteenth, was first employed at cadences. The earlier period had only permitted dissonance as a minor incident of texture: it was confined to the weak part of a beat. This method remained a standard procedure (the quavers of Example 18 provide examples) but the

use of prepared dissonances became more and more important as their expressive effects were explored. By the end of the century they could pervade the entire texture. Zarlino wrote in his *Foundations of Harmony* (1558) that

a dissonance causes the consonance which immediately follows it to seem more acceptable. Thus it is perceived and recognized with greater pleasure by the ear, just as after darkness light is more acceptable and delightful to the eye, and after the bitter the sweet is more luscious and palatable.[1]

Chromaticism (the use of notes extraneous to the diatonic scale) was another important device in the technique of the later composers of the period, though as far as the majority

1. Strunk, *Source Readings in Music History*, p. 272.

were concerned its employment remained occasional and incidental. The term 'chromatic' could also refer to the written appearance of the music. Madrigals were frequently described as *cromatici* because they used notes of short time-value (crotchets and quavers) which, being filled-in black, were thus 'coloured' in contrast to the 'white' open notes, semibreve and minim. Example 19 is fairly representative. Some composers experimented more freakishly. One of the most controversial figures was Vicentino (1511–72) whose *Ancient Music Adapted to Modern Principles* (1555) urged the adoption

GALLUS 'Mirabile mysterium'

[TRANS: 'Nature is made new']

of what he imagined to be Greek principles of tuning and modulation. He distinguished five divisions of the whole tone and devised signs for large and small major and minor seconds. In his fifth book of madrigals (1572) he employed such rarely-used accidentals as D sharp, and D flat. Another composer, Matthaeus Greiter, published in 1553 a piece called *Passibus ambiguis* ('proceeding by doubtful steps') which begins with an F-major triad and finishes on an F-flat triad; several passages, when transcribed into modern notation, require the use of double-flats.

WORDS AND MUSIC

The Renaissance humanists wished to revive the music of classical antiquity, but, since practically none of it had survived, were confined to speculations based on musical treatises. Since these treatises revealed the importance attached by the ancient writers to the text and to the close imitation of the verbal rhythm and metre by the music, composers attempted to recreate at least the spirit of the classical art by devising settings of classical poetry. Josquin, for example, set passages from the *Aeneid*. Experiments such as these led to increasing emphasis on questions of word-setting in all fields of vocal music. The German composer Hermann Finck remarked in his *Practical Music* (1556) that 'the newer composers are superior to the older in the matter of euphony and are specially eager to fit the notes to the words of the texts in order to render their meaning and mood with the greatest clarity.' As the century progressed 'the meaning and mood' of words came more and more to influence the composers' criteria of melody, rhythm, harmony, and texture. Example 16 illustrates the correspondence of verbal and musical rhythms. Word-painting of two kinds is shown by Examples 18 and 19: the first depicts 'painful melancholy' by piling up suspended dissonances; the second conveys the astonishment of the world at the birth of Christ by using an 'innovatory' technique. Thomas Morley, writing at the end of the century, sums up the prevailing attitude in a charming passage of detailed advice on 'dittying' (i.e. the setting of words to music).

It follows to show you how to dispose your music according to the nature of the words which you are therein to express, as whatsoever matter it be which you have in mind such a kind of music must you frame to it. You must therefore, if you have a grave matter, apply a grave kind of music to it; if a merry subject you must make your music also merry, for it will be a great absurdity to use a sad harmony to a merry matter or a merry harmony to a sad, lamentable, or tragical ditty.

You must then when you would express any word signifying hardness, cruelty, bitterness, and other such like make the harmony like unto it, that is, somewhat harsh and hard, but yet so that it offend not. Likewise when any of your words shall express complaint, sorrow, repentance, sighs, tears, and such like let your harmony be sad and doleful. So that if you would have your music signify hardness, cruelty, or other such emotions you must cause the parts to proceed in their rhythms without the minim, that is, you must cause them to proceed by semibreves with major thirds, and major sixths and such like (these intervals being reckoned from the bass); you may also use cadences with suspended fourths or sevenths which, being in long notes, will exasperate the harmony. But when you would express a lamentable passion then you must use rhythms proceeding by minims with minor thirds and minor sixths, which of their nature are sweet, especially being taken in the true tune and natural air with discretion and judgement.

Morley then notes the different effects produced by diatonic and chromatic writing. The diatonic 'serves to express cruelty, tyranny, and bitterness' and the chromatic 'grief, weeping, sighs, and sobs'. He continues:

If the subject be light you must cause your music to go in rhythms which carry with them a quickness of time; if it be lamentable the notes must go in slow and heavy rhythms; and of all this you shall find examples everywhere in the works of the good musicians ... We must also have a care so to apply the notes to the words as in singing there be no barbarism committed; that is, that we cause no syllable which is by nature short to be expressed by many notes or one long note, nor no long syllables to be expressed with a short note.

Morley gives here only general recommendations: neither he nor any other composer of the period would express 'cruelty' invariably by semibreves and major intervals any more than they would always use minims and minor intervals for 'lamentable passions'. Nevertheless his remarks present an accurate picture of the general manner in which composers sought to illustrate verbal images and descriptions by musical means. The principles he states hold good in reverse: if a piece employs chromaticism and so forth, this is nearly always because the composer intends to express extra-musical ideas. For example, the work by Greiter mentioned previously may seem at first sight perversely ingenious. But when it is seen to be built on a phrase from a *chanson* by Josquin entitled *Fortuna desperata*, the meaning of the enharmonic and chromatic devices becomes clear: they symbolize the changes of Fortune and the effects of these on men's lives.[1]

INSTRUMENTAL WRITING

The technique of imitative counterpoints represents only one pole of sixteenth-century development. The other is the influence and growth of instrumental music. Throughout the period, dance, lute, and keyboard music focused attention on homophonic texture and chordal writing. In the compositions produced during the second half of the century, contrapuntal and homophonic textures are to be found both blended and contrasted in styles increasingly idiomatic for the different instruments. Though detailed discussion is best deferred to the sixth section of this chapter, the presence of instruments and the influence of instrumental techniques should not be forgotten during the survey of what are called (largely for convenience of classification) 'vocal' forms.

1. cf. Edward E. Lowinsky, 'Matthaeus Greiter's *Fortuna*', in the *Musical Quarterly*, vol. 42, p. 500.

4. Chanson, Madrigal, and Allied Forms

FRENCH VERSE AND CHANSON

THE reign of Francis I (1515–47) witnessed the commencement of a period of fruitful exchange between the arts of Italy and France. Francis's love of Italian painting and sculpture was equalled by his admiration for Italian music. Many Italian musicians were employed at the French court, and Italian musical publications were consequently in great demand among the nobility and wealthy bourgeoisie. The resulting interaction of French and Italian musical styles was of primary importance in the complex development of the sixteenth-century *chanson* and madrigal, in which four main strands may be distinguished: (1) the movement among French poets towards simpler and more direct forms of expression, and the effects of this on lyric poetry; (2) the influence of the Italian *frottola* and *strambotto*, whose chordal style and syllabic treatment attracted composers setting the new verse; (3) the overriding influence of the great Flemish composers, many of whom wrote both *chansons* and *frottole*; (4) the dissemination of *chansons* in Italian publications and the influence of their style on that of the first madrigals.

Clément Marot (1496–1554) was the foremost of a new generation of poets whose work displayed the influence of popular verse. Abandoning previous attempts to imitate classical poetic forms, he employed short stanzas without (generally speaking) any stereotyped scheme. His language was colloquial, sometimes almost rustic, and included traces of Provençal dialect. An important result of his work and that of his contemporaries was the establishment of the alternation of masculine and feminine rhymes as a prevailing feature of French verse. Such poetry found a ready response from composers who were reacting against the mensural complexities and canons of Josquin's generation. They set it to music which emphasized the colloquial rhythms of speech and the simple organization of the verse.

The leaders of the new school of *chanson* composition were Claudin de Sermisy (*c.* 1490–1562) and Clément Janequin (*c.* 1490–1561). Although, like the vast majority of the composers of this period, they wrote both religious and secular works, they gained their greatest fame from their *chansons*. Claudin entered the royal service at the age of eighteen, becoming assistant director of the Royal Chapel on the accession of Francis I. Over 200 of his *chansons* were published during his lifetime. They are mainly chordal in style, the voices having simple melodic lines with syllabic treatment of the text. Frequent repeated notes convey the colloquial rhythm of the verse, though a strong syllable near the end of a phrase is often set to a group of rapid notes. Imitation is employed sparingly, being confined for the most part to the longer *chansons*. Many pieces commence with the rhythm ♩ ♩ ♩ (a feature of the *strambotto*) which came to be regarded by later Italian imitators as a characteristic *chanson* opening. The musical form frequently mirrors the rhyme-scheme: a typical method is to give the third and fourth lines of a seven-line stanza (rhyming *ab ab cc d*) the same music as the first and second and to repeat words and music of the final line. Such simplicity is well suited to the amateur performance for which so many of these works were intended. Musical repetition is a characteristic of the sixteenth-century *chanson* and, while its use varied with the individual composer, forms one of the chief marks that distinguish a true *chanson* from a madrigal. *Chanson* form is modelled on its verse structure: the madrigal is shaped by following the *ideas* expressed in its verse.

Janequin's popularity was even greater than Claudin's. After many years in the service of princes and ecclesiastics he was given in 1555 the title of 'composer-in-ordinary' to the king, being the first recipient of this honour. Altogether 286 of his *chansons* survive, most of them in Attaingnant's publications. They display great variety of treatment, some being of the Claudin type, others using frequent imitation and even canon. His most striking works are the so-called 'programme *chansons*'; one famous piece, *La Guerre* (a description of the Battle of Marignan, which the composer witnessed) inspired numerous imitations and arrangements. It employs vivid tone-painting, including onomatopoeic effects such as the imitation of trumpet fanfares and galloping horses, and symbolizing the confusion of the fighting by mingling binary and ternary rhythms. These devices appear in other programmatic pieces: *The Song of the Birds*, *The Hunt*, and *The Cries of Paris*. Passages like Example 20, from *The Lark* (occuring frequently and often continued for long stretches), may seem dull to the modern listener since they possess little melodic or harmonic interest,

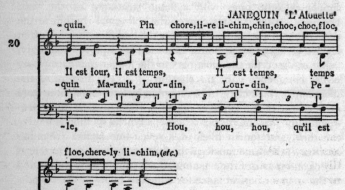

but are full of excitement for the performers. To take part in any of Janequin's programme *chansons* is a very enjoyable experience, not less so when the text (as not infrequently happens) includes passages reminiscent of Rabelais. Rabelais mentions both Claudin and Janequin in a catalogue of famous composers in *Gargantua and Pantagruel*, Book IV.

CHANSONS BY FLEMISH COMPOSERS

During the first half of the century Flemish composers maintained their position as the leaders of musical culture, being found in all the chief musical establishments throughout Europe. Consequently, although the work of Claudin, Janequin, and their followers was important, especially in relation to the development of more consciously national French art and of Italian instrumental music (cf. Part V), it had very little influence on the tradition of *chanson* composition represented by Josquin. This tradition continued unbroken till Lassus, in whose works the polyphonic *chanson* achieved its greatest heights and culmination. Josquin's pupils and successors developed his method of combining polyphonic treatment with clear-cut formal organization. The *chansons* of Nicholas Gombert (*c.* 1480–1556), who became director of Charles V's Chapel in 1529, show a fondness for imitation at very close rhythmic intervals producing a closely woven texture similar to that of his motets. Occasionally he uses canon, in which he is followed by Willaert, Arcadelt, and Rore. Lassus (1532–94) writing later in the century and influenced by madrigal styles, wrote only one *chanson* in canon, preferring to employ a remarkably free and varied technique of imitation which he combined with homophonic elements in the Claudin manner. His *chansons* range from simple chordal pieces like *Bonjour, mon cœur* to settings of poems such as Du Bellay's *rondeau, La nuict froide et sombre,* from humorous jingles to biting satire. Some were among the most popular pieces of the time: one in particular was reprinted in pirate editions several times, each time to a different text, and appears in Shakespeare's *Henry IV, Part 2* (V, 3) as a song called 'Samingo'.

THE LATER FRENCH CHANSON

Towards the middle of the century a reaction developed against the poetry of Marot. Ronsard and Du Bellay, leaders of the group of poets called the Pléiade, sought 'to glorify and ennoble' the French language by fostering the imitation of classical styles, purifying grammar and avoiding colloquial diction. Above all they desired the restoration of the lyric ideal of the Greeks: the combination of verse and music in expressing emotion. Ronsard, describing his poems as 'marvellously suited to music', desired polyphonic settings. Seldom, if ever, have composers taken a poet so promptly at his word: the greatest composers of the day, including Janequin and Lassus, vied in setting Ronsard's verse, some publishing collections entirely devoted to his work. Guillaume Costeley (c. 1531–1606) who set amongst other poems by Ronsard the well-known *Mignonne, allons voir*, and Claude Goudimel (d. 1572) both based the formal structure of their music on that of the verse; for example, the two quatrains of a sonnet's octave would have the same music, while the sestet would be through-composed. Other composers experimented with chromatic and enharmonic devices (including quarter-tones) in their efforts to match the force of the poet's inspirations.

Du Bellay and Ronsard stressed the essential characteristic of French when they wrote that it 'has not long and short syllables'; Baif, a younger member of the Pléiade, disagreed. In 1570, Baif established an 'Academy of poetry and music' (in imitation of the Italian *Accademie*) which aimed at the production and performance of *musique mesurée*, a setting of

CLAUDE LE JEUNE

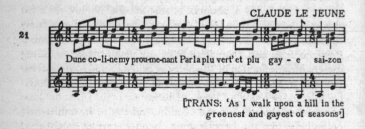

21

Dune co-li-ne my prou-me-nant Par la plu vert' et plu gay - e sai-zon

[TRANS: 'As I walk upon a hill in the greenest and gayest of seasons']

what he called *vers mesuré* in which the 'long' and 'short' syllables of the text were matched by long and short notes, each long note being exactly twice the length of a short. The text, since it decided the music's rhythm and form, had to be pronounced simultaneously by all voices. Claude Le Jeune (c. 1525–1600) was the most brilliant composer of the group centred round the Academy. Example 21 is fairly typical of his work in this style. He was, however, too versatile to confine himself to so limited a means of expression; he wrote several books of polyphonic *chansons*, some of which reveal his interest in the word-painting devices of the later Italian madrigalists.

GENESIS OF THE ITALIAN MADRIGAL

The first madrigals represent the convergence of two lines of artistic development, literary and musical. During the fifteenth century Italian vernacular literature had declined in prestige under the weight of the vogue for neo-classical Latin prose and verse. Its return to favour was largely the work of Cardinal Bembo (1470–1547) who strove by his writings and patronage to restore the standards of taste current in the times of Dante and Petrarch. Through his efforts and under the influence of his ideals, the new generation of poets at the beginning of the sixteenth century gradually abandoned the sentimental style and weak rhythms characteristic of earlier *frottola* verse and initiated a return to the older lyric forms of *canzona*, sonnet, and *ballata*. The poetic madrigal (so named in conscious archaism although it had nothing in common with the fourteenth-century form) was a *canzona* of one stanza, having no fixed rhyme-scheme or number of lines, but maintaining as a fairly constant feature a seven- or eleven-syllable metre for its verse. Between 1520 and 1530 settings of the new *canzone* revealing the growing influence of the *chanson* replaced the more serious types of *frottola*. The first madrigals were published in part-book form by Valerio Dorico of Rome in 1530. Most of these were either chordal like the Claudin *chanson* or intermittently polyphonic like the later *frottola*. Later examples established the characteristic features of the form, which was designed to express in detail the meaning, mood, and imagery of a poem having some literary importance, particular attention being given to the accurate declamation of the text. Hence the strophic forms of the *chanson* were abandoned since different verses could not be adequately expressed by the same music. The texture, composed of a combination having voices of equal importance, could be either chordal or contrapuntal, imitation, though frequent, being employed more to stress the independence of the voices and for textual illustration than for purely musical reasons.

Many early madrigals were designed as serenades addressed to the *madonne* (i.e. courtesans) of the larger Italian cities by noblemen and wealthy merchants. As the century advanced, the ideal 'lady' of the madrigalists became more refined; coarseness disappeared from the texts, and expressions of 'Platonic' love took their place. Although erotic themes formed the subject of the great majority of poems set by the madrigalists, philosophical, moralistic, and descriptive poems were frequently chosen for the opportunities they presented for word-painting.

Twentieth-century performances of madrigals are generally completely misleading. The choral singing of madrigals bears as little relation to the composer's intention as the performance of a string quartet by a string orchestra. Madrigals are chamber music requiring one voice (or instrument) to a part; any additions merely thicken the texture and obscure detail.[1]

THE FLEMISH MADRIGALISTS

Flemish composers were the leaders in the first period of madrigal development. Verdelot (d. 1540) shares with the Italian Costanzo Festa the distinction of being the first to write pieces expressly designated as madrigals; both are represented in Dorico's publication mentioned previously. Verdelot's first works exemplify the retention in the early madrigals of such *chanson* features as repetition of the final line of the text with its music and predominantly chordal movement. In his later madrigals, which include many for five and six parts in addition to those in three and four, contrapuntal writing and imitation become more prominent. His works were so popular that in 1536 Willaert published arrangements of twenty-two for solo voice and lute. Jacques A. Arcadelt (c. 1504–67), first active at Florence and later at Rome, where he joined the Sistine Choir in 1539, also reveals *chanson* affinities

1. Ceremonial madrigals of the type described in the first section of this chapter are exceptions to this general rule.

in his early madrigals; his later books develop a more characteristically Italian style, especially noteworthy for its melodic sweetness, combined with typically Flemish employment of contrapuntal devices. The four-part *Voi ve n'andat' al cielo*, published in 1539, contrasts a motet-technique of imitation at the opening, with later use of chords in triple time to express a change of mood. In *S'infinita bellezza* (from his third book, 1544) the soprano and tenor move in canon throughout while the other parts imitate them closely. His popularity surpassed Verdelot's: his first book of madrigals was reprinted thirty-three times in the century following his death.

Adriano Willaert (*c.* 1500–62), who as *maestro di cappella* at St Mark's, Venice, profoundly influenced all later Italian composers, was the first to use chromaticism extensively in the madrigal. His works reveal the typically Venetian love of colour in their expressive use of harmonies and contrasts of vocal texture. A contemporary description of a performance of Willaert's madrigals emphasizes this expressiveness: 'the music so wonderfully adorns the words that I confessed not to have known what music was in all save for that evening.' Cipriano de Rore (*c.* 1516–65), who studied with Willaert at Venice, followed his master in the search for expressive techniques. He began a fashion which continued to the end of the madrigal period for illustrating as sharply and clearly as possible not only the emotional qualities of the text but the meanings of important words. Some of his methods can be seen in *Da le belle contrade* for five voices: in Example 22(*a*) the chromaticism expressing 'cruel love', in Example 22(*b*) the use of reiteration for 'repeated embraces'. *O morte, eterno fin*, designed for the end of a tragedy performed at the court of Ferrara, shows his more usual serious style and his customary employment of close motet-like polyphonic texture. Rore is one of the first composers to disregard the structure of the poetic line and the rhyme scheme in his settings: the delineation of the verbal content overrides all other considerations. Some of his contemporaries and pupils employed the device known as 'eye-music' whereby the ideas expressed in the text are conveyed by the written appearance of the music. Thus 'day' would be set to semibreves and minims ('white' notes) and 'night' to crotchets and quavers ('black' notes).

In the widely-varied compositions of Lassus and Philippe de Monte (1521–1603) the 'Italo-Flemish' madrigal reaches its culmination. Both men were extraordinarily prolific, but whereas Lassus's madrigals form a comparatively small part of his output, Monte published a total of 1,100 in forty-one volumes. *Verament in amore*[1] is fairly typical; it was one of Monte's most popular works.

THE ITALIAN MADRIGALISTS

Music in the Low Countries was unfavourably affected in the later years of the century by the troubled social and political conditions resulting from Spanish repression and Calvinist intrigue. The Italian pupils of the Flemish émigré composers therefore came to the fore as the new leaders of musical

CIPRIANO DE RORE

22

[TRANS: (a) 'Ah cruel love, uncertain and brief are thy joys'
(b) 'Repeating embraces in so many coils']

1. *The Golden Age of the Madrigal*, selected and edited A. Einstein, No. 5 (Schirmer).

development. In their hands the madrigal tends to become more and more dramatic in its concern for colourful representation of the text and vivid representation of personal emotion. The composer Mazzone summed up the prevailing feature of the later madrigal when he wrote: 'The notes are the body of the music, but the words are the soul.'

The Venetian, Andrea Gabrieli (1520–86), who studied with Willaert and became organist at St Mark's in 1564, was one of the first to emphasize these trends. Though his youthful efforts are sometimes conservative – *Ecco l'aurora* (1556) is written in the manner of a narrative *chanson* – his later madrigals employ *cori spezzati* (double 'choirs'), passionate rising progressions of chromatic harmonies, and choral recitative, techniques even more frequent in his religious works. His nephew, pupil, and successor at St Mark's, Giovanni Gabrieli (1557–1612), developed his polychoral style still further, displaying a fondness for the rapid melodic movement of one part over block harmonies. Though the textures of his madrigals are generally less polyphonic than those of his contemporaries, he can use contrapuntal devices with brilliant effect: one madrigal (written at the age of eighteen) for twelve voices has a preponderance of elaborate twelve-part counterpoint.

Luca Marenzio (1553–99) was the supreme master of the Italian madrigal. He excelled in highly detailed and literal word-painting; a typical example (Example 23) occurs in the

six-part *Cedan l'antiche* where he depicts the pillars of ancient Roman architecture by chords and the arches by descending and ascending scales: symbols which are not only immediately obvious to the ear but visible in the graphic layout. His word-painting, however minute in its details, is always at the service of the musical organization by reason of the malleability of his motifs. An analysis of the opening lines of the epithalamium *Scendi dal paradiso* illustrates the employment of varied motifs to build a musical development that is formally satisfying.

Scendi dal paradiso Venere (Descend from Paradise, O Venus)	downward leap of fifth on the first word, followed by a descending scale in crotchets, the whole motif being treated in imitation;
e teco guida I pargoletti amor (and bring with you your little Cupids)	block harmonies with rhythm ♩. ♪ ♩ ♩ on *pargoletti*;
le gratie e'l riso (may the Graces and Laughter)	rising two-quaver motif for *gratie*, descending four-quaver motif for *riso*, repeated polyphonically;
oltre l'usato rida (laugh more than usual)	*rida* is set to a motif of semiquavers and quavers bound together by ties into a rapid tangle of close imitation leading to a cadence.

The increase of rhythmic excitement, the brief but important contrast of homophony with counterpoint, and the manner in which the melismas of *rida* lead logically to a cadence marking the end of the poem's first section, are all typical of Marenzio's virtuoso technique.

Madrigals by Luzzasco Luzzaschi (d. 1607), a pupil of Rore, illustrate the increasing use of chromaticism towards the end of the century. The most famous is *Quivi sospiri*, a five-part setting of lines from Dante's *Inferno* describing the state of those 'sad souls who in life earned neither praise or blame'. Whereas Luzzaschi's chromaticism is conceived melodically, that of his contemporary Gesualdo (c. 1560–1613) depends more often on the block contrast of unrelated harmonies. A passage such as Example 24 almost seems to have been

[TRANS: 'Ah, pitiless heart']

discovered at the keyboard. Gesualdo's vocal writing is frequently awkward: leaps of augmented and diminished intervals increase the difficulties of intonation present in all his chromatic passages. His experiments were not continued by other composers, though they were much admired.

Several of the later madrigalists devised series of madrigals that presented narratives in quasi-dramatic form. One of the first, *The Chattering of the Women at the Laundry* by Alessandro Striggio (1535–87), appeared in 1567. Much more famous was *L'Amfiparnaso* by Orazio Vecchi (1550–1605) which contained fifteen pieces, all save one for five voices, grouped into a prologue and three acts. The characters of the tale were reminiscent of the traditional figures of the *commedia dell'arte*. Stage production was not intended, for as Vecchi observed in his preface, 'this drama is observed with the mind, which it enters through the ears and not the eyes'.

The trend towards dramatic expression, which is evident also in religious music and which led at the beginning of the seventeenth century to opera, reaches its peak in the madrigals of Monteverdi. Whereas his early books contain examples of all the chief Renaissance madrigal styles (perhaps the best known being the setting of Tasso's *Ecco mormorar l'onde*), Book IV emphasizes *parlando* rhythms and choral recitative. In Book V Monteverdi provides a *basso continuo* accompaniment, an overt sign of the new Baroque styles. Book VI, the last to contain true madrigals, includes an arrangement of the

aria *Lasciatemi morire* from his opera *Arianna*; its opening bars
(Example 25) show a treatment of dissonance that is wholly
alien to the older style.

THE LIGHTER FORMS

The lighter type of *frottola* was superseded by a variant of the
strambotto originating at Naples called the *villanesca* (later,
villanella) which may be regarded as a less sophisticated and
more folk-like counterpart of the early madrigal. It gave rise
to many subsidiary forms, nearly all of which preserved the
sectional repetitions, the chordal style, and syllabic rhythms
inherited from the *frottola*. Later in the century, versions of the
villanella to various dialects became extremely popular; some
of these, such as the *bergamasca* and *moresca*, later developed
into dances. Another type, the *villota*, generally based on street-
songs, used refrains of nonsense syllables. At the end of the
century came the *balletto*, 'a slight kind of music devised to

be danced to voices' (Morley), presenting precise rhythms disposed in two sections, each being repeated and ending in a refrain to such syllables as 'Fa-la'. The most famous composer of *balletti* was Gastoldi; several of his pieces were closely imitated by Morley. Madrigal composers wrote in these forms also: commencing with Willaert's publication of four-part *villanesche* a steady stream of *villanesche*, *moresche*, and the rest was maintained by the leading musicians of Italy.

THE GERMAN LIED

German polyphonic song continued for the first half of the century in the tradition established by Finck and Isaac. The leading composer of this period was Ludwig Senfl (*c.* 1490– *c.* 1556) whose *Lieder*, though their technique remains heavily indebted to the older Flemish style, have a great range of emotional expression. Many use a *cantus firmus* method of construction and close if sometimes free imitation in the other voices.

A new period commenced in 1556 with the publication of *canzonas* by Scandello (a member of the Dresden Chapel), the first collection of Italian vocal music to appear in Germany. In the following year, Lassus, resident at Munich where he remained till his death, published the first of six books entitled *New German Songs for five voices . . . to sing and use on all sorts of instruments*. These included both secular and religious works. The former reveal many characteristics derived from the madrigal, such as chromaticism and word-painting; the influence of the *chanson* and *villanella* is seen in the large proportion of monophonic writing. But the German language is set to music in a manner worthy of a native-born composer.

The last great *Lied* composer of the century, Hans Leo Hassler (1564–1612), studied with Andrea Gabrieli at Venice. His Italian madrigals (published 1596) are worthy to stand beside those of his master. Though, like Lassus, he incorporates madrigalian devices in his *Lieder*, he returns for the most part to the older German habit of keeping the main melody in the top voice. The *New German songs in the manner of madrigals* (1596) are rather too chordal for the most part to have a truly madrigalian flavour, and the same holds true for his collection of vocal and instrumental works of 1601, *A Pleasure Garden of new German songs, ballets, galliards, and intradas*. His melodies are distinctive and easily memorized; one love-song which rapidly became very popular was *Mein gmüth ist mir verwirret*, later adapted to the Passion chorale *O Haupt voll Blut und Wunden*.

5. Church Music

THE FORMS OF MASS AND MOTET

Music for the Ordinary of the Mass continued to develop along the lines established by Josquin and his contemporaries, the forms most frequently employed being those which depended on the use of pre-existent material. These comprised:

(1) The tenor *cantus firmus* Mass, which tended to drop out of fashion as the century advanced, though examples occur as late as 1600 (e.g. Palestrina's *Missa Octavi toni*, published in that year).

(2) The 'paraphrase' Mass, based on the material of a monophonic model freely developed by imitative techniques; the chief types were:

(*a*) plainsong paraphrases, in which each movement was built on material taken from the corresponding movements of a Gregorian Mass, there being thus no thematic connexion between the movements;

(*b*) plainsong paraphrases, all of whose movements shared the same material derived from a Gregorian hymn, sequence, or antiphon;

(*c*) 'alternation' Masses, in which alternate sections of a Gregorian Mass were replaced by polyphony based on the material of the displaced plainsong sections;

(*d*) paraphrases based on secular tunes.

(3) The 'parody' Mass, built on a polyphonic model. Apart from these was the so-called 'free' Mass, constructed with entirely new material.

'Parody' technique holds an important place in sixteenth-century Mass composition: Lassus and Palestrina, for example, employ it in three-quarters of their Masses. Whereas Josquin's parody Masses rely mainly on the elaboration of the melodies of his models, the later composers concentrate more and more on the expansion of all aspects of the model, including harmonic and textural elements in addition to melodic patterns.

Secular and religious models continue to be used in equal proportions.

The term 'motet' covers not only motets properly so-called but includes polyphonic settings of the Proper Mass and Office texts, the canticles, and the psalms. The 'classical motet style' of the sixteenth-century motet developed in all these forms, but while the motet proper was always polyphonic throughout, the settings of Proper chants and psalms generally involved alternate use of chant sections. Many motets were divided into two parts, each part being complete in itself; the second part often began with a change from duple to triple time.

RELIGIOUS POLYPHONY AFTER JOSQUIN

Gombert is the leading composer of the generation succeeding Josquin. In his motets the technique of continuous imitation so characteristic of the rest of the century is present in full force. Whereas Josquin generally uses a motif only once in each part Gombert often reworks it several times before proceeding to the next. His dislike of strict forms and repetitions (already mentioned as a feature of his *chansons*) is shown by his infrequent use of *cantus firmus* methods of organization, as also by his asymmetrical numbers of motif-entries in different voices. In *Super flumina Babylonis* (Example 26), a typical example of

GOMBERT

26

Su - per flumina Babylo-nis. illic se - di - mus

In sa-li-ci-bus Et qui ab-du - xe-runt nos.

his motet style, another characteristic trait can be seen: a cunningly varied development by means of rhythmic shifts and suspensions of motifs that nevertheless preserve a fundamental family resemblance. Gombert's Masses are rather more conservative than his motets: several depend on *cantus firmus* technique. His parody Masses begin and end each movement with the corresponding material of the model. If the model is a two-section motet, the second section's material is used for the *Christe eleison*, the '*qui tollis*' of the *Gloria*, the '*et in spiritum sanctum*' of the *Credo*, the *Hosanna*, and the final *Agnus Dei*.

Jacobus Clemens[1] (*c.* 1510–55) shares with Gombert a general liking for note-against-note counterpoint which avoids melismas. Both have the same fundamental attitude to the treatment of dissonance, which approximates fairly closely to that of Palestrina described on p. 175 (though Clemens quite frequently jumps away from a dissonant unaccented note, a process avoided by Palestrina). Clemens, however, habitually employs freer imitation than Gombert, i.e. the intervals of the motif are not always copied exactly. Moreover, he frequently dispenses with imitation for several bars in the middle of a motet. Thus *Vox in Rama* (Example 27), although commencing with strict imitation, includes passages in which the parts have almost unrelated melodies. The rhythms of his melodies

are often derived from the text with a consequent gain in expressiveness. Canon he employs rarely, another feature in which he resembles Gombert. In his parody Masses (several of which are built on his own chansons and motets) he treats the borrowed material with great freedom.

1. Generally known as Clemens non Papa to distinguish him from a contemporary poet, Jacobus Papa.

The growing 'internationalization' of the Flemish style is illustrated by the works of the German Ludwig Senfl (*c.* 1490–1550) who studied with Isaac, and the Spaniard Cristòbal Morales (*c.* 1500–53). Senfl's use of imitation is often even freer than Clemens's: as long as the general shape of the motif is perceptible, he allows himself to vary the intervals considerably and to distort the rhythm. Morales combines imitation technique with devices characteristic of the fifteenth century. His motet to celebrate the peace treaty between Charles V and Francis I (see p. 124) has the tenor repeatedly singing '*gaudeamus*' ('let us rejoice') to the notes of a plainsong while the remaining voices sing another text to unrelated music. This device is employed with striking dramatic effect in *Emendemus in melius*, which combines the four-part setting of a responsory for Ash Wednesday with six statements of a (modified) chant to the words used by the priest while sprinkling ashes on the penitents: 'Remember, man, that thou are dust, and to dust thou shalt return.'

The importance of Willaert's influence in Italy has already been mentioned in the survey of the madrigal. His work in the field of religious music firmly established Flemish techniques as an integral part of the Italian style. He combined the use of imitation with accurate declamation of the text, insisting on the equal importance of this in religious and secular music. One of his innovations was the composition of psalms for alternating choirs in chordal style, a practice suggested by the existence of two choir lofts at St Mark's. These *salmi spezzati* did not involve eight-part double-choir writing: each psalm could have been sung entire by one four-part group. But Willaert's use of this device led in the hands of his successors to polychoral composition, a technique of great importance in the works of the Gabrielis and the composers of the early Baroque.

VIEWS OF THE REFORMERS ON MUSIC

From the beginning of the Reformation movement the various reformers differed on the part music should play in religious worship. Luther, an enthusiastic lover of music and accomplished amateur, favoured all branches of the art. 'He who despises music, as do all the fanatics, does not please me. Music is a gift of God, not a gift of men. Music drives away the devil and makes people happy; it induces one to forget all wrath, unchastity, arrogance, and other vices. After theology I accord to music the highest place and the greatest honour.' He insisted that all Lutheran churches should maintain a *Kantorei* (choir-school) and emphasized the importance of music in education. He defended the value of polyphony. A quotation from his preface to Johann Walther's *Wittemberg Song Book* of 1524 is typical of his many writings on this subject:

These songs are set for four voices for no other reason than that I wished that the young (who, apart from this, should and must be trained in music and in other proper arts) might have something to rid them of their love ditties and wanton songs and might, instead of these, learn wholesome things and thus yield willingly to the good; also, because I am not of the opinion that all the arts shall be crushed to earth and perish through the Gospel, as some bigoted persons pretend, but would willingly see them all, and especially music, servants of Him who gave and created them. So I pray that every pious Christian may bear with this and, should God grant him an equal or a greater talent, help to further it. Besides, unfortunately, the world is so lax and so forgetful in training and teaching its neglected young people that one might well encourage this first of all.[1]

What may be called the extreme left-wing of popular Protestantism tended to regard all art, including music, as an 'ungodly vanity': it was this spirit that led the Huguenots to burn down Orleans Cathedral and the Cromwellians to deface the statues on the west front of Wells Cathedral. Zwingli, although a cultured musician, ordered the destruction or silencing of the organs at Zürich in 1524, and three years later imposed the omission of singing from the services. But generally speaking the Puritan leaders drew a distinction between secular and religious music, distrusting, even forbidding, the former, while permitting the latter so long as it did not mar the 'purity' of worship. Calvin, in his preface to the *Genevan*

1. Strunk, op. cit., p. 342.

Psalter of 1542, not only recognizes the value of religious music, but emphasizes its indissoluble connexion with prayer.

As for public prayers, there are two kinds: the ones with the words alone, the others with singing. And this is not something invented a little time ago. For from the first origin of the Church, this has been so, as appears from the histories. And in truth we know by experience that singing has great force and vigour to move and inflame the hearts of men to invoke and praise God with a more vehement and ardent zeal. Care must always be taken that the song be neither light or frivolous: but that it have weight and majesty, and also, there is a great difference between the music which one makes to entertain men at table and in their houses, and the Psalms which are sung in the Church in the presence of God and His angels.

A year later he added another nine hundred words to this preface, which were printed in the second edition of the *Psalter* (1545); these refer to the use of music outside the church.

And yet the practice of singing may extend more widely; it is even in the homes and in the fields an incentive for us, and, as it were, an organ of praise to God ... Among the other things which are proper for recreating man and giving him pleasure, Music is either the first or the principal; and it is necessary for us to think that it is a gift of God deputed for that use. Moreover, because of this, we ought to be the more careful not to abuse it, for fear of soiling it and contaminating it, converting it to our condemnation, where it was dedicated to our profit and use ... What is there now to do? It is to have songs not only honest but also holy, which will be like spurs to incite us to pray to and praise God.[1]

During the period in which he was virtually the spiritual ruler of Geneva, Calvin forbade dancing and all secular music; polyphonic settings of translations of the psalms were encouraged as domestic music, but within the church only monophonic psalm-settings unaccompanied by the organ were permitted.

1. Translated by Charles Garside, in *Musical Quarterly* XXXVII (1951).

EARLY LUTHERAN MUSIC

Though from the beginning of his reform Luther stressed the importance of the vernacular in liturgical worship, this should not be taken to imply that vernacular singing was unknown in the churches of pre-Reformation Germany. In the four centuries before Luther a large body of popular religious song had developed which, although not officially recognized as part of the liturgy, was an inalienable part of parish worship. (Indeed, the Catholic Church in Germany still uses vernacular songs during Mass in very much the same way as in pre-Reformation times.) The songs consisted of translations of non-liturgical Latin songs, macaronic songs such as *In dulci jubilo*, and a large group of purely German songs of which the Easter hymn *Christ ist erstanden* is a famous example. (Luther and his followers rewrote the texts of some of these to conform with Protestant ideas.) In the first years of the Reformation, many Latin hymns were translated (chiefly by Luther) and fitted to adaptations of their old melodies; in addition, religious texts were written for secular melodies on the principle that 'the devil should not be allowed to have all the good tunes' (e.g. Luther's Christmas song for children *Vom Himmel hoch, da komm ich her* is based on the love-song *Aus fremden Landen komm ich her*). To these was added a fourth group, which became the most important of all, of songs specially written to texts by Luther himself: these include the well-known *Ein' feste Burg* ('A stronghold sure'), which has been called 'the confessional hymn of the Reformation', and the paraphrase of Psalm 130 *Aus tiefer Not*.

In the sixteenth century the chorales were sung by the congregation unaccompanied. Under the elastic schemes provided by Luther for services, they could be introduced freely at many points in the liturgy. Luther's 'German Mass' offered the following variations: a service could be held entirely in Latin or German; a German translation could replace any Latin prose text, and a chorale could replace both; both before and after the sermon and before the

Communion, chorales could be added at the discretion of the clergy.

Consequently German Lutheran composers continued to write Latin church music for Lutheran use, a practice which still survived in Bach's day. This music continued to be strongly influenced by Flemish and, later, by Italian styles. Only in the polyphonic settings of the chorales for schools and private music-making did the first beginnings of an indigenous German choral style appear. Walther's *Songbook* mentioned above keeps the chorale tune for the most part in the tenor; the other voices either move against it in quicker rhythms or proceed quasichordally in note-for-note style. Some of Walther's contemporaries, while maintaining a generally chordal texture, employed canonic treatment of the tune. Later settings developed the imitative elaboration of the tune. Example 28(a) shows the beginning of *Ein' feste Burg* from Kaspar Othmayr's *Spiritual Songs* (1546); the freely metrical rhythm of the *cantus firmus* tenor is not only imitated but ornamentalized in the outer voices. Example 28(b), from Hassler's *Psalms and Christian Songs* (1607), a setting of the third and fourth lines of the hymn, has a more motet-like character; such treatment led in the hands of the German organists of the early seventeenth century to the chorale-prelude.

THE GENEVAN PSALTER

French metrical psalms had already been written by Marot for the use of the court of Francis I. In 1539 Calvin published a Psalter at Strasbourg whose eighteen psalms included twelve (slightly modified) of Marot's versions. Marot became a Protestant for a short time and visited Geneva, where he seems to have found Calvin unsympathetic; he left Geneva two years later and ultimately returned to Catholicism, a fact which doubtless explains Calvin's description of him as 'a man in whom we take little interest'. His psalms were also incorporated (though with further modifications) in the complete *Genevan Psalter* of 1545, the rest of the psalms being translated by

Calvin's friend Théodore Bèze (or Beza). These metrical versions transform the psalms into hymns: each psalm is divided into stanzas which have the same structure throughout.

Louis Bourgeois (c. 1501–1601) was responsible for the musical organization of the *Genevan Psalter*. Although he wrote many of the tunes (e.g. *The Old Hundredth*) he also adapted French and Gregorian melodies. His tunes invariably conform to the hymn-structure of the psalm, the music of the opening stanza being repeated for subsequent stanzas. Like Marot, he soon became dissatisfied with Calvin's régime at

Geneva, being particularly incensed by Calvin's refusal to allow polyphony or accompaniment in church services. He was forced to publish his volume of harmonized psalm-tunes in chordal style in Lyon instead of Geneva, shortly after which he left Geneva for Paris.

POLYPHONIC METRICAL PSALMS

Claude Goudimel (c. 1505–72) wrote over sixty settings of metrical psalm texts in motet style. He also made two collections of four-part harmonizations of the entire *Genevan Psalter*; the first of these (1564) employed a chordal style with occasional ornamental passages: the second (1565) followed a simple note-against style similar to that of Bourgeois's settings. The 1565 volume exerted great influence throughout the Protestant world, continuing to be reprinted as late as the nineteenth century. It accompanied the monophonic Psalter in its progress to America, where its style permeated that of the hymns written for early American colonists.

Baif made metrical psalms in *vers mesuré* which were set by Le Jeune and the Catholic Mauduit (1557–1662). Both men imitated Goudimel in composing motet-style settings of metrical texts. Some of Le Jeune's are very long, each verse of the psalm being treated as a separate polyphonic section. Most of these have the psalm tune in the tenor with long notes characteristic of the older *cantus-firmus* technique. In Psalm 35 the tune is shifted complete from one voice to another, each of the thirteen verses providing fresh polyphony around it.

THE COUNCIL OF TRENT AND THE COUNTER-REFORMATION

The sessions of the Council of Trent (1545–63) aimed chiefly at correcting abuses in the administration of the Catholic Church and defending traditional doctrine against the innovations of the Reformers. In decrees promulgated in binding form on 17 September 1562 the Council restated the traditional attitude of the Church with regard to the place music should have in the celebration of the liturgy, though its recommendations were more negative than positive:

All things should be so ordered that the Masses, whether they be celebrated with or without singing, may reach tranquilly into the ears and hearts of those who hear them, when everything is executed clearly and at the right speed. In those Masses which are celebrated with singing and with organ, let nothing profane be intermingled, but only hymns and divine praises. The singing should be arranged not to give empty pleasure to the ear, but in such a way that the words may be clearly understood by all, and thus the hearts of the listeners be drawn to the desire of heavenly harmonies, in the contemplation of the joys of the blessed.[1]

A year later two Cardinals proposed that the 'scandalous noise' of polyphony should be forbidden. The Council therefore appointed a Commission to study Masses written in a 'reformed' style that emphasized the pronunciation and meaning of the text. Performances of works by several composers, including Palestrina and Lassus, supported by much public and private pressure from polyphony-loving princes, finally secured the retention of contrapuntal styles for liturgical use. This is the origin of the myth that Palestrina 'saved' contrapuntal music by composing the *Missa Papae Marcelli*.

Although the Council's recommendations were not fully observed, they influenced church music to some extent in all Catholic countries. In insisting on correct word-setting and intelligibility the Council was but supporting a trend already established by the humanist taste of the age. Four years before the publication of the decrees quoted above Zarlino had written: 'Since our minds are much moved by singing, there is no doubt that songs will generally be heard with greater pleasure when the words are pronounced clearly than in the learned compositions where the words are heard interrupted in many parts.' The works of the later composers of the century reveal a noticeable tendency to pay more attention to the effect produced on the audience and to extend the use of homophonic styles involving increased importance for the upper voices. Moreover, the part played by sacred music in inducing suitable

1. Reese op. cit., p. 449.

dispositions for worship came to receive more and more emphasis by ecclesiastics in their furtherance of reforms. The glowing fervour of the music of Palestrina and Victoria has its analogies in the other arts: the ecstatic distortions displayed in the paintings of El Greco and Zurbarán; the religious ardour of Tasso's epic *Jerusalem Delivered*; the adoption of new styles in church architecture which, by replacing the circle by the ellipse (i.e. a 'static' by a 'dynamic' shape) as a basic figure for the construction of a ground-plan, directed the eyes and bodily movements of the spectators towards the central altar. All reflect the enthusiasm of the Counter-Reformation, a rebirth of the Church's missionary zeal which not only strengthened and purified the spiritual life of those areas that had remained true to the old faith but won back vast areas of Central Europe that had yielded to the Reformers. The new trends in art were deeply influenced by religious practice: the *Spiritual Exercises* of Ignatius Loyola, the founder (in 1540) of the Society of Jesus, provided a discipline of imagination allied with intellect that influenced religious art for over a century.

The Council, while not condemning the use of the vernacular, had deemed the time inopportune for its introduction into the liturgies of Western Christendom. (The liturgies of the Eastern Churches have always retained their vernaculars, though they vary in the proportion of vernacular used.) But, following Protestant practice, vernacular religious songs and hymns were collected, composed, and published in countless volumes in Germany (chiefly), Austria, Switzerland, Belgium, and Poland. Though these tunes, like those of the Calvinists, had little, if any, influence on the composers of liturgical music, they remained an inalienable part of the popular tradition in Central Europe. Closely related to them in purpose, and often based on similar tunes, were the collections of polyphonic *laude spirituali* to Italian and Spanish texts. This development of the *lauda* genre was chiefly inspired by the Congregation of the Oratory (a body of priests organized in 1575 by St Philip Neri).

THE CULMINATION OF THE FLEMISH STYLE

Religious music in the later years of the century shows the influence of the secular styles of *chanson* and madrigal. Not only is the text set with greater attention to the details of its speech-rhythms and with regard for its emotional and spiritual content but the texts themselves (so far as the motet is concerned) tend to be chosen for the opportunities they offer for pictorial and emotional expression and for their relevance to the more purely personal side of life and religion. The music either favours syllabic over melismatic writing, or employs only short melismata; continuous imitation is freely permeated by homophonic writing; the texture consequently sounds more obviously harmonic (considered from the viewpoint of later ages), verging towards the beginning of functional harmony.

In the Masses of Monte, Imperial *Kapellmeister* from 1568, the parody technique produces a complete synthesis of musical elements from religious and secular styles. Every element of the model (usually a madrigal or *chanson*) is employed and developed. In addition to Gombert's practice of commencing a movement with the corresponding section of the model, Monte quotes important sections of the model in prominent places, and develops all the main material in free contrapuntal expansion. Moreover, the chordal and harmonic layout, the *resonance* of the model's texture, appears over and over again. Example 29 shows the first two bars of a madrigal *Cara la vita* by Wert and Monte's treatment of its material in the *Sanctus* of his *Missa super Cara la vita*. The harmonies of bars 2–4 in the Mass are those of the madrigal excerpt, one minim of the Mass being (harmonically) equivalent to one crotchet of the madrigal. The melody of the madrigal's treble part (a) occurs in diminished values in the top part of the *Sanctus*, followed by its inversion in the treble and alto; in inversion at the beginning of the bass; and in long notes reminiscent of *cantus firmus* technique in Tenor 2. The subsidiary motif (b) beginning in the tenor part of the madrigal is transferred to the treble of the

Sanctus in bar 3. These are but a few of the extraordinarily varied devices used. The succeeding bars provide a contrast to the melismas of the opening by syllabic treatment of *Domine Deus Sabaoth*. Only one of Monte's Masses is predominantly chordal: the rest preserve a polyphonic texture.

Ca - ra la vi -ta mi — a,

Monte's music may have influenced the early development of Byrd. When Monte visited England in 1555 as a member of the Chapel of Philip II, he met Byrd's father and the composer, then a choirboy of thirteen. The older man seems to have corresponded regularly with Byrd; a MS of one of his works in the British Museum marked 'Sent by him to Mr Wm Byrd, 1583' is accompanied by an eight-part motet 'Made by Mr Wm Byrd to send in to Mr Phillip [*sic*] de Monte, 1584'.

Lassus's forty parody Masses are not always as interesting or as varied as Monte's: the unchanging texts of the Ordinary do not seem to have inspired him very strongly. Secular models, consisting of *chansons* and madrigals by himself and other composers, predominate; his religious sources include two German *Lieder*. He tends to employ syllabic treatment of the text more frequently than Monte, with the result that most of his Masses are shorter than Monte's and generally a good deal shorter than Palestrina's. Although there are many beautiful passages even in the least interesting examples, the general level of inspiration lies far below that of Josquin's and Palestrina's Masses. In his *Requiem*, however, stimulated by the text's combination of Ordinary and Proper chants, Lassus produced one of the great masterpieces of the late century. The Introit (in paraphrase style) is typical of the work as a whole in its blend of free imitation and homophony: the treatment of the central versicle shows chordal writing influenced by Willaert's *salmi spezzati*.

It is in the field of the motet that Lassus reveals his supreme mastery, a mastery which is unchallenged by any other composer of his time. Commencing with the so-called *Antwerp Motet Book* (published when the composer was only twenty-three) and concluding with the posthumous *Magnum opus musicum* (containing 516 motets) his production embraces an amazing range of subject, style, and expression allied to a corresponding variety of technique. To talk of any one example as typical is utterly misleading; the following description of *Scio enim quod Redemptor* (the third section of Lesson VIII in Matins of the Dead, being the famous passage from the Book of Job beginning 'For I know that my Redeemer liveth') is intended only to illustrate his characteristic approach to a text. The previous two sections of the Lesson have depicted Job's misery and wretchedness; this third portion, in which he affirms his hope in an ultimate resurrection, begins with a strong proclamation of faith: a downward leap of a fifth on *Scio* ('I know') in imitation by tenor and bass rising on a triumphant melisma to the confident assertion of the Redeemer by all voices in chordal style (Example 30a). Chromatic inflexion of a

close contrapuntal passage suggests the awe of the Last Judgement for *et in novissimo die* ('and on the last day'); an upward leap of an octave or fourth initiates the next motif *surrecturus sum* ('I shall rise again'). The following passage, 'Again I shall be clothed with my skin' depicts by closely-spaced harmony in the lower registers of the voices the warmth of donning one's body like a cloak as it were at the general resurrection, rises again in triumphant fourths for 'in my flesh' and sinks to a sudden chromatic chord for the end of the phrase 'shall I see God' (Example 30b). This use of chromatic

block harmony to convey a sense of profound awe occurs again towards the end of the motet, where the voices emphasize the last words of 'whom my eyes shall behold, and not another'.

Lassus's motets include polyphonic psalm-settings (those of the penitential psalms are the best-known), responsories, Proper Office-chants, Magnificats, and Offertories. These last are, together with Palestrina's Offertories, of historical importance as the first Offertories to have been composed in free motet style without the use of plainchant.

Both Monte and Lassus were described by their contemporaries as master of *musica reservata*. The meaning of this term is still the subject of dispute among scholars because the available evidence is both conflicting and confused. There seems to have been a distinction drawn, even in works by the same composer, between compositions in *reservata* style and those that were not. The chief weight of the evidence favours the description of *reservata* as 'music expressive of the emotions delineated by the text', a definition which, whatever its degree of accuracy, does sum up a prevailing characteristic of late sixteenth-century music.

THE VENETIAN SCHOOL

The *cappella* of St Mark's was one of the largest in Europe. It normally included at least thirty singers and twenty instrumentalists, all holding salaried posts. On festive occasions (of which there were many in Venice) the choir-schools and fraternities swelled the number of musicians to nearly a hundred. 'To have such forces regularly employed must have meant that few courts in Italy could have equalled this, and it is not surprising that Venice should give birth to a school of composers adopting a style different from that of ordinary sixteenth-century music.'[1] This special style, whose primary feature is the combination of groups of voices and instruments and whose origins are exemplified by the *salmi spezzati* of Willaert, was typical of the ceremonial music written for St Mark's between 1570 and 1612. By the last years of the century it had been adopted (for occasional use) by the larger *cappelle* of Italy and southern Germany: Lassus, for example, wrote double-choir motets for the Ducal Chapel at Munich. Andrea Gabrieli was the first leading composer to specialize in polychoral works. While his earlier motets are written for the more normal four- and five-part choir, the *Salmi Davidici* of 1583 (which, like the previous works, require the use of instruments) are for six parts, showing an interest in the contrast of groups of different vocal range within the choir. Later compositions include a motet *Deus misereatur nostri* for three four-part choirs, and a Mass that has four choirs in the *Gloria*.

Giovanni Gabrieli uses choirs of differing range: a three-choir work will often require a high-pitched group, a middle group, and a bass group. Only the middle is likely to be fully choral in the sense that voices are employed for all the parts: the other groups, though they may include voices, will consist of string or trumpets for the high-pitched group, and trombones

1. Denis Arnold, 'Ceremonial Music in Venice', in *Proceedings of the R.M.A.*, vol. 82, p. 47.

and lower woodwind for the bass group. In many of his works Giovanni employs solo voices against an instrumental or vocal background, such voices often being required to perform elaborate *coloratura*. Modern performances of these works frequently ignore the spatial effects intended by the composer: in a concert-hall the music sounds from one direction only, whereas in St Mark's at the end of the sixteenth century it more often sounded from two, and, when large polychoral works were being played, from all sides of the building. Gabrieli's later works not only require differing tonal groups but give the soloists, instruments, and choir distinctive idioms which antici-pate some of the aspects of the Baroque styles of Monteverdi, Gabrieli's successor at St Mark's. *In ecclesiis*, written for a group of soloists (Choir I), a full choir (II), and instruments, begins with a soprano solo accompanied by the organ; this is answered by a choral 'Alleluia' that dovetails with the soprano. A tenor solo to organ accompaniment is answered in the same way. Then follows a six-part instrumental sinfonia for three cornetti, viola, and two trombones, which leads to a tenor and alto duet accompanied by the same instruments; this section also concludes with an 'Alleluia' similar to the two preceding but this time strengthened by independent six-part writing for the instruments. The third section commences with a soprano and tenor duet accompanied by organ, which proceeds by the close imitation of short motifs; this too leads to an 'Alleluia', after which the two choirs and instruments are contrasted and blended in the final section, ending with twelve-part writing involving colourful harmonies.

PALESTRINA

Until quite recently it was almost impossible to view Palestrina in historical perspective: his virtual canonization as the exemplar of Catholic church music plus the adoption of his style (more or less misunderstood) as a model for the teaching of counterpoint had effectively prevented an unprejudiced examination of his work. A reaction developing in the opening decades of the present century expressed partly the resentment of composers expected to write 'like' Palestrina[1] and partly the annoyance of scholars at the neglect and undervaluation of Palestrina's contemporaries. As a result of this, his position in musical history is now seen more clearly. Palestrina was, of course, one of the great composers of all time. But in the larger aspects of his style considered in relation to the main development of the century he was a conservative. His music conforms to the Roman preference for *a cappella* performance; he has left no instrumental music and his only secular works, two books of madrigals, are not particularly important for the development of the form. His virtual restriction to religious music (towards the end of his life he felt it necessary to apologize for the subjects of his secular madrigals) is an atypic trait which he shares only with the composers of the so-called 'Roman' school. In his systematic treatment of the dissonance (see p. 159) he was fully 'modern', but in his avoidance of chromaticism reactionary. The 'spiritual serenity' of his style derives from these characteristics and from his famous principle of the 'melodic curve' by which the opening gradual rise of a melodic line is balanced by a fall of equal distance and duration. For classical restraint and noble simplicity combined with a contrapuntal virtuosity that has ever since been regarded as flawless, Palestrina stands unsurpassed by any composer of his age. His music reflects the more austere side of the Counter-Reformation in its avoidance of secular elements, though it should be remembered that modern performances omit the habitual extempore embellishment of the upper voices[2] practised by the Roman choirs of his day.

Of Palestrina's 105 Masses, fifty-two are 'parodies' (twenty-seven on his own models, including three based on madrigals), thirty-four use paraphrase technique, eight have tenor *cantus firmi*, five are canonic throughout, and the remaining six are 'free'. From this list it will be seen that the *Missa Papae Marcelli*, although so well known, is not representative of

---

1. Ecclesiastical and other 'advice' of this sort has been largely to blame for the appalling decline of Catholic church music in recent years.

2. Manuscripts of written-out *abbellimenti* survive for some works.

Palestrina's methods of Mass composition. Nevertheless it resembles the majority of his Masses in the contrast of quasi-homophonic texture in the longer movements with melismatic polyphony in the shorter, a feature most probably inspired by liturgical considerations (Example 31). His paraphrase Masses are all built on plainsong models, taking each phrase of the plainsong in turn as the basis of an imitative section. The parodies exhibit even greater ingenuity than Monte's in the variation and development of the model. Example 32 shows the beginning of the second part of his motet *Assumpta est Maria* (in its turn partly derived from a plainsong antiphon) compared with the *Benedictus* of the parody Mass of the same name.

Palestrina's motets frequently employ repetition of sections either exactly or modified. Some of the themes are derived from plainsong but most are free. Word-painting is much more in evidence in the motets though of a less emotional kind than Lassus's. Example 32(a) has a typical illustration in the ascending scale for 'Who is she that goes forth?' Several of Palestrina's motets require antiphonal choirs, as do two of his parody Masses and the famous *Stabat mater*. This reflects Venetian practice while avoiding for the most part the vivid colouristic effects of the Gabrielis.

THE ROMAN SCHOOL

Several composers were especially influenced by Palestrina's work. Nanini (1545–1607) and Felice Anerio (1560–1614) exhibit contrapuntal mastery in a style largely similar to Palestrina's. Both, however, occasionally employ techniques and devices that Palestrina avoided, particularly chromaticism. Some of Anerio's works require organ accompaniment. The greatest composer of the Roman school was the Spaniard Victoria (*c.* 1540–1611), a close friend of Palestrina. He confined himself to church music, but within this field he ranks almost equal to Palestrina for the polished beauty of his style. Eleven of his twenty Masses are parodies of his own motets; none have secular models. His most famous work is the *Office*

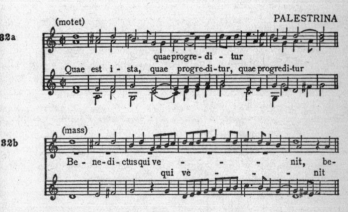

of *Holy Week* (1585) polyphonic settings of all the Proper chant-texts from Palm Sunday to Easter. Much of the music of this volume displays a mystical passion which has been compared with that of the writings of St John of the Cross; it appears in the rich harmonies of his polyphony, which are often more 'tonal' in their orientation than even Palestrina's. Moreover, his use of chromatic harmonies lies in the direction of what later periods called 'passing modulations' rather than sudden chordal contrasts. Another striking characteristic is his use of repeated notes (a quasi-dramatic device used effectively by the early seventeenth-century composers, particularly Monteverdi) to stress the importance of a word. The well-known motet *O vos omnes* contains many examples of this practice.

Victoria, like Palestrina, strove to write religious music that should truly serve the purposes of the liturgy, providing a stimulus to prayer and an accompaniment to ritual while remembering that music was not the most important part of worship. This attitude endured in Rome when the rest of the Catholic world yielded once again to the sensual brilliance of art in the Baroque church music of the succeeding century.

6. Instrumental Music

DANCE FORMS

In the first years of the century the *basse danse* was superseded by the *pavane*, a slow dance in duple time with solemn movements and dignified gestures suggestive of the peacock (*pavo*). Some think that '*pavane*' (= *pavana* in Italian) is a corruption of '*padovana*', a Paduan dance. Both appear in the early lute books, but by the middle of the century the *padovana* had become a quick triple dance. On the other hand some early Spanish *pavanes* are in triple time. The *pavane* was 'intended to express not charm and lightness but ceremonial dignity. In its step and rhythm princes walked. The piper played a *pavane* when a bride of good family proceeded to the church, or when priests, or masters and members of important corporations, were to be escorted in dignified procession.'[1] When used simply for dancing it was followed by a quicker dance in triple time, generally a *galliard*, consisting of leaps. Such pairing of dances was a constant practice throughout the century. *Pavanes* and *galliards* usually consisted of three sections, each section being repeated, the *galliard* often being a rhythmical variant of the *pavane* (Example 33). About 1540 the

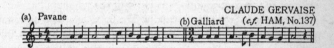

(a) Pavane   (b) Galliard   (*c.f.* HAM, No.137)   CLAUDE GERVAISE

passamezzo replaced the *pavane*. Like its predecessor it was in duple time, and was linked to the *saltarello* (leaping dance) in triple time. By the end of the century the *passamezzo* was ousted by the *allemande* and the *saltarello* by the *courante* (at first not distinct from the *saltarello*, but later developing into two forms, French and Italian).

1. Curt Sachs, *World History of the Dance* (Allen & Unwin, 1937), p. 356.

The *passamezzo* was normally composed over one of two bass patterns: the *passamezzo antico* (minor mode) or *passamezzo moderno* (major mode). These basses were treated freely, often being represented in a composition by nothing more than their implied harmonies. With the *romanesca* and *folia* they provided the chief ground-bass themes of the next century. Sometimes tunes accompanying these basses were used without them.

FORMS DERIVED FROM VOCAL MUSIC, AND 'FREE' FORMS

Some of the earliest printed instrumental music consisted of transcriptions of vocal compositions: motets, *chansons*, and so forth. The title page indicated instrumental performance by the direction *da sonar* (in opposition to *da cantar*): thus, for example, the first printed Italian organ music was described as *Frottole intabulate da sonar al organo*, i.e. '*frottolas* arranged for playing on the organ'. The term *ricercare* was first used in Petrucci's lute books of 1507, where it described a 'free' piece, partly improvisatory, partly preludial; by 1523, it was used exclusively for pieces that employed the imitative techniques of the motet. The *canzona*, originally an arrangement of a *chanson*, maintained the short sections, repetitions, and basic rhythms of the Claudin type of *chanson*, thus providing a contrast to the contrapuntal structure of the *ricercare*.

Madrigals were not normally arranged as instrumental pieces because their forms, being so closely dependent on the text, lacked the clear-cut sectional structure of the *chanson*. Lute composers adopted the term 'fantasia' to describe pieces in contrapuntal style which by reason of the limitations of their instrument could not be followed in the full motet-manner of the *ricercare*. *Toccata* (*toccare* = 'to touch') although applied at first to a few early lute pieces, came to mean exclusively a keyboard composition in 'free' style. In addition to these there were variations on psalm-tones, songs, and dances.

LUTE MUSIC

The popularity of the lute in sixteenth-century Italy is attested by the great quantity of surviving music. While the first publications consisted mostly of arrangements of vocal works, later prints emphasized dance-suites and variations. Dalza devised a suite of three dances: *pavane*, *saltarello*, and *piva* (a rapid triple-time dance). Other composers favoured the *pavane-galliard* 'pair'. In later decades another suite appeared: *passamezzo*, *galliard*, and *padovana*, these being frequently followed by variations. The first lute-dances were very simple, consisting mainly of a tune with chordal accompaniment, but later examples included much ornamental elaboration and contrapuntal writing. Two virtuosi, Terzo and Molinaro, developed a variation-suite, in which a *passamezzo* and *galliard*, having several sections constructed over the same harmonies, were repeated in division-technique with frequent passages in imitation. Another virtuoso, Francesco da Milano (1497–1543) named '*il divino*' by his contemporaries, developed the idiomatic side of lute composition in fantasias and *ricercari* which combined imitative sections with rapid scales, broken chords, and numerous ornaments.

In Spain the *vihuela* (a species of guitar tuned like a lute) called forth some of the most beautiful compositions of the age. L. de Milan's *Instructor: a book of music for the vihuela* (published in 1536) includes fantasias, *tientos* (in the free *ricercare* style of the early Italian lutenists), dances, and songs with lute accompaniment. For the fantasias he requires a free tempo, 'the ornamented passages fast and the harmonies slow', the first occasion of such directions in musical history. Example 34 is a typical sample of his fantasia style. Two years

LUIS DE MILAN

etc.

34

later another vihuelist, Luis de Narvaez, published six books of music, of which the *diferencias* (variations) are remarkable for their variety of rhythm and contrapuntal texture. Valderravano's book of 1552 includes, besides transcriptions of eight Masses by Josquin and motets by Willaert, Verdelot, and Morales, *diferencias* on dance-tunes that have contrapuntal texture similar to those of Narvaez. One of these dances is a very famous song of the day, *Guardame las vacas*, constructed over a variant of the *passamezzo* bass (Example 35).

VALDERRAVANO

35

(+ = first 5 notes of *passamezzo antico*)

The lute remained a favourite instrument in France long into the seventeenth century. Attaingnant published the first French lute-book in 1529, following it in the same year with an instruction book. This latter includes advice for the amateur on the problems of transcribing vocal music. The lute was even more popular in Germany since it was the chief domestic instrument in all ranks of society. German lute compositions therefore tended to avoid the elaborate virtuoso ornamentation of lute music in other countries: most of the extant repertoire consists of dances and vocal transcriptions.

LUTE SONG

Songs to lute accompaniment first appeared in print in two books of *chanson* and *frottola* transcriptions published by Petrucci; the top voice-part of the originals was retained for the solo singer, the alto omitted, and the tenor and bass parts were arranged for the lute. Such publications continued to appear for the rest of the century: Willaert's transcriptions of Verdelot's madrigals have been mentioned previously.

Attaingnant published several of Claudin's *chansons* in similar arrangements. Later French lute-songs were known as *airs de cour*.

Spanish songs with *vihuela* accompaniment were usually not arrangements of polyphonic works. The songs in Milan's book have very simple harmonic writing; those of his blind contemporary Miguel de Fuenllana (vihuelist to Philip II) are sometimes more polyphonic though always keeping the interest subordinate to that of the voice.

KEYBOARD MUSIC

The chief keyboard instruments of the period were the organ and harpsichord. The clavichord was not popular since it was incapable of sharing in ensembles. Both fifteenth-century forms of the organ, church and chamber, continued in use, the latter often being preferred to the harpsichord for ensembles. Although all keyboard music could be, and probably was, performed on any of these instruments, the organ remained the chief instrument, save that dance-music was not considered suitable for it. The gradual rise in importance of the harpsichord during the century directly reflects the increase in keyboard transcriptions of dances.

The first Italian keyboard publication (1517) contained arrangements of twenty-six *frottole* with elaborate ornamentation applied to the upper parts. Marco Antonio Cavazzoni six years later produced a book of *Ricercari*, *motets*, and *canzoni*: the first are of the improvisatory type found in the early lute prints, being designed as preludes to the motets; the *canzoni* have well-defined repetitive forms on the French model, such as A–A–B. In 1542 Marco Antonio's son Girolamo published a collection of *Ricercari*, *canzoni*, *hymns*, and *Magnificats*. Girolamo's *ricercari* have the imitative technique of the motet but extend the working-out of each motif far longer than any motet. The *canzoni* are free paraphrases based on the themes of the *chanson* whose titles they bear, while the *Magnificats* consist of polyphonic variations replacing the odd-numbered verses. Another publication by Cavazzoni in the following year includes an 'organ Mass', alternate sections of the chant being worked in polyphonic imitation.

The further development of Italian music came largely from Venetian organists. Andrea Gabrieli arranged numerous *canzoni alla francese* and wrote several original pieces in the same style. Like all such 'arrangements' these are elaborate re-creations in idiomatic keyboard style (Example 36). Some

of his later *canzoni* include imitative sections derived from the *ricercare*. Andrea also wrote numerous *Intonazioni*: brief preludes of brilliant scale and *arpeggio* figuration ending on a chord whose top note gave the beginning of a psalm, canticle, or versicle. His music was the most idiomatic writing for keyboard that had yet appeared. Giovanni Gabrieli developed the use of figuration still more elaborately than his uncle in toccatas and fantasias: the former generally consist entirely of passage-work or have a middle, contrapuntal section; the latter either resemble *ricercari* or consist of two to three sections, the last being treated in toccata style.

Claudio Merulo (1533–1604) organist at St Mark's from 1557 to 1585, and the composer of much church music and several books of madrigals, took the combination of toccata and *ricercare* a step farther to produce a scheme of alternate toccata and imitative sections which, although avoiding repetition, occasionally included the reworking in a later section of subsidiary material from an earlier section. Merulo was recognized as the leading organist of his time; when he played in St Peter's, Rome, it is recorded that his audience 'crushed one another in their eagerness to hear him'. The Spaniard Antonio de Cabezón (*c.* 1500–66) wrote keyboard music of extraordinary contrapuntal richness, ranging from tiny polyphonic *versillos* (settings of psalm-tones) to lofty fantasias, *tientos*, and *diferencias* on popular tunes. Though blind, he served as organist in the courts of Charles V and Philip II, and visited England for Philip's marriage to Mary Tudor. No keyboard music equal to his in nobility, variety, and melodic beauty can be found before the English virginalists at the end of the century. Example 37 gives a hint of his versatility in a psalm-tone.

37

Psalm verse: Cabezon (The chant is in the alto) (*c.f.* HAM No.133)

In Germany organists after Schlick tended more and more to overload their compositions with 'coloration' i.e. ornamentation. Hermann Finck said of them in 1556: 'They produce an empty noise wholly devoid of charm. In order the more easily to cajole the ears of untrained listeners and to arouse admiration for their own digital skill, they sometimes permit their fingers to run up and down the keys for half an hour at a time.' Harpsichord music, on the other hand, since it was written for the amateur, was generally much simpler. Nicolaus Ammerbach's dance movements, published towards the end of the century, are representative of this new German style.

French keyboard music, at least that part of it which has survived, consists mainly of dances and vocal arrangements. Jean Titelouze (1563–1633) published variations on hymns and magnificats in the first decades of the seventeenth century which display polyphonic writing in a conservative style reminiscent both of the Spanish and Italian organists.

ENSEMBLE MUSIC

Apart from the keyboard, instruments were still classified according to the fifteenth-century groups of 'indoor' and 'outdoor' types. Viols *da gamba* (held between the knees) were used for chamber music together with the softer-toned wind instruments, viols *da braccio* (held much in the same way as a violin) being regarded as street instruments. All brass instruments and the harsher-toned woodwind came under the heading of 'outdoor' from the standpoint of chamber music, but were 'indoor' instruments for the separate genres of church and theatre music. As the century developed there was an increasing tendency to construct instruments in several sizes, thus facilitating the performance of all 'voices' of a polyphonic composition by instruments of the same tone-colour.

As in other branches of instrumental music, the earliest ensemble music consists of adaptations of vocal models. *Ricercari* in motet-style were published by Willaert and many other composers. But in the hands of the Gabrielis the *canzon da sonar* developed into an ensemble form with rich possibilities whose later development led to the Baroque *sonata*. Some of Andrea Gabrieli's ensemble *ricercari* blend an imitative style with the sectional form of the *chanson*. Giovanni expanded this technique in his *canzoni* which repeat sections in chordal style as a contrast to polyphonic sections, thus having a general structure A–B–A–C, etc. His sonatas, of which the *Sonata pian e forte* is famous for its precise specifications of instruments, usually consist of unrelated sections; their contrast of large and small groups, similar to those of Giovanni's motets, appears again as a principle of the late-seventeenth-century concerto grosso. Ensemble fantasias of the period have the same free application of motet technique that characterizes the keyboard fantasia: the motifs are developed separately, succeeding motifs growing rhythmically more elaborate as the composition proceeds, but there are no sectional repetitions. Fantasias were also written by French composers, following the Italian style closely. Germany, on the other hand, did not produce much ensemble music of importance till the following century.

DRAMATIC MUSIC

Although music had an important part in Italian and French stage productions very little of it now remains. What survives is mostly in the form of madrigals. While the *sacre rappresentazioni* were continued in Rome and Florence, the courts of the Italian princes favoured the *intermedi*, musical interludes in a spoken play mingling elements of spectacle and dance.[1] Their development during the later years of the century often led to protests by playwrights who resented the competition. Tasso's famous pastoral *Aminta* (1573) was provided with music by several composers. The resulting vogue for musical pastorals led directly to the first operas. Monteverdi's *Orfeo* (1607) has many pastoral features; its orchestra closely resembles those employed in the later *intermedi*.

1. See the description of Cosimo de' Medici's wedding on p. 114.

7. Music in England

ALTHOUGH foreign musicians found employment in England throughout the century, English music was slow to absorb the newer European styles. The brilliant musical life of the last two decades of Elizabeth's reign is not typical of the period as a whole: before 1580 'art'-music was for the most part confined to the court, the cathedrals and more important churches, and to the musical establishments of the greater nobility. Hence English musical development exhibits a time-lag when compared with that of the Continent. Much of the music written during the first half of the century was old-fashioned by continental standards. The influx of later French and Italian music that began in Mary's reign created a vogue that ultimately inspired an English renaissance. This culmination of sixteenth-century English music is far too often called the Elizabethan age when in fact it was just as much a Jacobean age; for music (as for verse and drama) the period extended at least to the year of Shakespeare's death (1616) while some of its representatives continued writing for another fifteen years. During the first twenty years of the seventeenth century English music expanded along lines established in the sixteenth, being influenced little, if at all, by the Italian Baroque styles of monody and *concertato*, and exerted a leadership in Germany and northern Europe second only to that of Italy in the south.

LATIN CHURCH MUSIC AT THE END OF HENRY VIII'S REIGN

The works of Taverner (1495–1545), Tye (1500–72), and Tallis (1505–85) for the Catholic liturgy show the influence of Fayrfax and his contemporaries. Taverner's Masses are either short, using mainly note-against-note texture, or very long, being built over repetitions of a borrowed melody. Such melodies, though used in a manner resembling *cantus firmus* technique (employed by Taverner in his motets) are not disposed in long notes but either maintain their original rhythm or pursue an even rhythm in beat values. The Mass on *The Western Wynde* displays the first method of treatment, repeating the melody in different voices against long lines of soaring melismatic counterpoint. An example of the second method is provided in the Mass *Gloria tibi Trinitas* which keeps the plainsong in the alto throughout. Imitation is not a marked feature of Taverner's style. Tye and Tallis share many contrapuntal features with Taverner, though with Tallis these are confined to his earlier work. Tye's *Western Wynde* Mass varies the

twenty-nine repetitions of the theme with elaborations and changes of time-signature, the other voices frequently imitating it. An early Mass by Tallis based on his own motet *Salve intemerata* begins each movement with the opening motif of the motet. In his later Latin music, imitation is used more and more frequently, till, in his last works, such as the beautiful *Lamentations of Jeremiah*, it becomes fundamental to the organization of the contrapuntal texture. The opening of the Lenten motet *In jejunio* is typical of this later style (Example 38).

THE ENGLISH REFORMATION

The Henrician and Edwardian religious changes affected music profoundly and, at the beginning, adversely. The suppression of the monasteries (1536–47) not only involved the dispersal of monastic musicians but often included the destruction of musical MSS. (in large quantities) by religious fanatics. The Edwardian Act of Uniformity struck at all remaining musical establishments by forbidding the celebration of Mass,[1] hitherto the chief feature of the daily musical life of cathedrals, churches, and colleges. Under Mary, Mass music reappeared with the official restoration of Catholicism for five years, but was again banned shortly after Elizabeth's accession. In the new type of service established in Elizabeth's reign, Latin motets could be used occasionally in place of the new form of church music, the anthem.

Cranmer, in a letter to Henry VIII, stated what was to become the basic principle for settings of the new English texts: 'The song should not be full of notes, but, as near as may be, a syllable for every note.'[2] Composers reacted variously to the new conditions. Taverner gave up composition to become an agent of Thomas Cromwell; Tye and Tallis wrote music for the Protestant services which, while attractive, did not match the technical interest and artistry of their Latin music; both continued to compose Latin motets but not Masses.

The promulgation of the *First Book of Common Prayer* (1549) was followed a year later by John Merbecke's *The Book of Common Prayer Noted*; this provided simple monophonic settings that attempted to follow the natural speech rhythms of the English language. Merbecke's work does not seem to have interested his contemporaries greatly. It became obsolete when the *Second Book of Common Prayer* was issued in

1. 'The word "Mass" was retained in the 1549 Book of Common Prayer, but disappeared in later editions' (*Oxford Dictionary of the Christian Church*, O.U.P., 1957).
2. Strunk, op. cit., p. 350.

1552, whereupon Merbecke joined the pro-Calvinists among the Reformers, condemning all music as 'vanity'.

ENGLISH CHURCH MUSIC

The Elizabethan religious settlement established a pattern of service in which the place of music was clearly defined. The main musical forms (apart from simple chants such as responses and the like) were: (1) the *Service*, i.e., settings of the *Venite*, *Te Deum*, *Benedictus*, *Kyrie*, *Creed*, *Magnificat*, and *Nunc Dimittis*; a 'short' service employed chiefly chordal texture or note-against-note counterpoint, while a 'great' service exploited elaborate imitative writing in motet-style; (2) the *Anthem*, replacing the Latin motet, could be either for choir alone (the 'Full' anthem) or could alternate solo and choral sections, the whole being accompanied (the 'Verse' anthem). Syllabic setting of the text predominated, so that melodic and rhythmic styles were intimately associated with the verbal rhythm and stress. Melismas were usually placed on a strong syllable, a trait equally evident in the European Latin church music of the second half of the century.

Tallis's anthems are mainly chordal with occasional use of imitation; Tye uses imitation much more consistently. The first great music for Anglican worship appears in the works of Byrd. He extended the employment of imitation to embrace occasional melismas much more elaborate than anything by his predecessors. His *Great Service* treats the doxologies of the canticles in rich imitative polyphony with much repetition of the text (Example 39). This style provided the starting-point for the development of Byrd's younger contemporaries. Weelkes (1575–1623), the composer of more than forty anthems, begins his seven-part *O Lord, arise* with a motif that illustrates the third word by a rising scale (Example 40). Such elaborate writing in the larger anthems was balanced by the chordal technique of the short anthems. The two types continued to be developed side by side to the end of the period.

The verse anthem was at first accompanied solely by the organ. Byrd added a quartet of viols. Orlando Gibbons

(1585–1625), one of the greatest composers of Anglican church music, wrote twenty-five verse anthems which have highly developed polyphony for the viols in the solo sections. Byrd does not repeat the text from a solo to a choral section, whereas

with Gibbons this is the usual method. *This is the record of John* divides the text into three parts; each is sung first by a counter-tenor accompanied by viols and is then repeated by the choir with the instruments doubling the voice parts.

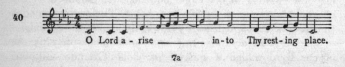

In addition to the strictly liturgical texts of the Prayer Book, several attempts were made during Elizabeth's reign to provide metrical psalters after the Genevan model. The most successful was published by John Day in 1562. It contained sixty-five tunes from various sources to which, in the second edition of 1563, were added thirty more in four-part harmony.

LATER LATIN CHURCH MUSIC

Several Elizabethan composers chose, as Catholics, to live outside England. Of these the most outstanding was Peter Philips (1560–1633). His religious music was entirely for Catholic use; hence, although it was highly thought of in Europe, none of it was printed in his native country. Byrd, though he wrote music for the Anglican Church, remained a Catholic; his Latin music shows some signs of the difficulties under which men who remained true to the old faith lived. His three Masses (which, of course, were not published) are all fairly brief, being thus suitable to celebrations of Mass where the former richness of ceremonial was no longer possible. Their contrapuntal style is remarkable for the variety of rhythms displayed. In this respect Byrd's music is much more interesting to twentieth-century ears than is Palestrina's. The *Gradualia*, a collection of polyphonic settings of Mass and Office chants in motet-form, were published in two books towards the end of his life. They constitute a profession of faith. Most of the texts chosen refer to doctrines attacked or watered down by the Reformers. The music affords many striking examples of contrapuntal virtuosity, word-painting, and original use of chromatic devices. In these works Byrd is revealed as the equal of Lassus and Palestrina.

THE ENGLISH MADRIGAL

The part-song type of Henry VIII's reign was continued by subsequent composers. Later examples, such as Thomas Whythorne's *Songs for 3, 4, and 5 Voices* (1571) show the growing influence of Italian music. Byrd's part-songs are designed for solo voice and four-part viol accompaniment, a texture which he applied later to the verse anthem. In 1588 he published some of these in *Psalmes, Sonnets, and Songs of Sadness and Piety*, describing them in a preface as 'songs originally made for instruments to express the harmony and one voice to pronounce the ditty . . . now framed in all parts for voices to sing the same'. On to the native tradition, represented by songs of this kind, the new generation of composers at the end of the century grafted the style of the Italian madrigal.

From 1560 manuscript copies of Italian madrigals circulated widely in England among the nobility and country gentry. This musical vogue was the counterpart of the literary Italianization evinced in the 'new poetry' of Sidney and Spenser.

Like this movement the English madrigal was a sudden growth for which models had been available for decades, a belated extension of a current already past its prime on the Continent. In fact, about seventy English madrigals are set to Italian texts . . . But the madrigal in England was more than a subtle importation of an Italian ideal : it was a unique nationalization of it; never before and perhaps never afterwards have English musicians adopted a foreign style with such wholeheartedness and intelligence, and at the same time added so much of their own and produced so distinguished a repertory.[1]

In 1588, the year of the Armada, appeared Nicholas Young's *Musica transalpina*, a printed collection of fifty-seven Italian madrigals. Another collection of Italian pieces, mostly by Marenzio, came out two years later, this time with English texts. The first completely English publication was Thomas Morley's *First Book of Madrigals for Four Voices* (1594).

Madrigal singing became very fashionable at the end of the century, so much so that, as Morley relates, if a man was unable to sing a madrigal part by sight it was accounted a sign of poor education. The madrigal appealed to a wider public than did its Italian counterpart; this is reflected in the choice of texts. Whereas the Italians strove to set verse which was recognized in its own right as fine poetry, the English were

1. Reese, op. cit., p. 814.

disinclined to use the great poetry of their day, preferring (with very few exceptions) to set verses specially written for them. They recognized that much of the poetry by Sidney and Spenser was too involved in meaning and syntax to make good material for music. Nevertheless, their works display as wide a variety as those of the Italians and as great a depth of expression, being in verbal delineation, rhythmic device, and subtle use of chromaticism in no way inferior to their models. Morley, Wilbye, and Weelkes are the equals of the Italian masters in imagination though not in copiousness of production.

THE AYRE

Later songs of the type arranged by Byrd in his 1588 publication were accompanied by the lute rather than a group of viols. The first published 'ayres' (as such songs were called) were by John Dowland (1563–1626). These ayres were very often designed both for accompanied solo performance and polyphonic performance by a group of voices.[1] As Thomas Campion puts it in the preface to his first book (1617), it appears that such performance might sometimes be improvised:

These airs were for the most part framed at first for one voice with the lute or viol, but upon occasion they have since been filled with more parts, which who so please may use, who like not may leave. Yet do we daily observe, that when any shall sing a treble to an instrument, the bystanders will be offering an inner part out of their own nature; and true or false, out it must, though to the perverting of the whole harmony.

Thirty volumes of ayres were published by 1622; most of the compositions they contained were simple, attractively tuneful, and delicately sensitive in details of word-setting. Dowland's songs, by reason of their passionate expression, stand out from the majority as some of the most beautiful compositions ever written for the solo voice. Their lute accompaniments often display an almost madrigalian contrapuntal

1. See p. 130 for an account of the lay-out of Dowland's book.

texture which underlines the meaning of the text by rapid changes of rhythm and frequent chromatic clashes. *In darkness let me dwell* has some particularly striking bars (Example 41). Several of Dowland's airs also exist as dances; the most famous of these, *Flow, my tears* is mentioned by its dance title *Lachrymae* many times in contemporary literature.

INSTRUMENTAL MUSIC

Lute music forms the largest part of the surviving instrumental repertoire. A recent survey has catalogued over two thousand pieces: three times the number of virginal works. Nearly half of these are dances (pavanes and *galliards*); arrangements of

41

Thus wed - ded to my woes, And bed-ded to my tomb,

O let me living die, O

vocal polyphony, fantasias, ground basses (including *passa-mezzos*), variations on popular songs, and short dances constitute the remainder. Dowland was the greatest of an imposing group of lutenist composers. As court lutenist to the King of Denmark his compositions became widely known in Europe, being 'printed in eight most famous Cities beyond the seas'.

Keyboard music for both organ and virginals antedates lute compositions. John Redford (1485-1545) is fairly representative of the earlier organists of the century. Most of his works, surviving in the *Mulliner Book* (a collection made between 1545 and 1585), are built on plainsongs with either imitative counterpoints or florid ornamental lines. The remaining pieces in the *Mulliner Book* consist of dances, settings of psalm tunes and chant melodies by Redford's contemporaries, and transcriptions of secular part-songs and anthems (many by Tallis); the selection thus includes music suitable for both virginals and organ. Later keyboard music tends to differentiate between the two instruments. The great collections of virginal music dating from the later years of the century (e.g. the *FitzWilliam Virginal Book*), though they still contain a few works suitable for organ performance, consist chiefly of the dance, variation, and fantasia forms that are to be found in the lute repertoire. In the variation, composers developed the art of building passages out of little short patterns (used either imitatively or ornamentally) to the degree where it became the beginning of a new technique in musical architecture. The English variation had an important influence on the work of the early seventeenth-century Dutch and north German organists. The style of John Bull (organist at Antwerp Cathedral 1617–28), for example, had a profound effect on that of Sweelinck, whose pupils laid the foundations of a development that culminated in the organ music of Bach.

Ensemble music in England relied little on vocal transcriptions, hence the forms of *ricercare* and *canzona* do not appear, being replaced by an almost wholly indigenous tradition. From the first years of Henry VIII's reign the leading composers provided a steady stream of fantasias for viols and other instruments. One fantasia form, the *In nomine*, was based on a melody from Taverner's Mass *Gloria tibi Trinitas*, where it is set to the words of the *Benedictus*, '*in nomine Domini*'. Taverner, the inventor of the form, treated the melody as a *cantus firmus*, in which shape it continued to be used by composers for another century.

The first printed book of ensemble music in England was Morley's *First Book of Consort Lessons* (1599), a collection of pieces for treble and bass viols, cittern and pandore (plucked stringed instruments of the lute type), lute, and recorder. This was the first publication to specify the instrumentation in detail: alternative performance is ruled out by designing each instrumental part for a particular instrument. The 'broken consort' (i.e. a group of different instruments, an unbroken consort being a group of similar instruments) was popular in England: its use by the London waits has been mentioned previously. Morley's book was the first of several such publications by leading composers. The most famous of all was Dowland's *Lachrymae* (1604), 'seven passionate pavanes' on his own tune with many other dances for 'lute, viols, or violins, in five parts'.

III · BAROQUE CHURCH MUSIC AND OCCASIONAL MUSIC

Henry Raynor

1. The Italian Concertato Style

THE utilization of the various Baroque styles by composers of liturgical music has led historians to speak perhaps too freely of the 'secularization' of music during the Baroque age, for whilst it is true that distinctions between religious and secular music were obliterated, the obliteration was not the composer's conscious aim. The new musical technique of *concertato*, balancing and opposing contrasted musical forces, made possible bigger forms and a more poignant dramatic expression as well as epigrammatic sharpness and brevity; composers naturally desired to exploit these new musical styles inside the church, and in doing so they created music that occasionally overrode boundaries of tradition as well as of taste and propriety.

During the earlier and evangelistic part of the Baroque period, forces within the church saw the popularizing and propaganda value of the new style, so that oratorio (non-liturgical religious music-drama) was encouraged by ecclesiastical authorities for its teaching value. That encouragement naturally led to further infiltration of the new dramatic style into the church itself. Oratorio was not a Jesuit invention, but it is significant that this most militant of teaching orders both fostered the new form and introduced it in their churches to countries where it was not previously known. In Italy, the birthplace of the form, it was the Jesuits who, for teaching purposes, encouraged the transformation of oratorio from a grave Latin composition into a theatrical Italian one. Thus composers who wished to bring the dramatic power and melodic attractiveness of the *stile moderno* into music for worship received a certain stimulus from within the church.

Oratorios were, of course, written by composers attached to a church or a cathedral, not by those whose duties kept them at court; the number of Italian oratorios is immense, and their composers kept closely in touch with the general public taste. In Austria and in Catholic Germany, however, where almost all the surviving music comes from court composers, few examples of the form can be traced. The French composer responsible for the introduction of oratorio to French listeners was the Italian-trained Marc-Antoine Charpentier, whose connexion with Louis XIV's court was comparatively short-lived.

Many musicians in Italy and Austria nevertheless regarded the new style as a somewhat ambivalent affair. Throughout the Baroque era, even the most revolutionary composers were ready to turn back to the *a cappella* style, although these efforts at writing music in the old manner are usually exercises in composer's counterpoint rather than religiously expressive masterpieces. This ambivalence has many causes. The go-ahead, missionary-minded clergy were prepared to encourage musical innovations in order to attract indifferent Catholics into church, and the new style became more and more the composer's natural language. But the centres of Catholic authority were conservative, and from time to time they set out to encourage a revival of polyphonic music, although by the time this style was in its final agony, composers had made of it a means of secularization perhaps even more scandalous than the unifying of instrumental and operatic styles in church music. It was a combination of antiquity with the purity of Palestrina's style and the fervent devotionalism of Victoria's which gave Renaissance polyphony a special sanctity in the minds of composers and ecclesiastical authorities.

Many of the earliest manifestations of the *stile moderno* were innocuous enough to pass by without arousing suspicion. By 1602, when Ludovico Grossi (1564–1645), named 'Viadana' after his birthplace, published his *Concerti ecclesiastici* (a collection of motets and psalm settings more revolutionary in title than in substance), numerous volumes of church works with organ continuo were in circulation. Some of these contained motets, in which a subjective, expressive attitude to the text and some freedom from strict liturgical principles was allowed, as well as movements from the Mass itself. They tended, like Viadana's *Concerti*, to base their claim to modernity on the use of the organ as an accompaniment rather than as part of a balanced *concertato*. Viadana's own compromise with fashion, the introduction of monody to the church, was simply achieved by writing what to all intents and purposes was four-part polyphony, treating the top line as a vocal solo and relegating the others parts to the organ. The Baroque balance of interest between melody and an expressive bass is not suggested, and the *basso continuo* in such cases had the utilitarian function of supplying music for churches in which the full choir was unavailable or defective.

MONTEVERDI

When Claudio Monteverdi (1567–1643) was appointed *maestro di cappella* at St Mark's, Venice, in 1613, he was charged with the duty of restoring the old style for the cathedral services. The Venetian composers had been the spearhead of the revolution for close on a century, and Monteverdi was already known as the man who had given musical autonomy to opera as well as the composer of the radically new *Vespers* of 1610. If it seems strange that a leader of the *avantgarde* should be appointed to a specially conservative task, it should be noted that Monteverdi was a master of both traditional and modern styles. His first published work, the *Sacrae cantiunculae* of 1582, was a collection of three-part motets in traditional style, and each of his succeeding volumes of church music – that of 1610 which includes the great Vespers, the *Selva morale et spirituale* of 1641, and a posthumously published memorial volume – contains *a cappella* music together with pieces that exploit the modern style to the full. Dramatic orchestration, massive *concertato* designs, eloquent monody and the excitements of what Monteverdi called *stile concitato* ('agitated style') come readily to his mind, but so does an expressively valid exploitation of the old principles of polyphony.

All Monteverdi's other church works are unfortunately overshadowed by the *Vespers* of 1610; a *Mass* and a *Requiem* in the *stile moderno* which might have rivalled them have failed to survive. The *Vespers* as usually performed nowadays include five items that form no part of the service at all. They were interspersed among the psalms by an enterprising publisher, his intention being to give an immediate impression of variety to a choirmaster browsing through the collection. The works were certainly not meant to be performed in the order in which they were printed, and the only genuine Vespers items are *Domine ad adjuvandum*, *Dixit Dominus*, *Laudate pueri*, *Laetatus sum*, *Nisi Dominus*, *Lauda Jerusalem*, *Ave maris stella*, and *Magnificat*. Of this last there are two settings, one a small-scale composition for First Vespers, the other a more elaborate and fully orchestrated setting for Second Vespers. The remaining items are in fact cantatas, with the exception of *Sancta Maria* (which is a petition from the Litany of Loreto) and they were meant to be performed, as the title-page tells us, 'in princely chapels and apartments'.

In the Vesper psalms proper, the *cantus firmus* is sometimes used fugally, sometimes against elaborate counterpoints of startling vocal virtuosity; sometimes it is hammered out in block harmony whilst the instruments weave lively harmonic and rhythmic patterns around it, as in the opening response. Every variety of ensemble that can be raised from amongst the forces he uses is called into action; solo voices, alone or in ensemble, appear against the choir, the orchestra, or selected bodies of instruments or singers. Expressive *arioso* monodies and duets rise upon the foundation of the traditional plain-song.

All the later church music which Monteverdi composed in the *stile moderno* is comparable to the Vespers in its range and dramatic force. The *Lamento d'Arianna* is taken from the opera to become *Il pianto della Madonna*; a *Salve Regina* for solo voice and continuo flares into drama for the words 'To thee do we cry, poor banished children of Eve', and is vividly graphic about 'our sighs, mourning and weeping in this vale of tears', which is set to a favourite Monteverdian device for lamentation – a chromatically descending bass which draws the voice into its fall. The jubilant rhythms of a *Gloria* are dramatically halted for the words '*et in terra pax*', whilst a setting of the Psalm *Laudate Dominum* (Example 42) ends in a carillon-like *Gloria Patri* interrupted by shouts of joy from the full choir and orchestra.

Monteverdi overshadows his entire period in Italy, but developments along the lines he laid down were common. Alessandro Grandi (d. 1630), his colleague at St Mark's, wrote monodic motets and Masses where the musical interest is fairly divided between the solo voice and a bass line of real expressive power, which often imitates the singer's melody. Tarquinio Merula wrote an entire Mass upon a single chaconne theme, and the Venetian Baldassare Donati in 1629 published a set of fifteen motets upon a single bass. The disciples of Monteverdi, however, rarely turned to such huge designs as the Vespers, and their delight in madrigalian word-painting to bring out the emotional content of the text led to the abandonment of the *cantus firmus*, although their master's genius had been able to satisfy the desire for both tradition and subjective expression.

ROME AND THE ORATORIO

The modern style enters unobtrusively in conservative centres like Rome; Francesco Soriano (1579–1621), Felice Anerio (c. 1560–1614), who succeeded Palestrina as composer to the Papal Chapel, his brother Giovanni Francesco (c. 1567–1621), and Gregorio Allegri (1585–1629), whose celebrated eight-part *Miserere* Mozart was to hear as a boy and set down from memory, moved towards the new style in their use of strongly pronounced rhythms and harmonically motivated writing. Special occasions, however, drew composers towards the vast, spatially organized designs inspired by the Venetian tradition which also suited the architectural magnificence of St Peter's, where Virgilio Mazzocchi employed extra choirs, one in the Dome and one in the tower above it. The 'colossal Baroque', as it has been called, reached a more than Berliozian magniloquence in the Mass written by Orazio Benevoli (1605–72) for the consecration of Salzburg Cathedral. This work was scored for two double choirs, each with its own continuo, and five separately organized accompanying orchestras (two of woodwind, two of strings, and one of brass) over a master continuo which reduces the whole work to harmonic simplicity and proves its complexity to be less a matter of organic substance than of the skill with which contrasted bodies of tone are played off against each other.

In the meantime, a further reconciliation of secular music and religion was taking place through the oratorio. This was at first a means of rousing popular devotion through sacred music-dramas which adopted all the new intensities of style possible in monody and *concertato* writing; it took its name from the *Oratorio* ('Prayer Hall') where devout laymen met together under the auspices of the Society of St Philip Neri in Rome for prayer and the singing of *laude*, or devotional songs. Such songs had no fixed stylistic order: Palestrina had written polyphonic *laude* to popular texts, while in 1619 Giovanni Anerio published a volume of popular devotional pieces in dialogue form with the significant title *Teatro armonico spirituale*, linking the dialogues with narrative choruses.

The earliest oratorios were either dramatic dialogues of this sort interspersed with reflective choral passages, or were close in style to the already popular chamber cantata. The first decades of the seventeenth century saw the appearance of numerous motets in dialogue form utilizing both monody and *concertato* style. Notable amongst dialogue compositions is the *Rappresentazione di anima e di corpo*, by Emilio de Cavalieri, first heard in 1600. At the same time, the development of *bel canto* singing naturally influenced the type of music used in sacred music-dramas, which differed from opera only in their employment of a narrator who is not one of the dramatic persons and in the importance they give to the chorus. From these roots oratorio grew in Rome, where it used Latin texts, and in northern Italy where colloquial language was the rule. Everywhere oratorio was designedly popular in style, but the closing of the Roman opera houses during Lent gave it an aristocratic audience whose patronage naturally accelerated its adoption of vocal bravura.

Oratorio becomes recognizably a form of its own in the sixteen surviving *Historiae sacrae* of Giacomo Carissimi (1605–74). Whilst his liturgical music has been more or less forgotten, Carissimi's oratorios and chamber cantatas are amongst the most important Italian works of their period. The cantatas, written for a musically educated audience, are sophisticated pieces which have a clarity of form and a subtlety of harmony absent from the oratorios. These, despite their Latin texts, are aimed at a 'mass audience'. Carissimi's stories – the Judgement of Solomon, Jephtha, Jonah, the Great Flood – are cast in brief dramatic episodes which lead up to big choruses. The choir is sometimes narrator, sometimes a participant in the action, and its music deals homophonically with impressive rhythms while the solo voices are used in a free *arioso* recitative (Example 43).

Although Carissimi's choruses are short they are often vividly descriptive, as in the sea storm of *Jonah* and the battle of *Jephtha*. The declamation blossoms out into *bel canto* richness over emotive words and phrases, for words are all-important. Carissimi is not concerned with the orchestral colours that delighted Monteverdi but with taut verbal drama that needs no extra decoration or propulsion, so that he is content with only two violins and organ for accompaniment.

Carissimi's majestic choral style was carried into Germany and France by his pupils: more typical of the development of Italian oratorio are the works of Alessandro Stradella (*c.* 1645–82), who, despite his success as an opera composer, regarded his oratorio *St John the Baptist* as his masterpiece. Stradella wrote his major works in Venice; and the greatness of his oratorios, apart from their skilful and unfailingly conscientious workmanship, is dramatic and lies in forceful operatic characterization. Stradella's rich, Italianate melodies motivate daring formal experiments; there is, for instance, an *aria concertante* where the orchestra is divided into *concertino* and *concerto grosso*, and a remarkable duet on a chaconne bass in which Herod expresses remorse for the Prophet's murder whilst his step-daughter rejoices in it.

The strands of oratorio and liturgy meet again in the work of the Sicilian Alessandro Scarlatti (1660–1725), who not only composed oratorios in which all the formal and expressive developments which found a place in his operas were used, but also used precisely the same idiom in much of his liturgical music. Eight of his ten surviving Masses look back to the *stile antico*, which, to the Neapolitan master (from 1684 to 1702 *maestro di cappella* to the Viceroy of Naples) was anything but a natural mode of expression. The other two Masses finally establish the form of the Cantata Mass, in which musical forms rather than liturgical necessities are the determining factors. Scarlatti uninhibitedly writes operatic music and perfects his crystallization of the aria as a large-scale vocal form by applying the design of a concerto movement, with extended and picturesque *ritornelli*.

In a sense, his fourteen oratorios have less to offer a modern audience than his liturgical music, and it would be easy to regard them as an excuse for operatic music during the Lenten abstinence. The importance of the chorus is sacrificed to vocal bravura and the dramatic exploitation of orchestral effects, but in reality the works are a sincere expression of a type of devotion with which our age is out of sympathy. The *Assumption Oratorio*, for example, ends with a duet in the rhythm of a *siciliana* for the Heavenly Bride and Bridegroom which, if we lose our grip upon its purposes, carries us straight into the love scene of a typical eighteenth-century opera.

Notwithstanding the extravagance of Scarlatti's church music, that of Antonio Vivaldi (1675–1741) was criticized by his Venetian contemporaries for its exaggerated devotionalism. Like Scarlatti, Vivaldi sectionalizes the liturgical texts – he breaks up the *Gloria* and distributes the fragments between soloists and chorus in much the same way as Bach does in the *B minor Mass*. A single psalm – Number 111, *Beatus vir* – is treated almost verse by verse in different styles; the opening is a conventionally Venetian movement for antiphonal choirs; the second verse becomes an operatic duet for two basses while the third is a *concerto grosso* movement for two sopranos and the lighter toned instruments. Yet despite the charge that this music is exaggeratedly fervent, it borrows from and lends to the composer's secular works. The '*Domine Deus*' of the *Gloria in D* refers to the slow movement of the Concerto,

Op. 3, No. 11; themes for *La Primavera* (Op. 8, No. 1) appear in the oratorio *Judith*, and Vivaldi makes use of sinfonias, *ritornelli*, and so on that would be perfectly at home in his concertos and operas.

2. Church Music Outside Italy

GERMANY AND AUSTRIA

THE revolution in church music, as in opera and instrumental works, began in Italy, and was rapidly carried across Europe. The Baroque period regarded the Italians as the natural masters of modern music, and it was to Italy that the promising young men of all countries were sent to study. The dramatization of church music proceeded in Austria and Catholic Germany through a long line of Italian composers who worked at the great courts and in the cathedrals, like Valentini (d. 1649) and Caldara (1670–1736) in Vienna, or Bonporti (1672–1749) in Trent.

The court musicians of Austria and south Germany were naturally called upon for numerous Mass settings and few oratorios. Between Carissimi and the end of our period, the Italians wrote comparatively little liturgical music, of which hardly any has been preserved, while their Central-European contemporaries were extremely busy with music composed within the framework of the rite.

Furthermore, the dramatically expressive style of the oratorio was slow to influence Central Europeans, who exploited *concertato* style with a lively sense of colour and an awareness of national musical idioms. In their works, trumpets (especially the high 'clarino' instruments that were the originals of the modern 'Bach trumpet') and drums stood for jubilation, trombones for splendour and solemnity, and an early use of the strings together with the organ continuo as the essential accompaniment is joined to a sense of form which compels Mass settings to accept a musical shape almost disastrously unliturgical. The opening *Kyrie* turns its central petitions – '*Christe eleison*' – into a solo or solo-ensemble piece between two choral movements in a way that quickly came to suggest affinities with the concerto, so that we find the *Christe* set in the dominant of the opening key or, in minor-mode works, in its relative major. The *Gloria* and *Credo* end with fugues, often,

211

in early days, upon the same subject; a straightforward *Sanctus*, demanding trombones for majesty, leads to a lively '*Osanna*', which is shortened in repetition after an extended slow-movement *Benedictus*. At the beginning of the period, the '*Dona nobis pacem*' which concludes the *Agnus Dei* (and the setting) often repeats music from the *Kyrie*; later, it became a separate, lively major-mode piece after the first petitions of the prayer had been set devoutly in the minor. In this way, composers found a satisfactory musical form even if its repetitions and its musical purposes worked against the spirit of the liturgy.

This Central-European style developed through the music of such composers as Christoph Strauss (1580–1631), who ended his life as *Kapellmeister* of St Stephen's Cathedral, Vienna; Johann Heinrich Schmelzer (*c.* 1623–80), a Viennese court chamber musician; Johann Kaspar Kerll (1627–93), a pupil of Carissimi who became court composer at Munich after spending the years 1674–7 as court organist in Vienna; Heinrich Franz Biber (1644–1704) of Salzburg; and Johann Joseph Fux (1660–1741), for nearly thirty years *Kapellmeister* at St Stephen's. Strauss, at the beginning of the period, employs a Monteverdian technique of *concertato* structures upon *cantus firmus* themes or in 'parody' Masses taking their main theme from a motet or other pre-existing work. His *Missa Veni Sponsa Christi*, for example, adapts the theme on which it is based to the different movements of the Mass with a lively sense of measured rhythm and, making the best of both musical worlds, brings in trumpets and drums to make a jubilant noise in the early clauses of the Creed. The *Requiem* which he composed in 1616 or 1617 is introduced by a '*symphonia ad imitationem campanelle*' in which the strings suggest the tolling of bells. The music is set out for two unequally voiced choirs – sopranos, altos, and first and second tenors on the one hand, tenors with basses in five parts on the other; the preponderance of low voices leads to effective antiphonal writing and interestingly varied ensembles. A more lavishly scored *Missa concertata in eco* colourfully exploits a favourite Baroque device.

In Schmelzer's work, a certain naturally Viennese type of expression appears; a human and relaxed pleasure in melodiousness seems to underlie much of his *Missa nuptialis*, in which the '*Osanna*' dances against a solemn trombone background (Example 44), while the '*Dona nobis*' is a sprightly

movement based upon *concertato* contrast effects. Schmelzer's music is by no means incapable of intensity, but in the *Requiem* of Kerll we find the continuo, reinforced by bassoon for the sake of greater definition, moving along lines almost Purcellian in their chromatic expressiveness. Contrasting sinfonias for strings divide the sections of the *Kyrie* of his *Missa cuiusvis toni*, of 1687, and the *Missa a tre chori*, composed in the same year, adds two clarino trumpets, two cornetts, three trombones, strings, and organ to soloists and three full choirs. From these forces it builds up remarkably contrasted ensembles as well as massively impressive climaxes.

Biber's violin music has ensured that he is not so completely forgotten as the other composers we have mentioned, and his *Missa Sancti Henrici* (1701) shows the *concertato* Mass coalescing into form; five soloists, five-part choir, five trumpets (two of them clarini), three trombones, timpani, strings, and organ naturally demanding to be used in block contrast group against group and in the various vocal combinations. In addition Biber allows his soloists moments of individual eloquence (but nothing approaching an extended arioso) away from the ensemble, while the *Gloria* and *Credo* end in vigorous fugues.

In the history books, Fux has become a symbol for arid scholasticism, largely through the authority of his textbook *Gradus ad Parnassum*. The Emperor Charles VI's influence, early in the eighteenth century, demanded a traditional *a cappella* style in court works and fortunately Fux (like Monteverdi) could turn to the old style and use it as a living language. He even displays expressive intensity in his use of scholastic devices, as in the *Missa Sancti Caroli* of 1718, written entirely in canon. Devotion to polyphony, evident in his operas, gives strength to his oratorios, which find dramatic validity in such things as big fugal structures, besides vitalizing his *concertato* liturgical works. Of all the Austrian composers before the rise of the symphony, none is greater than Fux in combining imagination with profoundly learned musicianship.

The development of the cantata Mass had little influence upon Austrian and German composers. Even Johann Adolf Hasse (1699–1783), a pupil of Alessandro Scarlatti, who became Director of the Opera at Dresden, never broke away from the idea of a solo ensemble set against a polyphonically treated choir, although he employs his orchestra for *ritornelli* in choral movements and for liturgically irrelevant *sinfonie*. It was the Italians employed in Vienna and elsewhere who brought the latest style northwards. Antonio Caldara, assistant *Kapellmeister* to Fux, was (like his superior) compelled for a time to write *a cappella* compositions, of which a highly intricate Mass – in double canon, inverted, contrary, and retrograde – is typical in its mathematical precision and expressive dullness. His later works, such as the *Missa dolorosa*, with its elaborate arias and *obbligato* instrumental solos, signal the victory of the cantata style over the *concertato* forms which the Austrian composers had used more than effectively.

Even in Italy, however, Austrian formal preoccupations had their influence, so that we find the Mass-form rounded off in works like the *Missa solenne* of Giovanni Battista Pergolesi (1710–36). Although Pergolesi's liturgical works do not show the charm and grace of such things as his *Stabat Mater* – he often seems to search for a grandeur of expression not naturally part of his musical vocabulary – his work for the church services has dramatic vitality combined with an operatic freedom of expression.

SPAIN

Despite the example of Frescobaldi and the fascinating organ works of such composers as Georg Muffat (*c.* 1645–1704), no important schools of organ composition established themselves in Italy and Austria, where composers could depend upon a church orchestra. In Spain, however, where a rigid conservatism in religious matters governed the provision of liturgical music, the custom of alternating plainchant with elaborate organ 'versets' in the psalms, canticles, and hymns, using the plainsong melody as a *cantus firmus*, was developed in a typically austere way. Spanish organ music of this period lacks the richness of texture achieved by organ composers in northern Europe, but it should be remembered that few Spanish organs of that time possessed a pedal keyboard.

Francisco Correa de Araujo (d. 1665) and the Portuguese Rodrigues Coelho (b. 1583), the early masters of the Iberian school, were both in touch with the organ style of English and Dutch composers, and in Araujo's music we find an interesting attempt to fuse the Anglo-Netherlands technique with traditional polyphony and a search for extremes of emotional expression. Coelho, in his versets and variations upon plainsong hymns, maintains traditional austerity in a more serene style. The master of the Spanish school, Juan Cabanilles (1644–1712), is known by about a third of his compositions, the rest having failed to survive. His work has less of the national austerity, but possesses a sturdy vigour of expressive counterpoint and a daring harmonic sense that leads him to startling 'modernisms'.

While Spanish composers wrote oratorios in the Italian style and popular *villancicos* ('carol' would be the most acceptable English equivalent) as well as traditional, folk-music-style pieces for religious dramas (*autos sacramentales*), such music had little influence upon their church work. The grandiose, multi-choral motets of Juan Bautista Comes (1568–1634) rarely approach anything comparable to *concertato* style, although his contemporary Juan Pujol (1573–1626) combined traditional techniques with real dramatic feeling and, at times, wrote a figured bass accompaniment for motets, rather in the style of the early Italian composers of the period who regarded the device as fashionable rather than functional or expressive.

The traditional style was continued by Cererols (1618–76) and Domenico Francisco Valls (1665–1747), whose unaccompanied *Missa scala aretina*, composed in 1715, created a ten-years' controversy because, in the *Gloria*, the second soprano of a five-part choir enters with the words '*Miserere nobis*' on A, against the B flat of the first sopranos and the G of the tenors and basses. The commotion caused by this unprepared but hardly shocking dissonance is typical of the conservatism that governed Spanish church life.

As the church orchestra began to gain ground in the Chapel Royal and the cathedrals during the latter part of the seventeenth century, the distinctive Spanish organ school declined, and we find, among the many *a cappella* works of Sebastian Duron, a *Requiem* for five unequally voiced choirs, each with its own instruments. Antonio Literes (d. *c.* 1572), the first major composer of the emancipation, composed a great deal of traditional work, organ versets and *stile antico* Masses and motets, but amongst his output are four Italianate Masses with orchestral accompaniment.

FRANCE

If a natural conservatism governed the development of Spanish religious music, church music in France was governed by the special conditions of French political and social life. While in the provinces the traditional ways continued in the hands of obscure musicians, the Absolutism founded by Cardinal Richelieu and developed by Louis XIV drew to the court not only the aristocrats who would otherwise have employed important artists in their own establishments but also all the first-class talent of the country. The unity of style that we find in eighteenth-century French music was, therefore, the creation of the King rather than of the musicians who served him.

As in Spain, throughout this period and on until the time of the Revolution, the alternation of plainchant with organ elaborations continued. Jean Titelouze (1563–1633), at the beginning of the period, was unable to escape the influence of the English and Netherlands composers, but this he wedded to a style which was never far from vocal polyphony. The musical revolution seems to influence his work in his feeling for tonality (a pedal A continues almost entirely throughout his *Ave maris stella*) and in sharp contrasts of registration that suggest *concertato* ideas.

Titelouze is a neglected giant of his period, and none of his immediate successors is comparable in stature. The new ideals found their way into the works of such composers as Nicholas Gigault (1625–1707), whose practical touches included the provision of numerous internal cadences, so that the priest should not be kept waiting, Nicholas Le Bègue (1630–1702), Guillaume-Gabriel Nivers (1632–1714), and Charles Couperin (1638–79). Although a decree of 1662 forbade composers to obliterate the *cantus firmus* or disguise it beyond recognition, André Raison (d. 1719) introduced dance-rhythms into his versets whilst insisting that they be played at a slow tempo to preserve 'the sanctity of the place'.

It was in accordance with their general musical culture that composers should tend to draw the *cantus firmus* into the modern tonalities they used for works outside the church, so that a modernized treatment of plainsong, called *plainchant musical*, became common and reached political importance during the struggles to establish the autonomy of the French church.

The five *Messes royales* by Henri Dumont (1610–84), in

whose work the Baroque choral style first established itself in the French church, are examples of *plainchant musical*, with their melodies given tonality and measured out into modern barred rhythm. His *Cantica sacra*, on the other hand, published nine years before his appointment as Master of the Chapel Royal in 1662, strikes for the first time the note of massive dignity that was to become typically French in a powerful *concertato* style. The Masses had few successors because, whenever possible, Louis XIV was in the habit of attending Low Mass, so that it became the composer's duty to provide elaborate motets with which to elaborate the simpler rite.

Lully's few religious works finally impressed the French church music of the period with the gravity and splendour of his operatic style. His motets become lengthy cantatas with fully-formed arias, sinfonias, and choruses, all of them accompanied by an orchestra used for purposes of magnificence. The *Te Deum* and *Dies irae* which Lully composed late in life are both of unquestionable greatness; their sinfonias have a massive strength matched by the exciting, hammered-out rhythms of the choir and the fierily dramatic declamation of the soloists. Except for a momentary quotation of the opening of the *Dies irae*, Lully has nothing to do with plainsong, and his one quotation, with a distorting accidental, is modernized *plainchant musical*.

Lully's music is magnificently ceremonial rather than devout: that of Marc-Antoine Charpentier (*c.* 1636–1704), who studied under Carissimi, brought an Italianate lyricism and a natural gift for polyphony to rival the French style worked out by the Italian Lully. Charpentier's church works – Masses, motets, psalms, and a fine *Te Deum*, all orchestrally accompanied, are closer than Lully's to the spirit of the liturgy, and his oratorios – the first French essays in the form – are closely modelled upon those of his teacher though they admit a richer lyricism.

Lullian grandeur combines with genuine fervour in the music of Michel-Richard de Lalande (1657–1726), who succeeded Lully in Louis XIV's favour. Lalande contrasts the massive homophonic style of his predecessor with passages of rich and fluent polyphony, and his harmony is often more adventurous than that of Lully.

François Couperin '*le Grand*' (1668–1733) was a greater musician than these in the range and finish of his work, but apart from the two organ Masses written almost at the beginning of his career, church music is a by-product of his genius. Both the Masses were written in 1689, when he was organist of the Church of St Gervais, the first, *à l'usage ordinaire des Paroisses, pour les fêtes*, apparently for his own use, and the second, *propre pour les Couvents des Religieux et Religieuses*, probably at the request of some religious community. They consist of organ versets intended to alternate with the plainsong of the Ordinary of the Mass, together with an organ solo at the Offertory. The music is of great strength and delicacy, sometimes fugal and sometimes sanctifying the contemporary theatre style. Occasionally they reach a chromaticism as startling as that of Purcell's more introspective works.

Couperin's motets belong to the last twenty years of the 'Sun King's' reign, during his melancholy and inevitable decline. They rarely aim at the grandeur of Lully or Lalande; Couperin's orchestra is smaller – some fine works require only two violins and continuo – and the choir is seldom used. Much of the loveliest of this music is for soprano solo or a duet of two sopranos. When Couperin is majestic, he achieves majesty through simplicity. The *Leçons des ténèbres*, the readings from the Book of Lamentations at Maundy Thursday Matins, the masterpiece amongst his church works, was probably – if the setting for two sopranos be taken as a guide – composed for a convent. Each verse of the Lessons is introduced by a letter of the Hebrew alphabet, and the traditional chant itself sets the composer off upon extremely elaborate, highly decorative vocal excursions, the decorations of which are in themselves highly expressive.

Two lengthy lessons are set for solo voice, employing all the devices of French vocal music – Lullian recitative, the fantasy of the *air de cour*, and a subtlety of ornamentation developed from Couperin's keyboard practice. The second voice enters only in the final lesson and demands the invention of new and elaborate music for all the recurrent features of the text – the introductory Hebrew letters and the verse '*Jerusalem convertere ad Dominum Deum tuum*' which closes each of the lessons.

The church compositions of Jean Philippe Rameau (1683–1764) round off the period. Despite Rameau's service as an organist at the cathedrals of Dijon and Clermont-Ferrand, he wrote only a handful of motets in a grand style of courtly magnificence. A setting of Psalm 69 for five-part choir and continuo is a work of rigorously austere counterpoint, contrasting strongly with the Lullian splendours of his other motets, in which orchestras and dramatic forms together with powerful choruses are built up in the manner of concerti grossi. This music, like much of Rameau's work, is impressive and finely wrought, yet in imagination and inventiveness it cannot compete with his operas and keyboard pieces.

3. The Chorale

WHILE the history of church music in the Catholic countries is to a large extent that of the composers' struggle to emancipate themselves from plainchant, the staple music of Lutheranism was the chorale, a hymn tune in modern tonality created for congregational singing in unison. The Calvinist churches abandoned all music except unison singing of the psalms in metrical translation, whereas the Lutherans rapidly built up a great body of fine tunes. Some of them were adapted folk tunes, some (like the Passion chorale *O Haupt voll Blut und Wunden*, one of the most famous) were taken over from secular compositions. To these tunes were set verses containing the essentials of Christian teaching and devotion.

It is impossible to exaggerate the purely musical importance of the chorales: from the very first they were subject to organ accompaniment and polyphonic elaboration, but their strong tonality helped them to avoid the musical shackles and almost insoluble problems (such as created the French *plainchant musical*) involved in their treatment as *cantus firmus*. In addition, as every chorale had its doctrinal or devotional significance for the congregation, its melody would be an infallible guide to the thought and purpose of the composer using it.

The Catholic artist's duty was to direct the thoughts of worshippers and to use music as a handmaid to the liturgy: the Protestant emphasis upon the Bible as the Word of God gave two duties to the composer; he could expound the Word and interpret it. Therefore the dramatic forms previously wedded to Catholic church music entered the Protestant field either as direct narrative accounts of Scriptural events or as introspective commentaries on the relationship between man and God. This searching and introspective attitude to religious music affected not only choral music but the organ pieces embedded in the Lutheran liturgy which were all in one way or another related to the chorale. Lutheran equivalents of the English 'voluntary', for instance, looked to an appropriately seasonal chorale for their foundation, while the organ's announcement of the tune to be sung became a fixed event in the service, and an opportunity for composers to disclose, through the chorale-prelude music, the underlying significance of its text.

The actual words of the service, which, in the Lutheran Church, at first included most of the Mass in a German translation, meant less to composers than the opportunities for drama and exegesis offered by organ treatment of the chorales or by the motets which developed rapidly into church cantatas. At the same time, it was natural that the new Italian styles (Italy being the Mecca of all would-be composers) should rapidly be converted to the use of the reformed churches. Jan Pieterszoon Sweelinck (1562–1621), who studied in Venice before settling down as organist of the Oude Kerk in Amsterdam, wrote a quantity of more or less conservative choral works while laying the foundations of the specifically religious organ style of the great Germans.

His organ toccatas, with their strong sense of form and rhythmic vigour, had profound influence on his successors, as did the fantasias, out of which developed the Bachian fugue; yet it is Sweelinck's treatment of chorale melodies which principally concerns us. He adopts the English variation style of increasingly elaborate ornamental figuration above a *cantus firmus*, building up with great skill to elaborate climaxes. The *cantus firmus*, however, is usually sacrosanct; whatever fantasy and richness go to the surrounding elaborations, it is rarely changed.

The types of vocal treatment possible in the chorale were codified by Michael Praetorius (1571–1621) in his collection *Musae Sioniae*, which discriminated between the 'chorale motet', where the melody appears fugally in all voices, 'madrigal style', in which the component motives of the chorale are set in *concertato* manner, and 'chorale – *cantus firmus*' style, a vocal parallel to Sweelinck's organ variations. Decoration of the chorale melody in a vocal setting is, however, governed by the sense of the words and not by the need for an architectural climax.

Praetorius, like Hans Leo Hassler (1565–1612) and Samuel Scheidt (1587–1654), was tentative in his treatment of the continuo, but Scheidt, a master of the organ variation comparable to Sweelinck, opened a new road in his *Cantiones sacrae* of 1620, which give a different contrapuntal variation for each stanza of the chorale. In addition, Scheidt developed the chorale-fantasia, which applied the principle of the chorale-motet to the organ.

Chorale-*concertato*, which developed from Praetorius's madrigal-style treatment of the chorale, was at first the most forward-looking principle in German music. Praetorius himself wrote multi-choral, lavishly accompanied works in this form, with vivid Italianate decorations of the melody. Johann Hermann Schein (1586–1630), one of Bach's precursors at the Thomaskirche, Leipzig, brought the full (sometimes extravagant) verbal expressiveness of the Italian madrigal school to works of this type in his *Geistliche Konzerte*. More revolutionary still are Schein's chorale-monodies; the early Italian monodists often descended to musical nullity in the interest of the text, but Schein gives rhythmic life and vigour to his monodies by binding their bass to the rhythm of the chorale. Other composers, notable amongst them Hieronymus Praetorius (d. *c.* 1629) and Thomas Selle (1599–1663), followed this lead with free compositions to biblical words in *concertato* style. Such works as these, with all the possible elaborations of the chorale, represent the composer's desire to present his own interpretation of religious truth.

SCHÜTZ

The greatest genius of the age, Heinrich Schütz (1585–1672), developed the free-style setting of scriptural texts: he uses chorales less than any other German composer of his age. His occasional references to chorale melodies are quite likely to be set to new words, and he is always ready to compose fresh music for chorale verses. A pupil of Giovanni Gabrieli, in Venice, from 1617 to 1672, Schütz was *Kapellmeister* to the Elector of Saxony, in Dresden, but the decline of his musical establishment during the Thirty Years War left him free to return to Italy to work under Monteverdi.

Schütz's earliest works were madrigals which applied Italian methods of word-painting to German texts with the utmost lavishness; the first German opera was his. The ability to utilize vivid illustrative themes within beautifully-wrought structures and the dramatist's power to convey character as well as the urgency of a situation inform all his work whatever its scale, from the large multi-choral *Psalms* (1619) to the monodies and small vocal ensembles of the *Kleine geistliche Konzerte* written during the war. Schütz is the one Protestant composer of his age whose music transcends sectarianism; it is not merely that in the *Cantiones sacrae* he set Latin texts with extreme poignancy: the complete individuality of his style gives his work a universal appeal.

Great multichoral structures, the excitement of Monteverdi's dramatic 'agitated style', and a startling melodic and harmonic inventiveness go hand in hand with the drama of such pieces as the account of St Paul's conversion from the *Symphoniae sacrae*, scored for six soloists, two choirs, two violins, and organ. First the soloists and then the two choirs, divided across the chancel, call out to the persecutor until the whole universe seems to be asking the accusing question that grinds through consecutive seconds to a cadence and from which a long *crescendo* and *diminuendo* are built up (Example 45).

The last movement of the *Musikalische Exequien*, which Schütz called 'A Concerto in the form of a German Requiem' (a compilation of scriptural and chorale words unrelated to the Catholic liturgy) ends with a setting of the *Nunc dimittis* across which two sopranos and a tenor (two 'Seraphim' and a 'Blessed Spirit') softly weave a romantic setting of the words 'Blessed are the dead who die in the Lord'.

It is natural that the dramatically minded Schütz should have composed the first German oratorios. The *Resurrection History* (1623) is given simply to a tenor narrator, singing a kind of plainsong recitative, and to a chorus whose contribution is polyphonic yet never complex. *The Christmas History* and *The Seven Words from the Cross*, published more than forty years later, tell their stories in recitatives and ensembles framed by big *concertato* choruses. The *Seven Words* uses chorale texts with Schütz's own music, and anticipates Bach's *St Matthew Passion* by accompanying the words of Christ with four viole da gamba instead of continuo alone.

The Passions according to St Matthew, St Luke, and St John (a fourth, according to St Mark, is generally regarded as

spurious) are austere works of the composer's conservative old age, in which he complained that the exploitation of modern devices led young composers to neglect the fundamental discipline of a training in counterpoint. The Passions employ only a quasi-plainchant narration, unaccompanied, and firm, unadorned choral writing. It was not until the next generation, with the works of Johann Sebastiani (1622–83) and Johann Theile (1646–1724), that Passion settings admitted orchestral accompaniment or non-scriptural interpolations.

FROM SCHÜTZ TO BACH

Of the composers who separate Schütz from Bach, only Dietrich Buxtehude (1637–1707) approaches their stature. The exploitation of chorale forms continued in the works of Franz Tunder (1614–67), who united all the accepted styles within single works, Matthias Weckmann (1621–74), and Andreas Hammerschmidt (1612–75), whose chorale arias and dialogues bring a new, somewhat sentimental freedom of expression into German church music.

Johann Pachelbel (1653–1706) and Georg Böhm (1661–1733) brought new virtuosity on the one hand, and a new infusion of grace and ease on the other, into German organ music. Pachelbel, in Nuremberg, was in close touch with the elaborately decorative organ style of the south, while Böhm was influenced by French keyboard music. Buxtehude's dramatic toccatas, his tight-knit chorale-partitas (which gave the old variation style a definite form), and his chorale preludes, coloured by a Schützian technique of illustration, left an indelible mark upon Bach's organ writing.

An official reform of church music in 1700 brought the cantata officially into existence; it was to be an extended work appropriate to the liturgical lessons of the Sunday or feast-day upon which it was sung, and it was to be the principal music of the church Sunday by Sunday. It could accept dramatization of biblical events, utilize the operatic recitatives and arias which had crept into chorale settings, and, of course, could build itself around the liturgically appropriate chorale. To the more radically Protestant wing of the Lutheran Church, this admittance of openly secular styles was a desecration of Sunday worship, and its official sanction was the cause of a good deal of *odium theologicum*.

Of the pre-Bachians, Buxtehude produced the most vividly imaginative, as well as the most profoundly musical works in this form. He never adopts a formal recitative and aria but clings rather to *arioso* styles of great eloquence and employs his choir in strong, gracefully wrought forms. At times, as in the cantata *Gott hilf mir*, choir and orchestra change roles, the players delivering the chorale *Durch Adams Fall* while the singers deal with illustrative figurations. More liberally accepting the new musical dispensation, Philipp Krieger (1649–1725) wrote new-style cantatas influenced by Italian opera, while Johann Kuhnau (1660–1728), Bach's predecessor at Leipzig, and Friedrich Zachau (1663–1712), Handel's first teacher, adopted a cantata form very close to that eventually exploited by Bach.

4. Johann Sebastian Bach

As very little of this music was in print, composers trained themselves in the local tradition of their birthplace, later adopting the new styles of the areas in which they worked. To know what Buxtehude was doing, it was necessary for the young Bach to visit Lübeck, as he could not buy scores of the great composer's work. It is worth noting that of some three hundred church cantatas composed by Bach between 1704 and 1744 (about two hundred of which have survived), only one, *Gott ist mein König* (No. 71)[1] was published in its composer's lifetime, and this owed its relative celebrity to the fact that it was written for a municipal thanksgiving service.

When, as a young man of twenty-three, Bach left Mühlhausen after disagreement with a puritanical parish council about the position of music in the church services, he declared that his final goal was 'a properly regulated church music dedicated to the glory of God'. Bach was, of course, an indefatigable systematizer; an exploration of fugal possibilities in all the major and minor keys, an investigation of the adventures of a single theme submitted to all fugal and canonic devices, and pieces written to study every aspect of keyboard techniques are an indication of his mind. His church music, though it was not intended to supplant all other liturgical work, was meant to stand as a model for the year's worship; the organ's contributions as well as the cantata were to be included in one comprehensive scheme.

Bach's early cantatas follow models set by his predecessors; at Mühlhausen, he tended to cling to concertato-style works like the funeral cantata *Gottes Zeit* (the *Actus Tragicus*, No. 106) which does not formally divide its sections or employ recitative and aria style. His work at Weimar and Cöthen after 1712 includes a number of introspective, intensely subjective works in which stylistic innovations are utilized. In *Komm du*

1. Bach's cantatas are not numbered chronologically; No. 71 is a very early work written while he was still organist at Mühlhausen.

süsse Todesstunde (No. 161), which relates its fervent longing for death to the sufferings of Christ through the organ's quotation of the Passion chorale, an *alto arioso* is accompanied by a representation of tolling bells from *pizzicato* strings and flutes, while in the simple closing chorale an *obbligato* flute soars above the voices.

Der Himmel lacht (No. 31) begins with an orchestral sonata that is really a Baroque concerto movement, while its tenor aria resembles a vocal concerto.

Bach's appointment to Leipzig in 1723 enabled him to create cantatas integrated into the liturgy of the day for which they were written. Since the chorales were connected with a particular Sunday or feast through their relationship to one of the day's lessons, the use of that chorale would bind a cantata into the liturgy. Bach never abandoned the forms won over from the opera house and from instrumental music, but he employed them more and more often for re-phrased or paraphrased chorale stanzas; whatever incidental poetry or biblical incident a cantata might contain, in Bach's later period it was the chorale, treated with a wealth of skill and feeling, that dominated the work. For a time in the 1730s, when his failures as a schoolmaster and his intransigence in dealing with his ecclesiastical and municipal superiors had depleted the choir, he composed solo cantatas such as No. 51 (*Jauchzet Gott in allen Landen*) for soprano, No. 54 (*Widerstehe doch der Sünde*) for alto, and No. 56 (*Ich will den Kreuzstab*) for bass, adopting for them a virtuoso vocal style. Whereas the pre-Leipzig cantatas had been mystically and almost agonizedly subjective, the bulk of his later works (that is to say, the bulk of his cantata output) represents a personal reflection on the liturgy in which intensity of imagination is balanced by a sense of liturgical fitness.

The chorale cantata thus reaches its apotheosis. When, in *Christ lag in Todesbanden* (No. 4), Bach returned to the old chorale-variation form, the variations consist not only of *concertato* movements but choruses and arias in concerto form accompanied by an orchestra which draws its figuration from themes illustrating the words of the text. The later cantatas are framed, usually, between an opening chorale-fantasia in any one of the possible forms – the very late *Jesu, der du meine Seele* (No. 78) has its vast introductory chorus built upon a chaconne bass, while concerto introductions abound – and a simple, four-part harmonization of the chorale at the end. The intermediate stanzas and any additional materials become recitatives, arias, and choruses in operatic or instrumental forms, always moulded to the chorale as a *cantus firmus* or as an elaborately decorated melodic line in *concertato* style.

A similar desire for liturgical validity informs Bach's organ music. In the *Orgelbüchlein* he set out to provide model chorale preludes for every service of the year, but he did not complete his scheme. What is often grandly extensive in these works from his Cöthen period becomes far more terse in the Leipzig years until, in the 'Catechism' Preludes (part III of the *Clavierübung*) we reach what may be the greatest of all works in this form. Each of a series of eighteen chorales dealing with the fundamentals of Christian dogma and devotion is given two treatments, corresponding to the Longer and Shorter Catechisms of the Lutheran Church, and surrounded with a wealth of illustrative thematic material that never slips beyond the composer's control.

The motets, which to Bach were primarily occasional pieces, seem permeated (like the cantatas) by the liturgical spirit, and both the Passions make use of chorale words and melodies to harness the congregation's imagination and gain its participation. The earlier *St John Passion*, tersely dramatic and apparently composed somewhat hurriedly for Bach's first Passiontide in Leipzig, takes some of its text from the Passion by Senator Brockes of Hamburg, and repeats several passages of music to different words. It is not in reality overshadowed by the epic grandeur of the *St Matthew Passion*, for each has its own approach and style. Part I of the bigger work, which was first sung in 1729, opens and closes with huge chorale-fantasias; in the opening movement, the chorale melody, 'O Lamb of God, pure, spotless', given to a separate boys' choir, strides across the great funeral procession of the double choir. In the later, the melody is presented in *concertato* style in a texture of richly expressive choral and orchestral figuration. In the *St Matthew Passion*, drama is embedded in contemplation; the action, performed in so many of the choral numbers with fierceness and horror, gives rise to soliloquies and choruses which permit the composer to speak directly through the rather turgid verse of his Lutheran pastor poet.

The *Magnificat*, written for Christmas 1723, and the *Mass in B minor*, composed ten years later, stand apart from Bach's other religious works by virtue of their Latin texts and their distance from the chorale. Each uses (at times) a plainchant *cantus firmus*; references to the old *tonus peregrinus* in the earlier work suggest the *Credo* and *Confiteor* of the later, in which plainsong melodies are used, just as the D-major jubilation of the *Magnificat* suggests the great choruses of rejoicing in the *Mass*.

Although the *Mass* was written for the Catholic court of Dresden, to win its composer the title of Court Composer, it is far removed from liturgical practicality; it is the longest and greatest of cantata Masses, with a minimum of *da capos* in the arias (and these instrumental) and the choruses (for example, the *Hosanna*), and the rich exuberance of Bach's counterpoint demands massive structures. Much of the work, like the *Crucifixus* – twelve variations on a chaconne bass adapted from the cantata *Weinen, Klagen* (No. 12) but ending, unlike its model, with a magical turn from minor to major – is adapted from other works, and it ends with a '*Dona nobis*' which repeats the stern counterpoint of the earlier *Gratias agimus*. The Protestant Bach was not concerned, in this work, with Catholic worship but with a statement of Christian doctrine more objective and impersonal than in any other of his works.

Like Schütz, Bach writes the direct expression of his own faith and devotion. In the *St Matthew Passion*, he takes away the halo of string tone from around the words of Christ for the agonized cry 'My God, why hast Thou forsaken me?' leaving only the continuo for support. The symbolism of Bach's work is endless and all-pervading; canon and strict counterpoint often represent the Old Testament rule of Law, free polyphony the liberating grace of the New Testament; evil is represented by a falling seventh and by snake-like figures associated with the serpent of Eden. Every suggestion in the text that is capable of illustration is likely to give rise to a figure upon which a powerful structure can be built.

46 Bach: *Magnificat*

Bach is always fascinated by music's power to express diverse ideas simultaneously; a choral prelude may present figures that illustrate phrases from different stanzas at the same time, and the use of chorale melodies as counterpoint to arias and choruses is another expression of the complexity of his thought clarified by its appeal to the congregation's own knowledge and musical experience. Musical puns are frequent; the 'ninth hour' of the *St Matthew Passion* demands a chord of the ninth; the Cross, in the same work, inspires music that forms an actual cross on the page of manuscript, just as in other connexions the word demands an accidental sharp, for a sharp in German is called a 'cross'.

The intellectual brilliance with which this complexity is developed into music of the most complete integrity has often been discussed; symbolism serves musical forms which grow from it, and never degenerates into mere vehicles of the composer's vivid imagination. Even so simple a matter as the putting down of the mighty and the exaltation of the humble and meek in the *Magnificat* creates a self-sufficient aria out of figures that are no more than symbols of physical movement (Example 46). Such illustration never obtrudes from the texture: it is always completely assimilated into a musical whole, and when Bach fails, it is not because the diversities he is apt to employ override his control, but because they cannot make a sufficiently convincing and attractive form.

The mysticism, the richness of emotion, and the amazing beauty of design and melody in Bach's music at its best, are an unending marvel. Like any other prolific artist, Bach was not always inspired, but a remarkable amount of his work has a ravishing grace and beauty of texture together with a romantic power of expression never surpassed by composers in whose works these qualities are most frequently noticed.

5. Developments in England

THE first fifty years of the Baroque period are, in Anglican history, the days of John Donne and George Herbert, of Lancelot Andrewes, Nicholas Ferrar, and William Laud, of Isaac Walton and Jeremy Taylor; that is to say, they are a period in which the comparatively new Church of England found itself a distinctive way of life and of devotion. This period ended with the Civil War and the Commonwealth, and the triumphant Anglicanism of the Restoration rapidly became a formal religion that in its public manifestations turned to a stately Erastianism. Through this period of change, the tradition of English church music, for all the impact of new continental styles and new ways of thought, persisted with a remarkable strength; not only Purcell but the naturalized Handel at times gained vigour and inspiration from the continuing influence of the Tudor masters; it was lesser, though often interesting, composers who seem to have broken completely with the mainstream of English music and to be dragged along almost willy-nilly by the new fashion.

Until the Civil War, the new style had little noticeable influence upon the group of composers, notably William Byrd (1543–1623), Thomas Tomkins (1572–1656), Thomas Weelkes (1575–1623), and Orlando Gibbons (1583–1625), who continued to develop the tradition. In the verse anthem, which had been established in the middle of the sixteenth century, the contrast between one or two solo voices accompanied by viols and the full choir, for which an organ accompaniment is usually implied even if in early days it is never independent of the choir, as well as in the traditional alternation of the two sides of the choir, there was ample material for further progress through the application of verse-anthem technique to service settings. Of all these composers, only Tomkins, in his later services, suggests that he expects an organ accompaniment, but he never emancipates it from the choir.

Nevertheless, while all these composers were exploiting the

excitements of block-harmony contrast with passages fluently polyphonic, the traditional English idiom was never lost; Gibbons and Tomkins exploit the piercing intensity of false relations in spite of the harmonically-based thought of their work. Henry Lawes (1596–1662), his brother William (1602–45), William Child (1606–97) and Christopher Gibbons (1615–76) – Orlando's gifted but lesser son – came closer to continental practice in their use of symmetrical measured rhythms, but became increasingly uncertain as they approached the massive dignity of the older style.

The Puritan revolution provided an interruption, but since none of the Puritan sects encouraged any church music beyond the singing of psalms, there was no change of direction. Although Cromwell had a deep love of music and enjoyed Anglican and Catholic music as well as psalm-singing in his own house, Puritanism added nothing to the spirit or the technique of church music.

With the Restoration in 1660, a spirit similar to that which dominated music at the French court began to govern music in England. The restoration of the cathedral choirs and the resuscitation of the old music (anthem books of the sixties consist principally of works from the Tudor and Jacobean periods) and the rebuilding under Captain Henry Cooke (1615–72) of the choir of the Chapel Royal meant a sudden intrusion of the French style to suit the taste of the new king. Cooke was a talent-scout of genius; starting from literally nothing, he had collected within a few years a choir whose boys included Pelham Humfrey (1647–74), John Blow (1649–1708), and in 1669 Henry Purcell (1659–95). Charles II's Francophile tastes led to the composition of anthems which extended the old verse-anthem into cantatas with orchestral movements and declamatory solo passages. To some extent, the Chapel Royal became a model of church music for which composers had to be found. Charles himself took the first step by sending Humfrey to study in France and Italy.

Humfrey became the revolutionary *par excellence*; a brilliantly gifted youth who never lived to realize his promise, the work he left is, at its best, suggestive of Purcell, upon whom he had considerable influence. The anthems aim at expressiveness above everything else, and exploit the latest fashions without (in most cases) achieving any real shape. Interesting harmonic audacities and passages of lively, expressive declamation rarely coalesce into a totally ordered work. Blow, whose work spanned the entire Purcellian period, and who resigned his post as organist at Westminster Abbey to Purcell only to resume it after his great pupil's death, seems at times to employ the fashionable devices of style with less than complete conviction, but there is a strength and vigour about his work almost always more impressive than Humfrey's usually fragmentary inspirations. Polyphonic anthems like his setting of Psalm 22, his pieces for one or two voices on ground basses – the English equivalent of chaconne style – and his solo songs (usually dealing with pathetic or tragic texts) show him at his greatest, capable of comparison with Purcell. The English tradition, to Humfrey, was something clumsily archaic, to be avoided at all costs; Blow's work does not entirely assimilate the traditional with the new but he wrote sometimes splendidly in either style.

PURCELL

As a choirboy in the Chapel Royal, Purcell was indoctrinated with the new style. First as copyist and then as organist at Westminster Abbey, he learnt the works of the Tudor composers and made copies of their music for his own use. Often he seems to be at his greatest in unaccompanied works whose polyphony is coloured by the extreme intensity of his chromatic harmony and marshalled by his sense of measured rhythm, as in his setting of the Funeral Service (Example 47).

Often even Purcell's genius fails to make a united whole from the fashionable anthem of the day with its numerous short sections. Sometimes his delight in illustrative figures exuberates at the expense of the design, but even when his music is at its least conclusive it has an amazing energy. At his greatest he marries the massive choralism of the English tradition to the vivid style of his period.

Although, like Schütz, Purcell is primarily a musical dra-

matist rejoicing in the words he sets with a consummate fidelity to the subtleties of English speech, what Purcell at his greatest finds in a text are the suggestions that enable him to construct for their transmission a movement of extraordinary shapeliness. There is no essential difference in musical idiom between his church music and the numerous court odes for royal birthdays and so forth, although the English of the

Prayer Book is far greater than the tawdry flattering verses of the odes, which, like the anthems of the period, are choral cantatas. As long as words provide Purcell with a sense of shapeliness and a type of language that excites his gift for vivid illustration and declamation, he can write great music. In works like the robustly happy *Yorkshire Feast Song* and the four *Odes for St Cecilia's Day*, he takes his text at its face value, as he does in church, and is diverted from his concentration upon it by no thought that religion needs a special tone of voice.

Technique, however, is not subject to verbal inspiration, and Purcell's endless inventive gift of melody is supported by a harmonic sense of remarkable audacity and a subtle feeling for rhythm that can accommodate all the complexities of English declamation without losing its forward thrust. It is only necessary to consider the intricacies of phrase length and stress that he can organize above a regular ground bass to see the masterly certainty that never deserts him.

Blow, not often Purcell's equal in church music, seemed to lack the power to draw inspiration for occasional works from the words they offered him. Jeremiah Clarke (1673–1707), another of the Chapel Royal boys, brought a neat workmanship and a pleasant melodiousness to works in these genres, but his music is at its most enjoyable when it means to charm rather than to impress. Daniel Purcell (1660–1717) the younger brother of Henry, wrote acceptably for the church but with few signs of his brother's genius.

HANDEL

The end of the period, in England, is dominated by Handel, who finally settled in London in 1712 and composed there a little service music, as well as a group of anthems and occasional odes. Handel was in all things a thorough-going professional; accepting the existence of national styles, he mastered those of Germany, Italy, and England and, at his greatest, fuses Italianate melody, German profundity, and the special harmonic intensities of English music into a tremendous integrity.

The German Passions (written before his English period) have a direct, dramatic vigour, and although the earlier of them, the *St John Passion*, was written two years prior to his visit to Italy in 1706, it shows his instinctive leaning towards Mediterranean melodic grace. The works on Latin texts, composed in Italy between 1706 and 1709, show considerable sympathy for their subject (the *Salve Regina* is a work of unusual intensity) together with an Italianate grace married to a German technique. The second German Passion (1716), a setting of the popular text by Brockes, paraphrases the words of the Bible and includes reflective verses in a heterogeneous mixture of styles. It is music that impresses by its worthiness rather than by its fervour or dramatic force.

In England, a setting of the *Te Deum* and *Jubilate* to celebrate the Peace of Utrecht and a *Birthday Ode* for Queen Anne composed in 1713, drew Handel's attention to the English language and (almost certainly) to the works of Purcell, whose types of melismata and command of massive chorale writing at once became part of Handel's repertory, to be used as required. The *Te Deum* and *Jubilate* are cantata-like settings, vigorous, extrovert, and much sectionalized. They are part of Handel's apprenticeship to a new language and style which, in the twelve Chandos Anthems composed between 1716 and 1718, show him to be not yet a master of the language although his much discussed insensitivity to English speech is usually caused by carelessness. The Anthems are short cantatas for a small three-part choir and an orchestra of oboes, strings, and organ. The introduction to each is often two movements in trio-sonata style. In the third, 'Have mercy upon me, O God', Handel achieves the chromatic intensity of Purcell. The fourth brings Italian style to English words, whilst the fifth has a clarity and directness reminiscent of Carissimi. The sixth, 'As pants the hart', is one of the few of Handel's works where a chorale appears as *cantus firmus*; *Christ lag in Todesbanden* is, however, in no way appropriate to the text although it appears as the foundation theme. The set as a whole has the gravity and dignity of the Anglican worship without any of the intensities of religious feeling found in the works of Bach.

The four anthems for the Coronation of George II in 1727 are all brilliant ceremonial music; the most textually direct of them, 'Zadok the Priest', is perhaps the finest in the unforgettable splendour of its opening. The deeper religious significance of the Coronation Rite means little to Handel. The *Te Deum* composed for the celebration of the Battle of Dettingen is much indebted to music by Urio; three other settings are proudly ceremonial music. The Funeral Anthem composed in 1737 for Queen Caroline, 'The Ways of Zion do mourn', is a masterpiece of classic gravity that stands four-square in the English choral tradition.

The long series of oratorios which followed his failure in the opera house are all, except the epic *Messiah* and *Israel in Egypt*, sacred dramas in which Handel's sense of character and dramatic situation functions often more freely than within the conventions of eighteenth-century opera. The international, eclectic Handel adds the seriousness of a native German style and the melodic grace he perfected in Italy to the English tradition, creating an amalgam of such power that, although it is inimitable, trapped the English for more than a hundred years into trying to use it as a model.

His English contemporaries in the field of religious music – William Croft (1678–1727), Maurice Greene (1695–1755), and William Boyce (1710–79) – all offered acceptable work. Croft was born too soon to feel the pressure of Handel's genius, and his work is that of a sincere, thoughtful, and gifted disciple of Purcell. Boyce's music has a robustness and vigour that is always likeable, and we owe to him a fine collection of the cathedral music of the sixteenth and seventeenth centuries, made when deafness prevented him from composing. Greene's work is much indebted to Handel's dignified style, from which, as well as from the music of his English predecessors, he developed a style of great strength and dignity far beyond the capacity of his un-Handelian contemporaries.

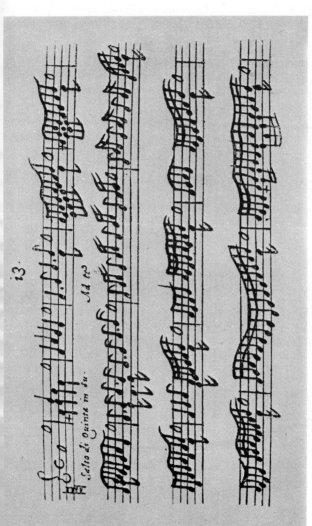

17. Giovanni Luca Conforto: a page from his treatise on ornamentation

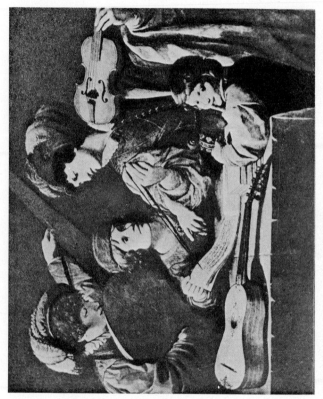

18. Vocal and instrumental music (Italian). Early seventeenth century

19. Tuning the chitarrone (archlute), much used as a continuo instrument

CAPO X.

Del diminuire, abbellire, o rifiorire
gli accompagnamenti.

SArei desideroso di mostrarti molte sorte di diminuzioni,
fioretti, abbellimenti, e maniere di dar grazia all'accompagnare; ma perche cio non si puo ben esprimere se non con intavolatura, dimostrerò solo qualche cosa in alcuni passi più frequentati, acciò possa lo Studioso applicar con qualche diletto. Si procuri dunque osservando questi Esempj di dar le Consonanze necessarie con la mano sinistra, e con la destra sonar la parte superiore, come quì si dimostra. V. Gr. ascendendo di grado, e in alcune Cadenze.

20. A page from Gasparini's *L'armonico pratico al cimbalo*

Extento fidenter brachio, Fides haud procul a posticulo sigillatim liquidéque vibrentur, genibus ne forte offendiculo sint, caute reductis.

Holding the Bow in this posture, stretch out your arm, and draw it first over one String and then another; crossing them in right angle, at the distance of two or three Inches from the Bridge. Make each several

String yeild a full and clear sound; and order your knees so, that they be no impediment to the motion of your Bow.

21. Illustration of correct playing posture
(Simpson: *The Division Viol*)

22. Town pipers (waits) in Germany during the Christmas season

23. Music to accompany a banquet in the Turkish Garden, Dresden

24. *La contesa dei numi* (Leonardo Vinci). Rome, Palazzo Polignac

25. Chamber music (flutes and viola da gamba)

26. Scene from *Teofane* (Pallavicino and Lotti). Dresden Opera, 1719

27. A view of the orchestra pit, Dresden Opera

28. Church musicians in Germany

29. Autograph of Bach's motet *Singet dem Herrn*

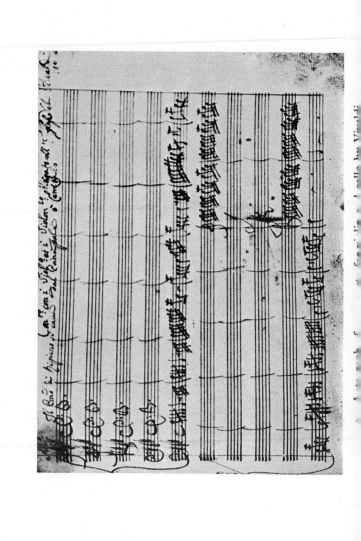

An autograph of a concerto for violin and cello by Vivaldi

31. Vocal and instrumental music (French)

32. Anthem with English and Latin texts by Tomkins.
London, 1668

IV · BAROQUE OPERA AND MASQUE

Alec Harman

1. Introduction: Theory and Practice

IT is impossible to state precisely when an artistic period begins and ends, because certain of its characteristics can be found in both the previous and succeeding periods, but for convenience we shall date the Baroque as extending from *c*. 1580 to *c*. 1760. Inevitably, as in any period of similar length, there was no one unvarying artistic aim or attitude to life, but the Baroque is singled out from all other periods by its variety, even dichotomy, of ideas, and from all earlier periods by an extreme desire to communicate.

That communication was of major importance is clearly revealed in many of the musical treatises of the period, most of them written by men who were also composers in their own right. Thus the first Baroque theorist, Vincenzo Galileo (1533–91), father of the astronomer, wrote in his *Dialogo della musica antica e della moderna* (1581) that the aim of composers should be 'to express the conceptions of the mind and . . . to impress them with the greatest possible effectiveness on the minds of the listeners'. Over 150 years later the German theorist Mattheson (1681–1764) stated in his *Der vollkommene Capellmeister* (1739) that 'what the composer thinks about while writing are the voices or the instruments, and especially the listeners'. There would have been little point in such statements if the opportunities of hearing music had been few, and it was during the Baroque that listening, both in private and in public, first became an integral part of the musical scene, though not to the same extent in every country.

The history of public musical performances begins in Italy, where the semi-private academies of the Renaissance, more numerous than anywhere else, continued to flourish in the seventeenth century. To one of these (the Florentine Camerata) Galileo belonged, and in it was sown the seed that eventually developed into opera. At first opera was a fairly exclusive affair, performed only in the residences of the richer nobility, most of whom, throughout the entire Baroque period, maintained their own players, singers, and sometimes composers. But such was the speed at which opera became popular in Italy that in 1637 the first public opera-house in Europe was opened in Venice, followed rapidly by others, also in Venice (the fifth was opened in 1649). They also appeared elsewhere in Italy and, more sparsely, north of the Alps.

From the latter half of the century onwards, many of the larger churches provided, from time to time, concerts of vocal and instrumental music. In Germany the tradition of music-making in the home established by the Mastersingers developed into '*Collegia musica*' which (like the Italian academics) were at first semi-private, but later expanded, being held in either house or church. Public concerts proper were first founded in Germany by Buxtehude, who, in 1673, organized a series of evening concerts, mostly of sacred works, in Lübeck on the five Sundays before Christmas; they were continued until the early nineteenth century and their fame was the cause of Bach's celebrated 200-mile journey in 1705. Other concert series were started by Bach's contemporary Telemann in Frankfurt (1713) and Hamburg (1720), and in 1743 semi-public meetings were held in Leipzig which eventually (1781) developed into the renowned Gewandhaus concerts.

In France, which musically speaking meant Paris, Philidor instituted 'Le Concert Spirituel' in 1725 for the performance of sacred vocal works, but towards the middle of the century the series began to include symphonies and concertos. It soon became internationally famous as one of the chief centres of pre-classical and classical music until its dissolution during the Revolution. French opera, however, had been public long before this, the first public performance coinciding with the inauguration of the Académie des Opéras in 1671. In Austria, dominated by Italian opera and the Imperial court at Vienna, there were no regular public musical performances of any kind until 1772, when the 'Tonkunstlersocietät' (now the 'Haydnverein') was founded.

As in Italy and France the ordinary Englishman (or rather Londoner) was able to hear opera as early as 1656. In 1672 the first regular series of public concerts in Europe was started by

John Banister, the leading violinist of the King's orchestra. These were essentially chamber concerts and included both vocal and instrumental music. On Banister's death they were continued by Thomas Britton (the 'musical small-coal man') until 1714, by which time a number of other public concerts had been founded, such as the Academy of Ancient Music (1710) and the two series organized by the famous flautist Loeillet in 1710, and by Hickford in 1714.

The increase in public concerts and operatic performances stimulated French, German, and to a lesser extent English, men of letters (as well as composers and theorists) to expound, explain, and criticize music. Italy did not contribute because music to the Italians was primarily an emotional entertainment, and they were not concerned to theorize about it, either on a philosophical or scientific level. Moreover, they were so completely enamoured of their own music – opera especially – that foreign works found no foothold, with the result that considered criticism, which is essentially comparison, was virtually non-existent, though opera audiences were usually critical enough in their own vociferous way. That Austria contributed nothing is explained by the lateness and scarcity of performances outside the Imperial Court. In Germany, France, and England, on the other hand, the invasion of Italian opera and operatic style provided a major topic for discussion, for in each country there was a native tradition in opera or semi-opera sufficiently strong to invite comparison and arouse opposition.

Musical writings in the Baroque can be conveniently divided into two classes, journalistic and didactic. The former was aimed at the man-in-street, the latter at the practising musician both amateur and professional. It was no coincidence that democratic England, with its waxing middle class and regular public concerts, was the first country to see popular musical criticism. Addison's articles in the *Spectator* (though he himself was no musician) greatly influenced Mattheson, who can be regarded as the first music critic in the modern sense. In the years 1722–5 he published the first periodical devoted entirely to music, *Critica musica*, which dealt chiefly with problems of musical taste. This was followed by a number of other German periodicals appearing with various degrees of regularity; Telemann's *Der getreue Musikmeister* (1728), Mizler's *Neu eröffnete musikalische Bibliothek* (1736–54), and the first series of *Der critische Musikus* (1737–40) by Scheibe (1708–76). In France, apart from the pamphlet war between the followers of Lully and Rameau in the 1730s, and the '*guerre des bouffons*' in the 1750s, popular criticism was limited to articles in periodicals of a general nature such as the *Mercure de France* and *Correspondance Littéraire* from 1750, and to those – mostly by Rousseau – in the *Encyclopédie*.

In the more learned publications the treatment of music can be roughly grouped under two headings, philosophic and scientific. The former ranged from the vague generalizations of Kircher (1602–80), whose celebrated *Musurgia universalis* (1656) links the five 'humours' (melancholic, sanguine, choleric, martial, and phlegmatic) with music of appropriate character, to the detailed classification contained in *Der General-Bass* (1728) of Heinichen (1683–1729), Mattheson's *Capellmeister*, and the second issue of Scheibe's *Der critische Musikus* (1745). Heinichen gives instrumental pieces that express (according to him) such activities as racing and fighting and such emotions as quarrelling, inconstancy, and the like, while Mattheson states that each dance movement has a definite emotion (minuet = moderate gaiety, rigaudon = flirtatious pleasantry, sarabande = ambition, passepied = fickleness). He translates Italian tempo indications into emotional terminology: adagio = sadness, andante = hope, allegro = consolation, presto = desire.

The scientific treatment of music had been popular ever since the days of Pythagoras, but most theorists, like the famous Greek, let their passion for numerical order override practical considerations. Thus even so outstanding a scientist as Kepler held fast, in his *De harmonice mundi* (1619), to the old astrological belief in the association between interval ratios and the structure of the universe, even of human society. The same delight in a neatly arranged system can be seen in the *Gradus ad Parnassum* (1725) of the Austrian composer Fux, where 'strict counterpoint' is classified into five species which, while logical enough, bear little resemblance to the late Renaissance style on which they are avowedly based. In his *Traité de l'harmonie réduite à ses principes naturels* (1722) Rameau, the most original Baroque theorist, rightly stressed the fundamental importance of the tonic, dominant, and subdominant chords and the basic character of the triad. But even he over-simplified matters in his desire for a system of harmony that was both neat and complete, by asserting that all chords are derived from the three primary ones, and that each is linked to the others by a *'basse fondamentale'*, for the discovery of which he gives largely arbitrary rules.

We may ridicule the excessive detail and unconvincing way in which certain Baroque theorists expounded the doctrine of emotions, but they were simply reflecting, albeit in a distorted manner at times, two of the basic traits of the period – communication, and a scientific-rationalistic approach to knowledge – and it is absolutely vital to the interpretation of Baroque music to grasp the significance of what they were driving at, namely the transmission of an emotion in terms of a musical idea, a speed indication, or a type. Such transmission was comparatively easy in vocal music where the words clarify the emotion, but in instrumental music it was (and is) impossible to suggest a precise emotional state, and it was this fact that caused writers like Mattheson to overstep the natural limits of instrumental expression in their attempts to provide an aesthetic system applicable to all music.

These attempts were mainly Germanic because they evolved naturally from the strong abstract quality of the German mind, combining a long tradition in instrumental music with an innate delight in systematized theory. To be sure, instrumental music was also popular in Italy and England, but both countries accepted it as such without trying to equate its expressive powers with vocal music, the Italians revelling in the sheer sensuousness of sound and in the emotional drama of the concerto, the English finding pleasure in freshness of melody and in the intimacy of polyphony. In France, however, owing to the rationalistic, realistic bent of the French mind, instrumental music was much less popular than vocal, unless it was of a functional nature, like dance music, or had extra-musical associations. Fontenelle's famous remark '*Sonate, que me veux-tu?*' may have been exaggerated, but it was certainly an indication of French reaction.

2. The Beginnings of Opera

THE association of music with drama in the early Baroque was not a new one, as it had existed ever since the so-called liturgical dramas of the Middle Ages, the forerunners of the Miracle, Mystery, and Morality Plays. In the basically secular culture of the Renaissance the association was continued in the revival of classical plays, when songs, duets, and choruses were sometimes included in the course of a play but more often relegated to the end of each act, where they provided a kind of commentary. These musical insertions were called *intermedii*, and were very popular, for, like the later Baroque intermezzi, they introduced a pleasing contrast and relaxation from the spoken drama.

The Renaissance delight in classical culture also led to a revival of the pastoral play. Because of its lyrical verse and the fact that Arcadia (with its shepherds and shepherdesses, fauns and satyrs) had always, from Pan downwards, been closely connected with music, it was frequently enhanced by songs and dances. To become opera, the *pastorale* needed only a musical style that would carry the action of the plot. 'Opera' here means a dramatic work set entirely to music, and for those stage works that include spoken dialogue the term will be qualified, for example 'ballad opera', or a different one used, such as *Singspiel*.

Monody was the answer to musico-dramatic problems, or so the earliest opera composers thought; and so enamoured were they and their audiences of the rapidity with which words could be delivered, and of the opportunities for expressive declamation, that their operas are almost wholly monodic.

The first opera was Peri's *La Dafne*, produced in Florence in 1597; it consisted of a prologue and six scenes and was wholly pastoral in character. The fact that it was the first opera and a very successful one makes it doubly unfortunate that the music is lost. The first surviving opera, then, is *La rappresentazione di anima e di corpo* by Cavalieri (d. 1602), another member of the Florentine Camerata, who poured into what is in effect a Morality Play the new wine of monody, spiced with frankly tuneful songs, simple choruses, dances, *ritornelli* (instrumental interludes preceding or following vocal items), and *sinfonie* (independent instrumental pieces that usually introduce but sometimes conclude an act or scene). The didactic religious nature of Cavalieri's opera, in which the soul is subjected to, but successfully resists, various temptations, reflects the atmosphere of the Counter-Reformation, and it was therefore natural that it should have been first performed in Rome (February 1600). It has sometimes wrongly been called the first oratorio because of its performance in one of St Philip Neri's oratories, but actually it is as much an opera as Peri's *Euridice* (Florence, October 1600). The latter is usually described as the earliest surviving opera, though in fact both necessitate a stage production with costumes, scenery, lighting, and machines, and both consist mainly of long and (to our ears) tedious stretches of monody. The same can be said for Caccini's *Euridice* (Florence, 1602), another setting of the libretto used by Peri.

The fact that Peri and Caccini were virtuoso singers, whereas Cavalieri was an amateur composer, can be detected in their operas. Yet *La rappresentazione* more than makes up for its mediocrity by including a wide range of dances and instrumental music. The distinction in approach between singer and composer is even more marked in the first opera by the first great opera composer, Monteverdi (1567–1643). Many madrigalian features can be found in his *Orfeo* (Mantua, 1607), which represents a fusion of both old and new elements effected by a musician whose craftmanship and sense of drama are of the highest rank. The score is full of imaginative touches, and the structure (particularly of the Prologue and Act I) is far more carefully planned than any later Baroque opera. The orchestra is a typical Renaissance one, consisting of continuo instruments – harpsichords, organs, gambas, and various plucked instruments – one or more of which accompany every single item in the opera. The rest of the orchestra is made up of members of the viol and violin families (fourteen), trombones (five), trumpets (four), cornetts (two)[1] and recorders (two).

One of the most remarkable things about the score is Monteverdi's association of a particular instrumental timbre with character. Charon, gloomy guardian of the Styx, is accompanied by the reedy nasal tones of a regal; sombre trombones are used in the *sinfonia* that precedes Act III (The Underworld), and they also accompany the chorus of spirits in this and the next Act. Trombones, as the result of their telling use in *Orfeo*, came to be traditionally associated with the infernal regions (Mozart's *Don Giovanni*) and the Olympian (Gluck's *Alceste*).

The most significant feature of *Orfeo*, as regards future development, is the number of songs and their treatment. These songs make the work more satisfying musically than the earlier monody-dominated operas. We can, in fact, discern the main solo vocal types of later Baroque opera; 'recitative', in which the lack of melodic and rhythmic organization leaves the singer free to declaim and act expressively; 'accompanied recitative' where the orchestra plays chords – sustained, tremolo, or arpeggiated depending on the text, which is always emotional; 'aria', always cast into some kind of repetition form, with the vocal line and bass organized and often sequential, with melody of prime importance; and lastly, *arioso*, which is best described as song-like recitative, fairly melodic but non-repetitive in form.

Despite its excellencies and its astonishing sense of overall structure and drama, *Orfeo* is too heavily weighted on the dramatic side, and in the amount of monody reflects the early enthusiasm for expressive declamation at the expense of melody. This state of affairs, being so untypically Italian, did not last long, but to trace the rise in importance of the aria and the development of opera in general we must return to Rome because only the last two of Monteverdi's operas after *Orfeo* have survived complete. Fragmentary, alas, is the beautifully expressive *arioso* '*Lasciatemi morire*' from *Arianna* (1608),

1. Woodwind instruments quite different from the modern brass cornet.

which set the fashion for operatic laments during the entire Baroque period.

OPERA IN ROME

Florence declined as an operatic centre after the first decade of the century, but Rome continued to enjoy a succession of works most of which were moral or religious in tone, like *La rappresentazione*, but more spectacular in presentation, and so reflected more faithfully the emotional realism of the Counter-Reformation. In opera, emotion and realism were present in mechanical contraptions that apparently enabled characters to defy the laws of gravity, and in stage settings that by faked perspective, elaborate construction, detailed painting, and changes of scenery aimed at as natural a presentation as possible. Parallel with these ran a clear division between the emotional aria and the realistic, narrative type of recitative. This division is clearly marked in Domenico Mazzocchi's *La Catena d'Adone* (1626), one of the few Roman operas on a secular subject, Landi's *Il Sant'Alessio* (1632), the first biographical opera, and Vittori's *La Galatea* (1639). The first two include comic episodes, and some of the minor characters are drawn from the contemporary scene, not from classical mythology, while in the last many of the arias show an attempt to underline structure by means of key relationship.

The main disadvantage of Rome, so far as opera was concerned, was the power of the Pope in cultural matters. So long as Maffeo Barberini was Pope Urban VIII (1623–44), opera, even comic opera, flourished, for he clearly took the line that art need not be sacred in order to be acceptable. The Barberini family were the chief patrons of opera in Rome, and in 1632 they celebrated the completion of a magnificent theatre seating over 3,000 with the first performance of Landi's *Il Sant'Alessio*. Seven years later saw the production in the same theatre of the first comic opera, *Chi soffre, speri*, with music by Marazzoli and Virgilio Mazzocchi, and libretto by Giulio Rospigliosi, the author of *Il Sant'Alessio* (among other works), who later became Pope Clement IX. Rospigliosi may be called the creator of

Italian comic opera, and when the Barberinis returned from Paris after their exile (1644–53) caused by differences with Urban VIII's successor, Innocent X (who, it seems, was averse to opera), he produced *Dal male il bene* with music by Marazzoli and Abbatini. Apart from continuing the distinction between recitative and aria, this work includes end-of-act ensembles that later became one of the most characteristic features of *opera buffa* and eventually of most operas from Mozart onwards.

After the middle of the century Rome ceased to be the main operatic centre, owing to the uncertainty of Papal approval and the growing secularization of the Baroque, which flourished more readily outside the headquarters, as it were, of the Counter-Reformation. Opera was the genre most affected by this secular trend because by its very nature it is theatrical, and theatricality implies exaggerated presentation that can easily become an end in itself instead of a perfectly legitimate means to that end. Although Roman productions were deliberately less spectacular than they could have been, in order that audiences should not be distracted from the edifying nature of the drama, the growing preoccupation of composers, singers, and producers with their own particular spheres meant that drama itself became less and less important.

OPERA IN VENICE

In painting and music, the two most directly emotional of the arts, Venice was the leading Italian city of the late Renaissance just as Florence was of the early Renaissance. In both arts the general aim was towards contrasts achieved through vivid colour, whether in the glowing canvases of Titian and Veronese or in the polychoral motets of Giovanni Gabrieli with their usually unspecified but (in practice) richly varied instrumental accompaniments. It is an interesting fact that in both the Renaissance and Baroque periods Venice 'emotionalized' a movement or an art form begun in Florence, and it is worth comparing the attention to line and the careful placing of objects of the early Renaissance Florentine painters with the all-important single vocal line and the realistic concern to convey the inflexions and overtones of the text of the Florentine monodists, for both are fundamentally similar in approach, and both contrast strongly with the emotionally coloured splendour of Venetian art and Venetian choral and instrumental music and opera.

Emotionalism through colour was, indeed, far more typical of Venetian culture than that of any other city or state, and the reasons are twofold: her geographical position and the fact that she was a republic. The former ensured constant communication with the Levant, its traditions of richly coloured mosaics and frescoes, and its instrumentally accompanied vocal music and antiphonal singing; the latter meant that unlike any other Italian city at that time (where the reigning aristocracy were the sole arbiters of taste) the likes and dislikes of the ordinary citizen constituted an important artistic factor. To the ordinary man, variety and colour, whether in sound or pigment, are more immediately attractive than line, whether single (as in monody) or in relation to other lines (as in a drawing or polyphony), and it is indicative of Venetian society and culture that monody-dominated operas were enjoyed by the élite, whereas it was not until opera had developed to the point where emotionally varied arias predominated and productions became spectacular that Venice took to the new genre. Venetian opera was *public* opera, and the first public opera houses in Europe were Venetian. From 1637 (when the San Cassiano was opened) until 1700 there were at one time or another sixteen similar establishments in Venice in which over 350 different operas were produced; in the following century the number rose to more than 1,600.

Monteverdi's first surviving public opera is *Il ritorno d'Ulisse in patria* (1641), notable for its profusion of arias, the majority in triple time, short, and through-composed. There is a clear-cut distinction between recitative and aria and, compared to *Orfeo*, a greater use of sequence and smoother melodic contours. Other important features are an orchestra that consists only of strings and continuo, the inclusion of comic scenes, a dearth of choruses, a fair number of ensembles, and a great variety of spectacle. Except for the last two, the main features of *Ulisse* are also apparent in *L'incoronazione di Poppea* (1642), Monteverdi's last and finest opera. It is dramatically more integrated than *Ulisse*, and the characters, once flesh and blood, really live; it is, indeed, the first great historical opera.

The reduction of the orchestra in *Ulisse* and *Poppea*, compared to *Orfeo*, was partly due to reasons of economy (public opera, unlike that of the nobility, had to pay its way), but also to a general artistic trend of the times – homogeneity. As early as 1624 Monteverdi had scored his dramatic cantata *Il combattimento di Tancredi e Clorinda* for first and second violins, viola, cello, double-bass, and continuo (harpsichord), and from then on the string family formed the unified central core of the orchestra, to which were added, at first very occasionally, later more frequently, woodwind and brass instruments. *Il combattimento* is also notable for the use of what Monteverdi called *stile concitato* or agitated style, where galloping horses and the fury of the fight are depicted by means of reiterated rhythmic figures, rapid repeated notes, and *pizzicato*.

The Venetian opera of Cavalli (1602–76), Cesti (1623–69), Stradella (1642–82), and Pallavicino (*c.* 1630–88), besides being full of spectacular scenes, are increasingly aria-dominated. Their melodies are more sequential, the contours larger and more expressive, the metre mostly triple, and the supporting harmony more and more crystallized round a central key. This new *bel canto* style could fully display the beauty of the human voice, the most emotional of all instruments; and as the Venetians greatly preferred a high voice to a low one, the majority of the main operatic roles were for sopranos and tenors. Furthermore, the hero's part was almost invariably written for a male soprano (*castrato*) whose powerful, flexible voice and boy-like purity of tone began to dominate the scene. From Monteverdi's *Poppea* until well over a century later practically every Italian opera and those composed in the Italian manner included at least one leading part for a *castrato*.

Although the *castrati* did not reach the height of their prestige until about 1725, when the more famous of them were treated by both managements and audiences like film stars of today, their waxing popularity during the late seventeenth century influenced the development of opera into becoming a musical entertainment for solo voices. Thus while Cavalli, who could be described as the first popular opera composer, saw to it that his libretti were reasonably integrated dramatically despite their provision for spectacular variety, and chose his musical type – aria, arioso, and recitative – according to the situation of the moment, he reduced participation of the orchestra and often dispensed with the chorus altogether, both for reasons of economy and because of the growing adulation of the solo voice. Not until the nineteenth century did the chorus again play a distinctive part in Italian opera.

The expansion of the aria during the latter half of the century, its greater variety, the prevalence of some kind of external structure, and the increasing sense of tonality are all linked together, for they all stem from the composer's wish to communicate. The greater variety in aria types, ranging from comic patter songs with wide leaps to highly expressive *bel canto* melodies, demanded internal repetition more than ever if the basic emotion was to be clearly presented. There soon arose the practice of beginning an aria either with a 'motto', a distinctive melodic phrase, or a series of chords which expressed succinctly the main emotion, and from which most or all of the ensuing material was clearly derived.

As regards external repetition the three principal forms were strophic, rondo, and *da capo*; of these the third became so typical of opera that it is often called 'aria form'. Its A–B–A structure provided more scope for contrast than strophic form and yet was simpler and shorter than the rondo. Owing to the idea of a basic emotion for each aria the middle section rarely contained any significantly new material, and this being so the only way to achieve a marked contrast was by development of the main material in various keys, ending 'out of key' so as to make the reprise of A obligatory. Baroque form, indeed, from *c.* 1650 on, is increasingly a matter of contrasts of key, not musical ideas.

The expansion of the aria and a firm grasp of tonality can be clearly seen in the later operas of Legrenzi, Stradella, and

Pallavicino; with them polyphony and counterpoint began discreetly to reappear, basses are more melodically distinctive and often imitative of the voice, not just functional, the voices are more independent in ensembles (though runs of thirds and sixths are still common) and the orchestra is given a more substantial share in the proceedings; otherwise the main features are similar to Cesti's operas.

ITALIAN OPERA ABROAD

It was inevitable, after the glories of the Italian Renaissance, that Europe should imitate whatever art form Italy produced, and it was natural that the Catholic countries that lay nearest to Italy should be first affected. Southern Germany, Austria, and Bohemia saw Italian opera before any other country – Salzburg (1618), Vienna (1626), Prague (1627) – and any native operatic talent quickly succumbed to the Italian invasion.

The most important centre of Italian opera north of the Alps was Vienna, the seat of the Holy Roman Emperor, and thus traditionally bound by close ties with Italy. Opera here was for the court, not the populace: hence the differences between Italian opera in Vienna and Venice. Cesti's *Il pomo d'oro*, written for Leopold I's wedding in 1667, is an extreme but not an unfair example; there were sixty-seven scenes involving twenty-four different stage settings (some of them of fantastic elaboration and all brilliantly executed by Burnacini, the greatest theatrical designer of his day), nearly fifty characters, an orchestra of strings, woodwind, brass, and continuo, with a special group of cornetts, trombones, and regal for the infernal scenes, besides many ballets and choruses. The size of the orchestra, the extent of its participation, and the number of choruses are in sharp contrast with Venetian opera and remained typical of Italian opera in Vienna during the seventeenth century, as evidenced in the works of her two leading composers, the Italians Bertali (1605–69) and Draghi (1635–1700).

The rise of native opera in northern Germany, Spain,

France, and England, its submersion by Italian opera – except in France – and its later re-emergence will be dealt with later, but it is convenient in this section to note the fact that only seven Italian operas were seen in Paris in the seventeenth century, four of them during the Barberini's exile there. Of these seven, one was *Orfeo* (1647) by Rossi (1598–1657), an important cantata composer, and the last was *Ercole amante* (1662) by Cavalli, both written expressly for Paris, and both attempting to appeal to French taste by making recitatives more declamatory and tunes more dance-like, and by incorporating numerous ballets, for which, in Cavalli's opera, the music was composed by a young expatriate Italian, Lully.

3. Neapolitan Opera

THE impact of Italian music abroad was strongest from *c.* 1690 until *c.* 1760, when sonata, concerto, and opera became crystallized, even stereotyped in structure, so reflecting one aspect of the times – the desire to plan and formalize. In Italy opera remained the most popular as well as the most important genre, bequeathing more than she assimilated, and forming the main span between the Baroque and Viennese classical styles. The centre of this next stage in the development of opera was Naples, where Alessandro Scarlatti (1660–1725), the greatest Italian operatic composer of the Baroque, spent most of his creative life.

Naples, situated between Vesuvius and the sea, enjoying a wonderful climate and position, had for centuries been a pleasure resort. From 1522 to 1707 she was a dominion of Spain, ruled by Spanish viceroys, and although during this period she produced little of musical importance until the last decade of the seventeenth century, what she did produce has a definite relevance to the type of opera that bears her name. Fundamentally it was for solo voices (choruses were infrequent, very short, and chordal in texture) and structurally it was very formalized, with recitative and aria following each other in regular succession, and the aria almost invariably in *da capo* form. Scarlatti did not, as is sometimes stated, create Neapolitan opera single-handed, for it arose from a combination of Neapolitan taste, libretto reform, and Scarlatti's genius for writing eminently singable melodies wedded to clear tonally-centred harmony.

As we have seen, most Venetian opera in the latter half of the seventeenth century paid scant attention to drama. This produced a reaction, notably in a young Venetian poet Apostolo Zeno (1668–1750) who published his first opera libretto *Gl'inganni felici* in 1695. Influenced by the classicism of the French dramatists, especially Racine, he restored something of the unity and dignity of the earlier Florentine libretti by concentrating on a central theme, reducing the number of subsidiary plots and irrelevantly spectacular scenes, and largely eschewing comedy. The above libretto, an important step towards *opera seria*, quickly became popular, as did subsequent ones from his pen, and in 1718 he was appointed Court Poet to the Emperor Charles V at Vienna. His libretti were soon imitated by other poets, the most distinguished of whom was Metastasio (1698–1782), a more imaginative dramatist and a finer poet than Zeno. Over 1,000 operas were based on his libretti, some being set as many as seventy times. Neither Zeno nor any other poet came anywhere near such popularity.

The standard Zeno-Metastasio libretto consisted of three acts, each divided into scenes distinguished by changes of mood and characters rather than of stage setting. Each scene consisted normally of a recitative which unfolded the action, and an aria which commented on it. The recitatives were frequently dialogues between two or more characters, whereas the arias were almost invariably solos, the chief exceptions being duets for the principal lovers. Choruses and solo ensembles other than duets are rare, though the final number is often a concerted ensemble. On paper the recitatives are far longer than the arias, but in performance the two roughly balance, as the former were commonly set as *secco* recitatives sung at a conversational speed while the arias, apart from the natural lengthening that results from a lyrical setting involving many repetitions of phrase, are constructed of two verses, the first of which was meant to be repeated.

With Zeno's reforms opera became fully Baroque in character, the basic emotion of the aria already present in Venetian opera being even more clearly defined, and the resultant unity within each scene was extended to cover the entire work through the concentration on a central plot. This soon became very conventionalized in its dramatic situations, relying on a *deus ex machina* to resolve the tangle of affairs and provide the invariable happy ending. Such regularity and simplicity of structure and presentation were more immediately acceptable in Naples than anywhere else, but the acceptance only became complete when the libretti were clothed with melodies that matched each emotion, enabling the singer to display fully the resources of his art. Naples became the 'Singing City', and her four conservatories together with a number of private singing schools were famed throughout Europe. Here, during the late seventeenth and eighteenth centuries, generations of singers and composers were trained, and the slant given to their training was typically Neapolitan; in other words the singers concentrated on display, the composers on ingratiating melody.

The growing esteem of the singers in Venetian opera reached its zenith in Neapolitan opera, with the *castrati* reigning supreme. The chief of these were Grimaldi or Nicolini (1673–1732), Bernacchi (1685–1756), Bernardi or Senesino (*c.* 1680–*c.* 1750), Maiorano or Caffarelli (1703–83), Carestini (*c.* 1705–*c.* 1759), Conti or Gizzielo (1714–61), and, the greatest of them all, Broschi or Farinelli (1705–82). All but Bernacchi and Senesino (both Bolognese trained) were products of Naples, and their popularity was such that they could alter an aria or demand a new one if they so desired; so could some of the 'natural' singers, such as the renowned *cantatrici* (virtuoso women singers) Bordoni (1693–1781) and Cuzzoni (1700–70), and the bass Boschi. Such interference in the composer's domain persisted to the end of the eighteenth century (Susanna's '*Al desio di chi t'adora*' in Mozart's *Figaro*) but it was the *castrati* who first established the practice.

The power and prestige that the leading singers enjoyed were not lightly achieved, however, for the training involved before they became fully professional was more arduous and comprehensive than it is today. In addition to rigorous exercises aimed at developing control, flexibility, and power, they received instruction in the theory and composition of music, as well as in acting and elocution. This all-roundness must always be borne in mind when assessing Neapolitan opera from the score, for the usually arid recitatives come to life when delivered with expressive clarity accompanied by appropriate gestures and mien, and the repeat of the first part (the reprise) in the invariable *da capo* aria is not anticlimactic when it is suitably embellished. Such embellishment was axiomatic in Neapolitan opera, expected by composers and audience alike, and it spread to the whole field of Italian vocal music; it was, indeed, the exact musical parallel of the highly elaborate ornamentation of Baroque architecture, and it served the same end – to heighten the emotional impact of the main structure. Although this Baroque practice has always been known it is only very recently that a few enlightened singers have departed from the habit that should in any case have offended their artistic sense: the exact repetition of the first section.

Even with a centralized plot, internal simplicity of form, and superb singing, Neapolitan opera would not have appealed as it did to the Neapolitans had it not offered a wide variety of mood. The arias were generally so arranged that each one represented a different emotion from the preceding and succeeding ones, and were sung by different characters. This was primarily the function of the librettist, and in Zeno's (and more especially Metastasio's) libretti the arrangement is skilfully done. Moreover the composer, besides writing music that underlined the basic emotion of each aria, increased the variety by drawing on a number of aria types, no one of which occurred successively. These types ranged from the *aria d'agilità* or *bravura*, a virtuosic show-piece, to the *aria cantabile*, the *bel canto* aria which was in slow triple metre, sentimental, and ideal for displaying the technical and musical accomplishments of the singer.

It was in this type of aria that embellishments could most effectively be incorporated because of the slow tempo. Embellishments were applied not only to the reprise but also to the middle section, though less elaborately, and there was accordingly a heightening of interest as the aria progressed. The 'star' singers improvised their embellishments, a feat only possible after a grounding in composition, but the lesser lights either wrote them out beforehand or got someone else to do it for them. Undoubtedly many of these embellishments were in extremely bad taste, being mere vehicles for virtuosity, just as are many of the cadenzas interpolated by players into Mozart's piano concertos, but in both cases the principle is perfectly satisfactory, and at its best Neapolitan opera provided a feast of variegated and often memorable melodies, marvellously executed and sensitively embellished, together with a unified plot set in elaborate and colourful scenery and communicated with a wealth of gesture and inflexion at almost conversational speed.

The main criticism of such opera is based on the premium it placed on immediately attractive melody, and its reliance on the singer. Inevitably, considering the vast quantity that was written in order to satisfy the craving for variety, much of the music was second-rate, or worse, although this could be transmuted by the greatest singers. If not, there was precious little left to appeal, as the harmony was largely functional and essentially diatonic despite the occasional use of chromatic chords such as the so-called 'Neapolitan sixth'; the accompaniments were mostly for unison violins and continuo, and the plot thoroughly conventional in structure and situation.

The above description is of what may be termed the standard type of Neapolitan opera, but in the hands of its greatest exponents it developed in various ways.

ALESSANDRO SCARLATTI

The first opera to be performed in Naples was Monteverdi's *Poppea* (1651), but the earliest operas that can be called typically Neapolitan were by Provenzale (1627?–1704), whose two surviving works were produced in 1671 and 1678. Provenzale enjoyed considerable popularity in Naples, and when in 1684 the young Scarlatti was summoned from Rome and appointed over his head as music director of the Spanish Viceregal Chapel, he resigned in protest. Scarlatti's name was not new to Naples, as three of his operas had already been performed there; these three, in the late Venetian style of Stradella and Legrenzi (then the dominant influence in Rome) are particularly noteworthy for the polyphonic richness of many of their orchestral accompaniments.

During the next eighteen years Scarlatti's operatic style underwent a remarkable change. Compared with his earlier Venetian style, melody became more sequential, harmony smoother, and more tonally centred, and the *da capo* form gradually ousted all others. The importance of the orchestra waned also, the most striking accompaniments being those in which a solo instrument concertized with the voice, and the number of solo ensembles dwindled to a few duets. By 1702 Scarlatti had established the standard type of Neapolitan opera, though few of his successors could match his melodic gift or his delight in orchestral colour and polyphonic texture. This delight persisted all his life and appeared from time to time in most of the operas of this first Neapolitan period, even in those (generally regarded as his worst) written during the last six years.

Many of the operas written before 1702 exhibit four noteworthy features; the first two assumed some importance in later *opera seria*, the third helped to prepare the way for *opera buffa*, and the fourth became the structural starting point of the classical symphony. The first feature is the 'mixed scene' in which either one or two characters express different emotions. The second is the accompanied recitative which came to be reserved as an introduction to the emotionally climactic arias. The third is the introduction of two comic figures – usually an old woman (sung by a tenor) and an old man (bass) – who often have a scene to themselves at the end of Acts I and II, nearly always finishing with a duet. The fourth, the so-called Italian overture or *sinfonia* that precedes the opera, normally consists of three movements – quick, slow, quick, and is, like Neapolitan opera as a whole, fundamentally homophonic in texture.

It is quite plain that Scarlatti, during this first period at Naples, wrote to please popular taste, and that the type of opera he did so much to establish was in some respects alien to his own ideals. His growing irritation at not being able to write as he wanted came to a head in 1702 when, with his salary in arrears and the political future of the city uncertain, he asked for and was granted leave of absence. He first went to Florence where he was warmly received by one of the most enthusiastic patrons of opera, Prince Ferdinand de' Medici, but as the Prince offered him no permanent position he accepted an inferior post in Rome rather than return to Naples.

Rome, however, was still feeling the effects of the pontificates of her two great reforming popes, Innocent XI (1676–89) and Innocent XII (1691–1700), who had strongly condemned the worldliness that, as we observed earlier, gradually replaced the original religious spirit of Baroque art. As a result Scarlatti found little opportunity for his operatic talent, and before he returned to Naples in 1709, most of his operas were performed at Prince Ferdinand's private theatre or at Venice.

Much of what he wrote during this period has unfortunately been lost, but there is no doubt that it enhanced his prestige, and when he was reappointed to his old position in Naples he was sufficiently famous to write as he wished. In the remaining years of his life Scarlatti composed his greatest operas, most of them for Naples, but some, including *Griselda* (1721), his last and possibly his finest work, for Rome. Papal disapproval of opera being relaxed, he resided there from 1717 to 1722/3 before finally returning to Naples.

It is from the operas written after 1707 that Scarlatti should be judged, as they alone truly reflect his ideals. The vocal element still reigns supreme, with the *da capo* aria as the fundamental unit, and the chief vehicle of expressive melody. Integration is the most distinctive feature of these last operas compared to the earlier ones, for they reveal an almost complete cross-section of contemporary practices used in such a way as to communicate more vividly the meaning of the words, and by so doing impart a greater variety to the whole. The arias are supported by an orchestra ranging from violins in unison to the full string band plus woodwind and brass, the harpsichord being reserved for the *ritornelli* in contradistinction to previous practice.

Melodic figures clearly influenced by the solo concertos of Corelli and Vivaldi are common in the string parts of these operas and occasionally even invade the vocal line (Example 48). The texture is richer, more polyphonic, and is sometimes shot through with snatches of imitation, while woodwind and brass are quite often used for specifically coloristic purposes and harmony is more expressive, its wider chromatic excursions firmly anchored to a central key. There is, moreover, a greater dramatic sense in parts of *Mitridate* (1707), unusual for its political plot and deeply felt expression of brotherly and sisterly love, in the use of vivid accompanied recitatives (*Mitridate*, IV, *Griselda*, III), and in highly emotional mixed scenes (*Attilio Regolo*, III) where the heroine goes mad from hallucinations of Hades.

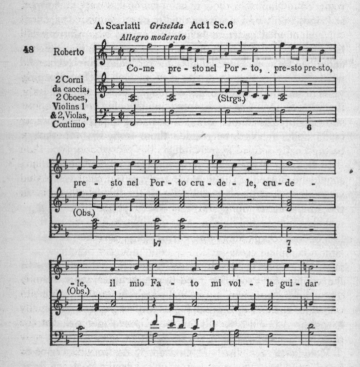

We know for a fact that Prince Ferdinand found much of what Scarlatti wrote for him too complex and not tuneful enough. It seems, therefore, almost certain that, even allowing for Ferdinand's poor taste (he preferred the operas of a comparative nonentity called Perti), most of Scarlatti's last operas were not fully appreciated by his contemporaries. As E. J.

Dent has put it, his 'real importance . . . lies not in his direct influence on his immediate followers, but in his relation to the whole of classical music'.

The operas Scarlatti wrote during his first Neapolitan period were more widely imitated than his later ones because their homophonic texture demanded little more than an ability to write attractive melodies. This standard Neapolitan type, primarily intended for the man in the street, provided excellent entertainment. On the other hand there was what we may call the polyphonic Neapolitan opera, represented to a certain extent by many of Scarlatti's later works, and which stemmed from late seventeenth-century Venetian opera. Roughly speaking, the former type was cultivated in the south of Italy, the latter in the north and across the Alps, but some Neapolitans, e.g. Feo (*c.* 1685–*c.* 1745), Leo (1694–1744), and Durante (1684–1755) – all three, significantly, church composers of some merit – tended more towards the polyphonic type than their fellows, of whom the most important were Vinci (1690–1730) and Porpora (1686–1766), perhaps the most celebrated teacher of singing and composition of his time (both Farinelli and Caffarelli were his pupils, as was Haydn).

NEAPOLITAN 'OPERA BUFFA'

Just as in the sixteenth century, when the *canzona alla Napolitana* reflected the need for a simpler more frankly popular art compared to the madrigal, so in the eighteenth century Naples created *opera buffa* to offset the lack of comedy in Zeno's and Metastasio's libretti. *Opera buffa* was not the same as comic opera: this, from *Chi soffre, speri* onwards, only differed from *opera seria* in the nature of the story, but in *opera buffa* the characters were fewer (usually only two) and were drawn, like the plot, from contemporary life. Only natural voices were used, no *castrati*, and the arias, sometimes reminiscent of folk-song, ranged from patter songs to sentimental ditties, but never essayed the heights of emotion. They were freer in form, harmonically limited, and expressed the words naturally, simply, and melodiously. Ensembles figured more prominently, especially at the end of each act. Everything was more life-like and less artificial than *opera seria*, though it resembled the latter in its recitative-aria structure and homophonic texture.

Opera buffa developed from the seventeenth-century intermezzi which, like the Renaissance *intermedii*, were scenes in lighter vein sandwiched between the acts of a serious work, in this case opera. They became very popular with the spread of public opera in the latter half of the century, for apart from their character they provided greater variety to an evening's entertainment, and as the main work was usually in three acts the intermezzi generally consisted of two scenes, which, by 1700, formed a continuous plot. This dovetailing of serious and comic works, which often involved startling contrasts, clearly appealed to the Neapolitans, and it was not until the late 1730s that intermezzi were performed as an entity; at this point, with what we may call 'buffo style' already established since the early 1720s, *opera buffa* was born.

The most famous *opera buffa* is *La serva padrona* (1733) by Pergolesi (1710–36), which created a furore in Paris in 1752 and has remained in the repertory ever since. Although a delightful work, it is a pity that its historical notoriety has distracted attention from the same composer's *Livietta e Tracollo* (1734) and similar works by Vinci, Leo, and others, which are little if at all inferior.

Opera buffa did not displace *opera seria* in popular esteem, for it neither catered for the delight in vocal virtuosity and embellishment, nor provided the emotional range possible in *opera seria*; in fact most composers from Pergolesi to Mozart wrote both types successfully, and towards the middle of the century the two styles interacted. In *opera seria* comic episodes began to reappear, written in a typical *buffo* style, while *opera buffa* tended to merge with comic opera by expanding to three acts, including a greater degree of love interest, and increasing the cast to include a group of comedians (usually three men and two women) and a pair of young lovers. The leading composers of this enlarged *opera buffa* were Logroscino (1698–after 1765), Jomelli (1714–74), Rinaldo di Capua (b. *c*. 1715), Traetta (1727–79), and Galuppi (1706–85), all Neapolitans except the last, a Venetian. Galuppi expanded the end-of-act ensemble into a series of five or six movements, and although there is little musical and no dramatic climax the idea soon spread to the whole field of opera, reaching a peak in Mozart's superbly climactic finales. Most of Galuppi's comic operas are on libretti by Goldoni (1707–93), the Venetian playwright, many of whose racy and topical comedies paralleled *opera buffa* in their portrayal of lower- and middle-class society.

NEAPOLITAN OPERA ABROAD

Neapolitan opera conquered virtually the whole of Europe, excluding France but including Russia, where a permanent opera house, founded at St Petersburg (now Leningrad) in 1734, was served by a number of distinguished Italian composers, including Traetta and Galuppi. In Spain the native *zarzuela* and *tonadilla*, both essentially comic and popular, and consisting of spoken dialogue interspersed with songs, gave way before the tide from Italy, though the *tonadilla* just managed to survive. Austria and southern Germany had already been subjugated, and now Vienna was joined by Munich as one of the main centres of Italian opera north of the Alps.

In Vienna, where Zeno and Metastasio were court poets, the leading composers were the Austrian Fux (1660–1741) and a group of Italians – Caldara (1670–1730), the Bononcini brothers, Giovanni (1670–1755) and Antonio Maria (1675–1726), and Conti (1681–1732). Here the northern type of Neapolitan opera was cultivated because Germanic aristocratic taste preferred polyphonic texture, so that Fux's operas in particular, though melodically much less captivating than the southern Neapolitan type, provide greater contrast in their profusion of ensembles and choruses, and in the variety of their orchestral accompaniments.

As in the seventeenth century, opera was staged with exceptional lavishness, especially after 1708 when the Josephine Theatre, the most magnificent opera house of its time, was created by the famous architect and stage designer, Bibiena.

But the War of the Austrian Succession (1740–8) had the disastrous effect of closing the theatre (it later reopened as a ballroom) and opera practically ceased. When it was revived in the latter half of the century its main features, though modified to some degree, persisted and played a considerable part in the operatic styles of Mozart and Beethoven, and it was no accident that Gluck's reforms of Italian opera were conceived and first successfully presented in Vienna, despite the new rococo taste from France, and the powerful Italian faction that later labelled Mozart's operas as heavy, confused, and dissonant.

In Munich, too, the northern type of Neapolitan opera predominated, largely through Steffani (1654–1728), a most brilliantly gifted man – ambassador, priest, singer, conductor, and a composer of outstanding talent, who fused traditional German polyphony with Italian *bel canto*. His basses are melodic as well as providing harmonic support, obbligato arias are prominent, and he included far more ensembles, particularly duets, than did Scarlatti. The last forty years of his life he spent mostly at Hanover, which, as a result, became the first major Protestant town to capitulate to Italian opera. It is to the Protestant states that we now turn.

The earliest German opera was produced in Saxony – *Dafne* (Torgau, 1627) by Schütz (1585–1672). Schütz, an ardent admirer, but far from slavish imitator of Italian music, had studied in Venice with Giovanni Gabrieli from 1609 to 1612, and it is most unfortunate that the score of his only opera is lost. The libretto is a translation of Rinuccini's mentioned earlier, and its secular character is untypical of early German opera which, like Roman opera (and for the same reason) was mainly moralistic or religious in tone. The first surviving example, *Seelewig* (Nuremberg, 1644) by Staden (1607–55) shows this clearly. The opera describes the unsuccessful attempts of the villain Trügewalt, aided and abetted by the Arts and Senses, to ensnare the Soul. *Seelewig* is actually a *Singspiel*, a play with songs, very similar to Florentine monody, and instrumental pieces scored for a fairly large orchestra.

The development of German opera in the Protestant states

was hampered by political divisions, and, more especially, by the Thirty Years War (1618–48), and the growing Italian influence from the south. It is, therefore, not surprising that the most important centre of German opera was Hamburg, the most northerly as well as the richest and most independent of the larger German cities. In 1678 the first public opera house in Europe outside Italy was opened in Hamburg with *Adam und Eva* by Theile (1646–1724), a pupil of Schütz. This, like *Seelewig*, was a moral opera, and while several others similar in tone followed, partially placating that strict and increasingly influential Lutheran sect, the Pietists, who equated the stage with the devil, the growing secularity of the Baroque atmosphere led to an increasing number of worldly plots, many of them direct translations from Italian and French libretti.

Complete Italian operas soon followed, some of them with the recitatives in German which made the story intelligible and hence gave an idea what the arias were about. The music, too, revealed Italian influence: whereas the operas of the first generation of Hamburg composers, of whom the most notable were Conradi (d. *c.* 1694), and J. W. Franck (*c.* 1641–after 1695), are characteristically German in their preference for *arioso*-like rather than *secco* recitatives, those of the second generation, led by Kusser (1660–1727), are more Italianate in every way. The cosmopolitan style of Kusser's operas is even more pronounced in those of his pupil Keiser (1674–1739), the greatest composer of German Baroque opera, who combined the native traits described above with French and Italian elements.

Under Kusser and Keiser, and the latter's distinguished though less gifted successors in the operatic field, Telemann (1681–1767), and Mattheson, Hamburg enjoyed a period of great brilliance; but the disapproval of the Pietists, the doubtful reputations of many of the women singers (*castrati* were forbidden until *c.* 1730), the patchwork shoddiness of most libretti, which pandered to the lowest taste of the audiences (except those by the admirable dramatic poet Feind, 1678–1721), and the growing admiration for Italian singers and the Neapolitan style, ended by 1740 in the extinction of German opera. A similar fate overtook native opera at the other main centres in northern Germany, Weissenfels and Brunswick, and Italian *opera seria* reigned supreme until the nineteenth century.

In view of the increasing numbers of Italian composers in all the major cities of Europe, except Paris, during the first half of the eighteenth century, it is strange that the two greatest exponents of Neapolitan opera were both German, Hasse (1699–1783), and Handel (1685–1759), who cultivated the southern and northern types respectively. Hasse, who spent most of his life in Dresden, possessed such a remarkable gift for beautifully constructed melody, supported by crystal-clear and seemingly inevitable harmony, that the Italians nicknamed him '*il caro Sassone*'. His operas reflect to near perfection that homophonic style which developed from *bel canto* and *opera buffa*, and which we now call *stile galante*. It can be found in embryo in Scarlatti's last operas, but it was not fully fashioned until the middle decades of the eighteenth century when it formed the foundation of the Viennese classical style. It is characterized by melody that is essentially lyrical, rhythmically simple, and mainly sequential, and which is frequently an extension, as it were, of the accompanying harmony; its other features are a bass that is primarily functional, a firmly centred tonality, and a fairly slow rate of chord change.

Hasse cultivated other styles besides the pure Neapolitan, and it is significant that he left his first teacher in Italy, Porpora, for Scarlatti, whose influence can clearly be seen in the German's later operas. In the best of these the arias are wonderfully matched to the basic mood, and achieve a most satisfying balance between drama and lyricism. *Secco* recitatives are carefully set, and accompanied recitatives, though sparingly used, are always highly emotional; in other words Hasse was, for his time, more than usually sensitive to the merits of the text, and this explains why he set all Metastasio's libretti at least once, and why he was the poet's favourite composer. In his handling of the orchestra, too, he learnt much from Scarlatti, and while most of his earlier operas are full of continuo arias, the later ones contain very few. The main differences between the two composers' later operas, apart from texture, are the expansion of the aria by means of one or two subsidiary ideas (paralleled in the concerto and presaging the dualistic construction of the classical first movement), and the greater degree of virtuosity demanded of the singer (Example 49). The *castrati* especially are given more opportunity for

embellishment and display through the introduction of an improvised solo cadenza heralded by a $^6_4$ chord, just as in the classical concerto which borrowed the idea direct.

4. England – The Masque

THE pre-Commonwealth masque was primarily an entertainment for royalty and the aristocracy, and consisted, like the French *ballet de cour*, of a succession of dances. Some of them were character dances that ranged from slapstick to the macabre (the 'antimasques' performed by semi-professionals) and some were conventional ballroom types (the 'revels' danced by members of the audience); they were accompanied by voices and instruments, and separated by dialogue and songs, the whole being lavishly staged and dressed. The chief creators of the early masque were Ben Jonson (1572–1637), Campian, Davenant (1606–68), and Inigo Jones, who achieved fame as a stage designer many years before his success as an architect. The chief composers were Campian, Coperario, Alfonso Ferrabosco II, Robert Johnson, and the Lawes brothers, Henry (1596–1662) and William (1602–45), the elder of whom was praised, in absurdly extravagant terms, by Milton as being the first to set English words correctly.

True to their native conservatism English composers only slowly assimilated the new ideas and styles from abroad, and while the first four composers mentioned above produced some attractive songs and dances in Renaissance style, especially Johnson, it was a Frenchman, Nicholas Lanier (1588–1666), who first introduced recitative into the masque in Jonson's *The Vision of Delight* (1617); indeed, Jonson's *Lovers Made Men* (1617) was wholly 'sung after the Italian manner, *stylo recitativo*, by . . . Lanier', according to the poet. The effect of the recitative style is more apparent in the compositions of the Lawes brothers, though, as usually happens when men are mastering a new technique, their music is distinctly inferior to that of their predecessors, for, like the Florentine monodists, they became over-concerned with the accurate setting of verbal rhythm at the expense of the melodic line, and both emotionally and harmonically the results cannot compare with the Continental counterparts, Italian *arioso* and French recitative.

This type of recitative, potentially moving, declamatory, and moderately lyrical, was the only one favoured by English composers, and it is probable that the rejection of *secco* recitative was due to that strong element of realism in the English character and physiognomy. Whatever the reason, the fact remains that English stage-works with music, from the early seventeenth century to the Savoy operas, have, with very few exceptions, consisted of musical numbers inserted into spoken dialogue.

During the last years of Charles I's reign the masque, less unified dramatically, and more reliant on spectacle, reached its apogee in *The Triumph of Peace* (1633) by the popular playwright Shirley (1596–1666) with music by William Lawes and Simon Ives (1600–62). It included a vast procession on horseback from Holborn to Whitechapel, and cost the Inns of Court who commissioned it over £21,000 (at least £200,000 in modern money). The extravagance of the times and the general laxity of morals, both reflected in the masques and other stage works, were strongly attacked by the voluminous pamphleteer Prynne (1600–69), whose puritanical attitude towards the theatre became 'official', as it were, during the Commonwealth. As a result, and also because they were staged privately and had to be less expensive, Commonwealth masques were less spectacular; this led to a greater emphasis on drama and music, an emphasis that persisted after the Restoration (1660). Fortunately England produced at this time a number of notable dramatists as well as three composers who laid the foundations of what might have been, given successors of comparable merit, a school of English opera.

The composers were Locke (*c.* 1630–77), Blow (1649–1708), and Purcell (1659–95). All possessed a keener dramatic sense, and assimilated foreign influences more successfully, than any Englishman before them. All were capable of writing vivid recitatives and attractive dance-like melodies, yet there are hints of a preference for polyphonic textures entirely typical of English seventeenth-century music as a whole. Although more complex than contemporary textures abroad it enjoyed greater tonal freedom and was characterized by harmonic asperities resulting from a linear approach. The last two features are more apparent in Locke than in Blow and Purcell, but they do not lessen the effectiveness of his contributions to the stage, the chief of which are *Cupid and Death* (1653) by Shirley (a few of the musical items are by Christopher Gibbons, son of Orlando), *Orpheus and Euridice* (1673), *Psyche* (1673) by Shadwell (1642–92), and the incidental music to Shadwell's arrangement of Shakespeare's *The Tempest* (1674).

Psyche is a semi-opera; that is, a stage work in which the main emphasis is almost equally divided between music and spoken text. *Orpheus and Euridice*, called, like *Cupid and Death*, a masque, is a little one-act opera, sung throughout, with dancing a minor feature. It indicates the rapidly growing influence of Continental models during the last third of the century. Similarly indicative is Blow's masque *Venus and Adonis* (c. 1682), though here again the work is in fact an opera. French influence is apparent in the overture, the pastoral prologue, the frequency of choruses and ensembles, and the type of recitative described above, while the predominance of airs over recitatives and the fairly regular construction of the melodies show Italian influence. The vocal lines, however, are still somewhat angular compared with those abroad, and the feeling for tonality is less strong. In addition to many charming numbers in this opera, there is one most impressive moment near the end that comes near to Monteverdi's lament from *Arianna*, when Venus, at the sight of Adonis mortally wounded, gives vent to her grief in an *arioso* of quite remarkable intensity.

Although *Orpheus and Euridice* and *Venus and Adonis* are the two earliest surviving English operas, Davenant had written three works during the Commonwealth combining entertainment with instruction (an idea unthinkable in France and Italy) in order to allay the Puritans' abhorrence of the traditional theatre. The three works were *The Siege of Rhodes* (1656), *The Cruelty of the Spaniards in Peru* (1658), and *The History of Sir Francis Drake* (1659); the music of all three has been lost. When the ban on the theatre was lifted at the Restoration Davenant made no attempt to repeat his earlier successes. It may be that he was more interested in the straight play, and merely used opera as a means of side-stepping Puritan prejudice, or he may have thought, as Locke did, that in normal circumstances his countrymen would not countenance an English opera sung in its entirety.

PURCELL

Blow unfortunately wrote nothing else for the stage after *Venus and Adonis*. This work, however, undoubtedly influenced his pupil Purcell, especially *Dido and Aeneas* (1689?), which has several features in common with the earlier piece, notably a climactic lament, Dido's 'When I am laid in earth'. This wonderfully poignant expression of grief exhibits Purcell's superiority over all other English composers of the Baroque, for it reveals outstanding gifts of melody and harmony that heighten the rhythm and mood of the text; both features are typical of his work as a whole, though he seldom approached elsewhere such intensity of feeling. Typical, too, are the richly polyphonic accompaniment and the use of a ground bass.

Although the very poorly drawn character of Aeneas in Purcell's opera is a major dramatic flaw, for which we can blame the librettist Tate (1652–1715), and the fact that it was written for a young ladies' boarding-school (the men, therefore, had to be imported), the all-round quality of the work is such that we can only regret its uniqueness in the composer's output. As with young Alessandro Scarlatti, though with very different results, popular taste could not be gainsaid, and apart from numerous songs, and instrumental pieces for various plays, all Purcell's subsequent contributions to the stage were semi-operas – *The Prophetess, or the History of Dioclesian* (1690), adapted from Beaumont and Fletcher, *King Arthur* (1691) by Dryden, *The Fairy Queen* (1692), adapted from Shakespeare, *The Indian Queen* (1695), adapted from Dryden and Howard, and *The Tempest* (1695?), adapted from Shakespeare.

The only one of these specifically designed to be set to music was *King Arthur*, the others being adulterated versions of the originals; because of this and the more or less haphazard intrusion of spoken dialogue, Purcell had little opportunity to plan on any extended musical scale. But when he did have the opportunity, as in the *Masque from Dioclesian*, the result is a consistent improvement on *Dido and Aeneas*. Indeed, this work so impressed Dryden that he invited Purcell, whom he had previously ignored, to compose the music for *King Arthur*, and although the score is uneven in quality it demonstrates the composer's remarkable dramatic and emotional versatility, from the highly original 'Frost Scene' with its shivering vocal and instrumental tremolos, to the rumbustious folk-song 'Your hay it is mow'd'.

The three semi-operas that followed *King Arthur* are much more even in quality, particularly *The Indian Queen* and *The Tempest* which as a whole represent the peak of Purcell's entire output. None of the individual items, however, is superior to his previous stage music, including incidental items to a host of plays. These last semi-operas reveal more affinities with French and Italian music than any previous work for the English stage, by reason of their smoother vocal line, a more regular construction of the air, and the increasing though still comparatively infrequent use of *da capo*.

The general level of Purcell's vocal and instrumental music in his stage works is remarkably high; higher, indeed, than in Lully's *tragédies lyriques*, or in contemporary Italian operas, including those of Scarlatti's first Neapolitan period. It should be remembered, however, that in each individual work Purcell was called on to contribute far less than the operatic composer abroad; moreover, because there was little continuity, he was largely unconcerned with having to plan a succession of songs so that they provided variety of music and mood. For these reasons alone fewer demands were made on his inventive fertility, and it was easier for him to maintain a high level of inspiration.

His exceptional melodic and dramatic gifts make it probable that, given another twenty years of life, he would have composed several full-scale English operas in which his flair for powerful declamation would have broken down the antipathy of his countrymen to sung dialogue. What is certain is that later audiences tolerated recitative in English or Italian provided that the arias were attractive enough. Thus *Arsinoë* (1705), 'the first Opera that gave us a Taste of Italian Musick', as Addison put it in the *Spectator*, was moderately successful because it consisted of a tolerably good selection of Italian arias collected by a very mediocre composer, Clayton (*c.* 1670–*c.* 1730), who added recitatives and adapted the whole to an English libretto. But Clayton's own setting of Addison's *Rosamond* (1707) was a complete fiasco, whereas that by Arne (1710–78) in 1733 was very successful. Arne, though he lacked Purcell's dramatic and emotional range, had a real talent for writing attractive if somewhat superficial melody, and had there been a flourishing native operatic tradition he would almost certainly have added to it more than he did; as it is he composed but one more English opera, an extremely successful setting of a translation of Metastasio's *Artaxerxes* (1762).

The only other successful English opera between *Arsinoë* and Arne's *Rosamond* was *Calypso and Telemachus* (1712) by Johann Ernst Galliard (*c.* 1680–1749), a work much admired by Handel; but in the period before Handel settled in England, a number of Italian operas proved very popular, the composers including Scarlatti, the Bononcini brothers, and Conti.

HANDEL

In 1710 Handel came to England and saw how the land lay; two years later he returned and conquered. He had already seen his *Almira* (1705) enthusiastically received in Hamburg, and had tasted to the full all that Italy had to offer on a visit that lasted from 1707 to 1710. During that visit he met Alessandro Scarlatti and his son Domenico, as well as Corelli and Steffani, and he had seen his opera *Agrippina* (1709) cause a sensation in Venice. Steffani, indeed, was so impressed by Handel that he recommended him as his successor to the post of chapel-master to the Elector of Hanover.

But Handel's experience of London must have convinced him that greater opportunities lay there, and when he returned to England in 1712 he almost certainly did so with the intention of over-staying his leave. One can imagine his feelings when he learnt that the Elector of Hanover was to become George I, but what might have been a distinctly unpleasant episode was saved by the King's recognition of Handel's genius, and by 1715 (one year after his coronation) George had attended a performance of Handel's opera *Amadigi*, and shortly afterwards doubled the composer's pension. The King also became one of the patrons of the Royal Academy of Music, an operatic company founded by Handel in 1719, and centred at the King's Theatre; other members included Giovanni Bononcini and the impresario Heidegger.

Except for three short visits abroad in 1729, 1733, and 1737, Handel spent the rest of his life in England, and did not keep fully abreast of the developments in Italian opera that took place after he left Italy in 1710. Thus *buffo* style, with which he first became acquainted during his 1729 visit, is only tentatively introduced into some of his later operas. Unquestionably he was profoundly influenced by Italian music, but he was much less Italianate than his younger compatriot Hasse, for his best operas incorporated only those Italian and French elements which could be satisfactorily fused with his native penchant for sonority and instrumental colour. His melodic gift was exceptional, greater than Scarlatti's or Hasse's, and this, combined with the fascinating variety of his orchestral accompaniments and richness of texture, a variety and richness superior to any earlier or contemporary operatic composer, made him the leading exponent of the northern Neapolitan type of opera, and the greatest operatic composer of the late Baroque.[1]

It is not possible here to give a full account of the riches contained in Handel's operas, but some idea of the variety of means and expression will be gained from the following summary:

1. For an account by E. J. Dent of the operas and the problems of reviving them, see *Handel, a Symposium*, edited by Gerald Abraham (O.U.P.).

1. Arias. In addition to the various categories mentioned on p. 262, the typical Scarlattian *siciliano*, and the rhythmically square-cut type first popularized by G. Bononcini, are those influenced by dances that stemmed mostly from France (see p. 285) – *bourrée*, *courante*, *sarabande* (for example, the well-known '*Lascia ch'io pianga*' from *Rinaldo*), minuet, and gavotte.

2. Accompaniments. These range from continuo alone (very rare) and continuo with violins in unison to six-part imitative polyphony (an independent vocal line plus strings and oboes, *Agrippina*, II, 5), two oboes, two trumpets, two horns, strings, and continuo (*Radamisto*, final ensemble), and two oboes, four horns, strings, and continuo (*Giulio Cesare*, first and last choruses). The influence of the fully developed concerto idea (which originally stemmed from the operatic aria) can be seen in *Agrippina*, III, 11, where the main body of the orchestra, the *ripieno* group (strings in this case), is contrasted with six soloists – two oboes, two violins, and two cellos (the *concertino* group).

3. Instrumentation. Of all Baroque composers Handel was the most imaginative orchestrator, partly because, like Bach but unlike Hasse, he gave full rein to the traditional German delight in instrumental colour, and also because, unlike Bach, he found in opera the most natural medium for experiments in instrumentation. For opera was essentially public entertainment, and the eighteenth-century public craved variety as never before, particularly if it were novel; moreover, opera presented a wide range of affections, many of which could be more or less vividly portrayed in the aria accompaniments, for example, the birds' song in *Rinaldo*, I, 6, which is scored for two treble recorders and piccolo (probably a sopranino recorder) supported by violas only. Other notable examples are, apart from those in 2 above, two 'violette marine' (viole d'amore) in *Orlando Furioso*, III, 8; two recorders supported by muted violins and violas and pizzicato cellos and basses with no harpsichord in *Agrippina*, II, 7; and the Sinfonia in *Giulio Cesare*, II, 2, where the vision of Parnassus is portrayed by two orchestras, the first comprising oboes, bassoons, theorbo, harp, viola da gamba,

and strings, the second of oboes and strings, the harpsichord being totally excluded.

4. Texture. Handel's texture was more varied than that of his contemporaries, for it ranged from pure homophony, for example, violins and voice in unison with continuo absent, to imitative polyphony in four to six parts. The latter was an essentially German trait and is revealed consistently in his overtures, all of which are based on the French pattern: a stately sonorous first section, dominated by dotted rhythms, is followed by a quick fugue, often rounded off by a coda similar in style to the first section, and sometimes succeeded by one or more dance movements.

5. Drama. Handel was as little concerned with the quality of the libretti he set as were his contemporaries outside France; indeed, he comes off rather worse in this respect than does Hasse, for Metastasio's libretti were, on the whole, the best the period produced. This being so it is all the more remarkable that Handel managed to infuse such a high degree of humanity into many of the stereotyped characters with which opera abounded. Scarlatti had done this occasionally (*Mitridate*, *Griselda*), but with nothing like Handel's frequency or impact. Compared to that of nineteenth-century opera, which was less tied by conventions and more subjectively emotional, Handel's characterization is slight, but for its time it is unusual, and it reflects, significantly, the marked individualism of English society noted earlier.

Up to 1728 Handel's operas enjoyed considerable success due to their intrinsic excellence, and to such international celebrities as the *castrati* Senesino, Nicolini, and Valentini, the sopranos Cuzzoni, Bordoni, Durastanti, and Épine, and the bass Boschi. More important still, Handel was virtually alone in the field.

THE BALLAD OPERAS

In 1728 the poet and dramatist John Gay (1685–1732) collaborated with a naturalized German composer J. C. Pepusch (1667–1752), and produced *The Beggar's Opera*. It was an instantaneous success, for it satirized the government in the person of the Prime Minister, Robert Walpole, as well as poking fun at the recent stage brawl between Cuzzoni and Bordoni in Bononcini's *Astianatte* (1727). The earthiness of its setting in the London underworld, and the popular simplicity of its songs interspersed with spoken dialogue, tickled the public palate, always avid for something new. It was the first of the so-called 'ballad operas', and while it contained a number of folk-songs, it also drew upon the works of Purcell, Lully, Handel, and others, with words rewritten or added, just as in modern pantomime.

Other ballad operas quickly followed by Colley Cibber, Fielding, and Coffey, with a greater proportion of newly composed music. For the next seven years, during which nearly fifty were produced, their success contributed to the decline in popularity of Italian opera, not so much by their satire of operatic conventions as by attracting many people who would otherwise have supported the Royal Academy of Music or its rival company, the so-called Opera of the Nobility. This was founded in 1733 by the Prince of Wales and the Duke of Marlborough, mainly for political motives in opposition to the King, and having acquired Senesino (recently dismissed by Handel) and persuaded Cuzzoni, Montegnana, Porpora, and later Hasse to join them, they seriously affected Handel's operatic fortunes.

In 1737 things came to a head, and the rivalry of the two companies, the decline in quality of both music and libretti, and public reaction against foreign importations brought about the collapse of Italian opera. Although this was only temporary the old enthusiasm never returned, despite Handel's attempts to revive it by writing four more operas in the next four years, and some successful new operas and revivals by Hasse, Leo, Galuppi, and Pergolesi.

While the part played by the ballad operas in the decline of Italian opera has been exaggerated, their compromise between song and speech, and their essential realism, reflected typical English traits, many of them almost exactly paralleled by Hogarth's pictorial satires. The mélange of song and speech persisted until very recent times, despite occasional successes with recitatives replacing spoken dialogue such as Arne's *Artaxerxes*. Moreover it gave birth to the German *Singspiel*, for *The Devil to Pay* (1731) by Coffey was performed in Berlin in 1743, and (with new music) in Leipzig in 1752. From this date *Singspiel* became increasingly popular, and eventually reached its peak in Mozart's *Die Entführung aus dem Serail*.

5. Opera in France

THE only European country that successfully resisted the tide of Italian music was France. Until the late Renaissance northern Europe, with France as the artistic centre, had dominated musical history, and it may be that, consciously or unconsciously, her long tradition of leadership strengthened an instinctive reaction against what we may term the purely musical characteristic of Italian music. In other words, the French favoured the descriptive, the narrative, the realistic, and rational, and because music is fundamentally the most abstract and irrational of the arts, France only cultivated those musical genres that had some concrete associations – song, opera, dance, and programme music.

The few *bel canto* Italian operas (including Rossi's *Orfeo*) produced in Paris about the middle of the century did not greatly appeal, except for the ballets specially introduced to please French taste, and the spectacular and elaborate scenery devised by Giacomo Torelli, the greatest theatrical designer of his day. Dancing and spectacle had dominated the *ballet de cour* since the late fifteenth century, with *récits*, usually spoken, introducing and sometimes linking each scene. From 1605 on, recitation increasingly gave way to settings in the Italian monodic style, almost wholly due to the presence of Caccini at the court of Henry IV from 1604 to 1605.

The stress on vocal ornamentation introduced by Caccini tended to overshadow the literary element in the *récit*, a tendency paralleled in the *ballet de cour* as a whole by an almost complete disregard for unity of plot. About the middle of the century, however, traditional traits re-established themselves, poetry and drama became less subservient, and with Benserade the *ballet de cour* once again achieved dramatic unity. The *récit*, now invariably sung but with less vocal elaboration, connected the various scenes. During the first half of the century the two chief composers of ballet music were Guédron (1565–1621) and Antoine Boësset (*c.* 1585–1643), and they were followed by Boësset's son Jean-Baptiste (*c.* 1613–85), Cambefort (1605–61), and the most famous (and infamous) of them all, Jean Baptiste Lully (1632–87).

LULLY

Lully, although Italian-born, was brought up in France from about the age of ten. His musical gifts were first revealed in his violin playing, and at twenty he so impressed the Dauphin (later Louis XIV), that he was made one of the Vingt-Quatre Violons du Roi. Four years later, he was allowed to form and train a select band of sixteen violinists (subsequently expanded to twenty-one) which soon outshone its parent. As a result Lully was appointed conductor of the Violons du Roi, and under his direction the band became internationally famous. As was usual at the time, Lully had to provide a good deal of the band music himself, but although he contributed to various ballets, beginning with Benserade's *La Nuit* (1653), it was not until 1658, when he wrote the complete score of Benserade's *Alcidiane*, that he achieved any real success as a composer. From then on, sure of his creative gifts and extremely jealous of anyone who might hinder his ambition of becoming the first musician in France, he never again collaborated with another composer. His jealousy, indeed, extended to his literary colleagues, and although he wrote the music for several of Molière's comedies, including *Le Bourgeois Gentilhomme* (1670), over half of the thirty ballet-scores that he composed between 1658 and 1671 were to ballets devised by the comparatively obscure Benserade. The same is true of his operas, or *tragédies lyriques*, as he called them, for he preferred the libretti of Quinault to those of more eminent poets.

It was Lully's jealousy also that caused him to transfer his attention to opera, for as long as opera (whether by Italians or by Frenchmen) was only temporarily successful he was not interested. When, however, in 1671 a minor composer named Cambert, and his librettist Perrin, produced *Pomone* – the first extant though unfortunately incomplete French opera, which achieved such a success that it ran for eight months to packed houses – and when they followed this with *Les Peines et les plaisirs de l'amour* in 1672, then Lully decided to step in. Within two months of the production of Perrin and Cambert's second opera, Lully had so used his influence with the King that he had obtained for himself a royal privilege giving him a monopoly of all French opera. This privilege had previously been granted to Perrin in 1669, but while in prison for debt he sold it to Molière, whose interest in the possibilities of drama with music had also been aroused by the success of *Pomone*. As a result of Lully's machinations Molière's purchase was worthless, Perrin died in misery three years later, and Cambert went bankrupt and fled to England, where he became court composer to Charles II until he was mysteriously assassinated in 1677.

Not content with the scope of his privilege Lully repeatedly petitioned the King to extend its powers, until by 1684 no opera of any kind could be performed in France without his permission, and no theatre could employ more than two voices and six violins. Fortunately, though in no sense a mitigation, Lully's unscrupulousness was more than matched by his genius, for he created a type of opera unique to France, and one that so appealed to French taste that it remained popular for over a century. From 1673 until his death he produced thirteen operas, the best of which are *Thesée* (1675), *Atys* (1676), *Isis* (1677), *Phaeton* (1683), and *Armide et Renaud* (1686), all on libretti by Quinault.

In many ways Lully's operas were the antithesis of the contemporary Italian model. In accordance with French literary taste (which was much superior to Italian) the libretto assumed tremendous importance, and this brought about recitatives that are models of correct declamation (unlike *recitativo secco*), and airs that are vocally simple and contain few melismas. There is, in fact, much less distinction than in Italian opera between recitative and air, because French recitatives, being more melodic, tend towards *arioso*. There were also differences in aim: French opera chiefly concerned itself with glorification of the king by means of extravagant allegory. Its less rigid division into scenes consisting of a recitative and aria, and application of the vocal and dramatic conventions described earlier, its avoidance of violence and passion (foreign to French *sensibilité*), its inclusion of numerous ballets, and the greater importance of the orchestra, were all general but important traits.

Lully's orchestra reflects the inherent north-European delight in sonorous texture, for more of his recitatives and airs are accompanied by strings, or by strings and wind, in comparison with Italian opera, and much of his dance and instrumental music is in five parts.

The importance of the dance and of the overture in Lully's operas had repercussions in other northern countries. Dances and dance songs became very popular, and in the hands of German composers crystallized into the suite. The overture in the so-called French or Lullian style proved more attractive than the Italian sinfonia in opera, and was also used as an introductory movement to a suite. The main distinction between French overture and Italian sinfonia is one of texture, not of tempo (slow-quick as opposed to quick-slow-quick): the rich, complex, and polyphonic French type reflected the intelligent and cultivated taste of those aristocratic audiences for which the operas were intended, whereas the clear-cut sinfonia appealed more readily to the man in the street, who was Italian opera's chief patron.

Lullian opera was, on the whole, more realistic and reasonable than Italian because the libretto, in addition to its literary distinction, had to be clearly enunciated, whether in recitative or air, and because the plot could be unfolded without hindrance by such Italian conventions that successive arias must not be sung by the same character, or transmit the same emotion. Moreover, because of the much less dominant role of vocal melody, rivalry and jealousy between singers hardly existed and solo ensembles appeared more frequently. The delight in sonority, as well as pageantry, found expression in many more choruses than were common abroad, sung by crowds who either formed part of the plot or were introduced to glorify king and realm. But if the construction of Lully's operas was less rigid and dramatically more realistic than Italian opera (despite the insertion of ballets and spectacular scenes that were not always justified by the action), vocally they were inferior. To assess one against the other is pointless, as they had different ends in view. It all depends on whether a well-written, credible, but emotionally circumscribed plot, enhanced by recitatives and airs whose main function is to communicate the text, is preferred to opera that is formally clear-cut, where vocal melody and art reign supreme, presenting a happily variegated succession of arias with a wide emotional range.

Although many of Lully's operas remained in the repertory for well over a century this did not mean that there were no changes in French musical taste during the period. The classical grandeur and nobility of Lullian opera was less typical of the general atmosphere at the court of Louis XIV than were the operas of his successors, notably Colasse (1649–1709), Destouches (1662–1749), Campra (1660–1744), and Rameau (1683–1761). All reveal the trend, already apparent in Lully's time, towards frivolity, sensuousness, and an insatiable craving for variety, a trend that gave birth to *style galant* and rococo. In music the former, like the Italian *stile galante*, is characterized by homophonic texture, slow harmonic movement, and melody constructed of short phrases, but unlike *stile galante* the melodic line is profusely ornamented, reflecting precisely the elaborately decorated architectural style known as rococo.

Post-Lullian opera, therefore, relied more and more on elegant charm of melody, and a variety both of mood and spectacle, with pastoral scenes increasingly favoured, these forming an idealized background for a highly artistic amorality, as well as satisfying a nostalgia for an existence more real, more earthy even, than courtly life, preparing the way for Rousseau's 'back to Nature' philosophy. The drama became less important, melody more so, with much ornamentation; this had been strictly controlled by Lully as it would have marred the classic simplicity of his vocal line, and hindered the clear communication of the text.

The pastoral element is first clearly revealed in a work by

Destouches – *Issé* (1697) – which was immediately popular and remained so for nearly eighty years. Almost as popular and more significant musically was Campra's *L'Europe galante* (1697), which, apart from being more Italianate in the lyricism and number of *coloratura* passages of its airs and the perfunctoriness of its recitatives (Campra was of Italian descent), shows for the first time in French opera the dramatic possibilities of the orchestra. This is particularly noticeable in the Italian-influenced accompanied recitatives where *tremolos*, rapid scale passages, arpeggios, and agitated rhythms heighten the emotional content of the text. The emotional range of post-Lullian opera widened, but at the same time became shallower, and the sensationalism of Voltaire's tragedies was hinted at not only in Campra's use of the orchestra, but also in his modulations (bolder than those of Lully), in his chromaticisms, and in his dissonances. Campra reflected in his operas one of the two basic attitudes to life of the French eighteenth-century aristocracy, namely that anything was permissible save *lèse-majesté* and boredom, and to prevent boredom any activity, any emotion was welcomed provided it was not expressed too deeply or violently; amorality, sensual but refined, was the ruling ethic. Yet in contrast to the craving for emotional variety came the strong rationalistic bent, desiring to collect and neatly classify, as typified by the Encyclopedists. Both these characteristics are shown, more clearly, perhaps, than in the work of any other Frenchman, in the compositions and writings of Jean-Philippe Rameau.

RAMEAU

Rameau's earliest published work was a book of harpsichord pieces which appeared in 1706. He did not begin to write for the stage until 1723, and not until ten years later did he become famous as a composer, with *Hippolyte et Aricie*. Earlier, he had achieved notoriety with the publication of his now famous *Traité de l'harmonie* (1722), in which music is discussed scientifically and philosophically, and harmony is neatly but not always convincingly derived from the three chords, tonic, dominant, and subdominant. The book aroused much opposition, because of its turgid and pedantic style, because most composers could not understand it, and because its author had yet to prove himself as a creative artist, in other words to put his theories into practice. Despite its faults, many of which Rameau later corrected in a series of treatises, the book is of great significance since it was the first to stress and demonstrate rationally the importance of something that had been accepted in actual composition for some time, namely, the tonally fundamental character of the three principal chords; and in addition the fact that chords like E–G–C and G–C–E are not separate entities but inversions of the same triad C–E–G.

Rameau believed that music 'depends on reason, nature, and geometry', that it is 'a physico-mathematical science', and that 'melody is born of harmony', which was certainly true of his time and later. His belief in the power of harmony was typically north-European: 'it is certain that harmony can arouse in us different passions, depending on the particular harmonies that are employed', and he equates concords, discords, keys, modulations, cadences, and chromaticism with various states of mind.

The importance of harmony in Rameau's theoretical exposition of music finds abundant expression in his compositions, and especially in his stage works. Rameau also relied to a greater extent than any previous composer on the expressive powers of the orchestra, depicting violent emotions such as suicidal grief (*Hippolyte*, V, 1), terrifying apparitions such as the emergence of a sea monster (*Dardanus*, IV, 3), cataclysmic natural phenomena such as an earthquake (*Les Indes galantes*, II, 5), and supernatural horror (the famous 'Trio des Parques' in *Hippolyte*, II, 5), as well as portraying languorous or bucolic pastoral scenes by means of exquisitely scored musettes and tambourins. His reliance on harmony is also shown in the number of ensembles and choruses, and it is in these, in the orchestral passages such as those noted above, and in the abundance of dance-music that the best of Rameau is to be found.

His recitatives are still typically French in their *arioso*-like

declamation, but his airs are much more Italianate than
Lully's (partly the fruits of three years spent in Italy as a
young man), and it was this obvious Italian element, together
with the highly emotional use of the orchestra, and his avowed
unconcern with the literary and dramatic merits of his libretti
that caused the first of several Parisian musical 'wars' when
Hippolyte was produced, the Lullistes consisting in the main
of a few cultured reactionaries and a strong bourgeois faction,
and the Ramistes, headed by Campra and Voltaire, of most of
the musical élite.

Hippolyte was followed by a series of operas (or *tragédies*)
and ballets, the most notable being *Les Indes galantes* (1735),
Castor et Pollux (1737), *Les Fêtes d'Hébé* (1739), *Dardanus*
(1739), *Platée* (1745), *Pygmalion* (1748), and *Abaris* (1764), of
which the first, third, fifth, and sixth are ballets. Ballets,
indeed, appear with increasing frequency in his later output,
for Rameau was yet another instance, like Alessandro Scarlatti and Purcell, of a composer who felt obliged to give the
public what it wanted, even if this conflicted with his own
desires. He has with justification been called a 'symphonic
dramatist', since the orchestra was his chief vehicle of expression and he was deeply concerned to create a *musically* dramatic
entertainment in which the chief characters are the orchestra,
song, and dance. The varied contrasts produced by their
succession and association, rather than the stereotyped stage
figures and situations, provide the real drama. Such a conception of the lyric stage was hardly appreciated even a century
later, and despite the support of most of the musical intelli-
gentsia Rameau's works, after *Dardanus*, became more fragmentary (the great majority were ballets or pastorales), with
the orchestra and chorus less powerfully expressive than in
his *tragédies*, but still of prime importance.

In the year *Platée* was written, Rameau was appointed court
composer; in the following year a performance by a visiting
Italian troupe of Pergolesi's *La serva padrona* caused no comment, but when it was again produced in 1752 it sparked off
the second of the Parisian musical wars, the *Querelle* (or
Guerre) *des Bouffons*. The Lullistes buried the hatchet and,

backed by the King, joined forces with the Ramistes against the invader. Opposing them was a pro-Italian group headed by the Queen and the Encyclopedists, notably Grimm, Rousseau, and d'Alembert, who decried French opera in general, and Rameau's in particular. After a bitter dispute lasting two years, during which Rameau's *Platée*, *Pygmalion*, *Les Indes galantes*, *Les Fêtes d'Hébé*, and *Castor* were pitted against *buffo* operas by Pergolesi, Leo, and others, French music won the day. The reasons why the Franco-Italian controversy flared up in 1752 and not in 1746 are three-fold. Firstly, in 1746 Paris was still too taken up with the novelty of Rameau's operas and ballets, and was either vigorously for or against them, but in 1752 the novelty and the opposition had considerably lessened and hence the public were ripe for some new diversion. Secondly, the simplicity of texture, melody, and harmony of *La serva padrona*, and the naturalness and humour of the story and its characters contrasted strongly with Rameau's rich and complex idiom and the conventional unreality and seriousness of his libretti with their spectacular and usually irrelevant episodes. Thirdly, Rameau himself, in *Platée* especially, (last performed only three years earlier), had to some extent whetted Parisian appetites for a more Italianate style, for not only was *Platée* his only comic stage work, but it was also simpler, melodically and rhythmically, than anything he had previously written. It was in fact described by two of his most violent detractors as 'a sublime work' (Grimm), as 'divine', 'Rameau's masterpiece', and 'the most excellent piece of music that has been heard as yet upon our stage' (Rousseau), while d'Alembert, during the *guerre*, pertinently asked 'whether *La serva padrona* would have pleased so greatly if *Platée* had not accustomed us to that kind of music?'

But although *opera buffa* was defeated in Paris it left its legacy, for Rousseau was inspired to write a French imitation, *Le Devin du village* (1752), which, despite the feebleness of its music, became extremely popular. More important still, he published a manifesto, *Lettre sur la musique française* (1753), which exalts vocal melody as the fount of all music, subordinates harmony and instrumental music to the position of expressive adjuncts of song, avers that homophony (melody with a simple accompaniment) is the only natural and correct style, and that polyphony and contrapuntal devices are uselessly artificial; the *Lettre* thus conflicted much more strongly with Rameau's conception of opera than with Lully's, and its implicit recognition of the importance of the libretti re-established a typically French characteristic. Together with *Devin* and a translation of *La serva padrona* by the brilliant playwright Favart, the *Lettre* played a major part in establishing the vaudeville and *opéra comique* of the latter half of the century; it also helped to prepare the way for Gluck's 'reform' operas. Gluck's librettist, Calzabigi, during his ten-year residence in Paris prior to *Orfeo ed Euridice* (1762), was undoubtedly influenced by the literary and dramatic tradition in French opera, and was also impressed by Rameau's powerful and wide expressive range, which he could hardly have failed to communicate to Gluck.

V · BAROQUE INSTRUMENTAL MUSIC

Denis Stevens

1. The Age of the Thorough-Bass

If the idea of a *basso continuo*, or thorough-bass, had not arrived on the musical scene when it did – at the beginning of the seventeenth century – it would have been necessary to invent it. The years that led up to its appearance had seen gradual but important changes in the art of music, not least among them being the growth in size of choral and instrumental bodies and the growth in range of instruments, either considered individually, or in groups. These parallel increases in size and range gave rise to a common effect, or rather defect, in texture; one that has made itself evident at more than one point in musical history – the lack of a suitably sonorous middle.

In the best polyphony all those voices between soprano and bass share in their importance, both functional and aesthetic: it was part of the composer's duty to spread musical interest throughout the texture. Duet sections, even those in which the paired voices were some distance apart, were no cause for embarrassment either to composer or singer, for the acoustic of the church helped to fill the void and make rich what looked austere on paper. A soprano voice and bass-line heard in some private apartment or princely music-room was another matter. The middle of this texture needed filling in, and the lute, theorbo, harp, or harpsichord were just the instruments to oblige. They compensated to some extent for the lack of reverberation in an intimate acoustic, and their gentle tones were ideally suited to the formation of arpeggic or chordal bridges between the gamba and voice.

Church acoustics remained unchanged for the most part; what did change was the size of ensembles and the variety of instruments pressed into service. They needed binding together by a continuous and powerful thong, and this came to be known as the *basso seguente*, the sinuous bass-line of organ or harpsichord which snaked its way from one bass part to another, providing a conflate of both when they happened to sound together. The Sienese choirmaster and composer,

Agostino Agazzari, set forth at an early stage in its history the theory and practice of *basso continuo* in his *Del sonare sopra il basso* (1607) and elsewhere. He discusses the usefulness of figures and accidentals placed above the bass line so as to show what chords must be played, but hints also at the need for aural astuteness. If the player does not possess a good ear and quick musical reactions to what is going on, then let him write the necessary figures into his part.

Bass parts were not at first published (or even written in manuscript) with figures, thus the term 'figured bass', which is often used as an alternative to *basso continuo*, cannot strictly be called its true equivalent. Indeed, the lack of figures gave the player considerable latitude in accompanying, for he could act as a kind of 'sub-composer' instead of a mere vehicle for the transmission of filling-in-chords. To quote Agazzari:

> No definite rule can be laid down for playing works where there are no signs of any sort. One should be guided by the intention of the composer, who may (and does if he sees fit) place on the first half of a note either a fifth or a sixth, the latter being major or minor as seems more suitable to him or to the text.

One of his strongest points is that more than one way exists of proceeding from one consonance to another. He is no hidebound academic, but a practical musician looking ahead and trying to help others understand the new art of *basso continuo*. His practical suggestions include remarks on registration, ornamentation, and discretion: the organist should never obscure the soprano line by playing high notes or distracting divisions. When other instruments are playing and giving support to a soloist, there is no earthly reason why the organist should merely double:

> There is no need for him to play the parts as written if he aims to accompany singing.

It was this creative aspect of continuo-playing that enabled each and every performance of a Baroque sonata, concerto, or Mass to assert its individuality in a way unknown to latter-day stereotyped interpreters. It persisted up to and even beyond the time of Bach, who was admired for his extempore accompaniment of a solo line. In the words of Johann Daube:

He knew how to imitate it so cleverly, either with the right hand or the left, and how to bring in a counter-subject against it by surprise, so that the listener would have sworn that everything had been carefully written out.

It was the custom in Germany for composers to supply careful and generous figuring for the bass lines of cantata, concerto, and trio-sonata. Bach himself was no exception; and the custom persisted far beyond the Baroque period into Haydn's time and even Beethoven's. The autograph of the *Emperor Concerto* contains several instances of figures added to the bass of the *tutti* sections, presumably in the composer's own hand. When a German commissioned a work from an Italian, misunderstandings sometimes ensued, as when the violinist Pisendel requested a concerto from his friend Vivaldi. On first seeing the manuscript, Pisendel pointed out the lack of figures in the bass part, whereupon Vivaldi took it back again, added a few figures for the sake of appearance, with the curt and somewhat impolite footnote: *per gli coglioni*. Typical as it was of the Italian to suspect the virility of those musicians unable to realize from an unfigured bass, his attitude was by no means unusual when viewed from the standpoint of a harmonically trained composer. If the theory and practice of figured bass originated in Italy, it was there that the inevitable demise first took place. But by then its task had, in the main, been satisfactorily accomplished, and the 'all-round' keyboard player had taken his rightful place in the hierarchy of musicians.

2. Virginals and Harpsichord

AT first glance, the changes in style between the keyboard music of Bull and Bach, of Frescobaldi and Rameau, seem much greater and of far more fundamental a kind than they really are. There was no gradual progress (as is sometimes stated) from loosely constructed fantasias, shapeless, inconsequential, and quasi-extemporaneous, to highly organized sonata forms in which musical logic and tonal sensibility went comfortably hand-in-hand. In point of fact, many of the apparently meandering fantasias obey symmetrical if not absolutely strict rules of tonal architecture, and at the other end of the scale may be found sonata movements concealing an almost primitive freedom beneath their formally four-square exterior.

The virginals, and its more sturdy offspring the harpsichord, were marvellously well suited for the spontaneous expression of free fantasy, a realm of musical thought in which they were excelled by only one other instrument, the organ. The harpsichord, like the organ, enjoyed some variety of tone-colour and dynamics, and these two were of value to the composer whether in pursuit of the purest *raptus* or the most down-to-earth imitation of nature. Rich in melodic as well as purely virtuosic possibilities, ample in harmonic resource, the harpsichord was the instrument *par excellence* for the creative artist. Armed with nothing more inspiring than a ground bass, composers turned out variation patterns of infinite choice and wide emotional range, certain that their experiments would provide the player (and possibly the listener too) with moments of genuine delight.

In Germany, a true harpsichord style hardly emerges from the early Baroque school, pre-occupied with organ-playing as it was; yet there are a few indications of interest in music by Melchior Schildt (1592–1667) and Heinrich Scheidemann (c. 1596–1663). The much-travelled Johan Jakob Froberger (1616–67) brought an Italian touch and a French veneer to the Imperial Court of Vienna's music, and it is clear that his playing – transparent as a lutenist and sonorous as an organist – set a new standard for harpsichordists throughout Europe, except perhaps London, which rejected him and never properly recovered from its insularity until Handel's time.

Alessandro Poglietti proved to be another powerful Italian influence in Vienna, combining charm with opportunism in a way that won him no little favour. When Leopold I was twenty-three years of age, Poglietti composed an *Aria sopra l'età della Maestra vostra* which dutifully presents a melody followed by twenty-three variations. Like Froberger's style, that of Johann Caspar Kerll (1627–93) echoes both Italy and France; a generation later and much farther north, Johann Kuhnau (1660–1722) played a more decisive part in the formation of an indigenous keyboard school by disguising the *sonata da chiesa* as a fit and proper solo item, and by drawing on dance-movements and hymn-tunes alike for his picturesque *Biblische Historien* (Example 50).

The harpsichord music of J. S. Bach, who succeeded Kuhnau at Leipzig, shows breadth of intellect as well as perfection of style, although much of it is didactic both by implication and by design. The *Inventions* and *Sinfonie*, the *Forty-Eight*, and the *Clavierübung* (containing the six *Partitas*, the *Goldberg Variations*, and the *Italian Concerto*) enshrine contrapuntal mastery of such an order that the *Chromatic Fantasia*

seems part of another world. Yet it was the world of Frescobaldi and Louis Couperin, and it was due to be re-explored and exploited anew by C. P. E. Bach in his incomparable *Fantasias*. There is nothing English in the *English Suites* of old Bach, and nothing exclusively French in his *French Suites*: these sets of stylized dance movements present a synthesis of many styles then current. The same is true, though to a lesser extent, in some of the harpsichord suites of Pachelbel, Buxtehude, Gottlieb Muffat, and Telemann.

Germany's regard for the artistic leadership of French composers brought about subtle yet lasting results, for the very good reason that *le goût français* came of strong stock and noble lineage. The charm and delicacy of French keyboard music often obscures its perfectly balanced structural power, which may be sensed as early as the work of Chambonnières (*c.* 1602–72) whose suites observe unity of key without however relating the themes of one movement with another. Louis Couperin's suites are of more majestic cast, the chaconnes in particular giving evidence of his firm grasp of variation-form and his lively invention. Transcriptions of operatic numbers, although less characteristic of the keyboard than Liszt's, proudly join the dance-movements of d'Anglebert's harpsichord book (1689). Both Louis Marchand and Jean-François Dandrieu affect the Italian vein, but Louis-Nicholas Clérambault (1676–1749) adds to this a distinctive French touch that came naturally to one who had grown up in the great days of the opera-ballet. In contrast to the stylistically broad-minded Élisabeth Jacquet de la Guerre, Gaspard le Roux recalled some of the improvisatory features of earlier French masters, excelling in dance-movements where fine interplay of rhythmic elements predominates.

The central and dominating figure of the French *clavecinistes* was François Couperin, member of a dynasty of musicians whose contributions to creative and practical keyboard art cannot be over-estimated. His four books of *Pièces de clavecin* (1713–30) provide extraordinary examples of the suite at its least inhibited: the title *ordre* (chosen by the composer himself) indicates that he felt the suite, as he inherited it, too cramping, and accordingly he provides his *ordres* with as many as twenty individual movements if there is a reasonable excuse. The unity of key is modified skilfully to allow contrast, even though restricted to relative keys, while ample variety of mood is assured by dances disguised by intriguing titles and cleverly constructed *rondeaux*. Couperin's treatise on harpsichord playing and musical ornamentation, *L'Art de toucher le clavecin* (1716), combines thoroughness and artistry in a way that set him apart immediately from lesser lights and imitators. Although it was left to Jean-Philippe Rameau (1683–1764) to prove the solid virtues of harmonic structure as against the lighter vein of the *air tendre*, Paris knew no greater master of the harpsichord, in all its variety of colour and expression, than Couperin le Grand.

The strong Italian influence on French music came mainly through the publications of Frescobaldi (1583–1643) and his immediate successors. In spite of the profusion of brilliant toccatas, cerebral *ricercari*, and sprightly *canzone*, the world at large could derive its greatest musical pleasure from the kaleidoscopic variations on well-known melodies – *Ruggiero*, *La Girolmeta*, *La Monica*, *La Follia*. In the elegance of his figuration and the broad sweep of his phrases Frescobaldi betrays the mark of the organist, yet such is the balance of his keyboard texture that clarity is never clouded by the mists of partially understood polyphony (Example 51).

Bernardo Pasquini (1637–1710) looked backwards to Frescobaldi in his numerous *partite*, forwards in his monothematic *ricercari*, which his often gauche pupil Bernardino Azzolino della Ciaja tried to imitate. Alessandro Scarlatti and Domenico Zipoli contributed towards the development of the partita and the sonata respectively, but it was the younger Scarlatti, Domenico (1685–1757), who made of the sonata what Couperin had made of the suite. In the fantastic variety of his hundreds of short yet tautly-constructed harpsichord sonatas, Scarlatti shows what magic can be drawn from a few simple and basic chords. The effects he obtains, whether brilliant, humorous, evocative, or pathetic, prove him an unrivalled exponent of the *appoggiatura* and *acciacatura*, the leaning-note and crush-note capable of changing the colour of a chord as quickly and dramatically as a shaft of sunlight in a dark wood. Although Scarlatti's sonatas are neatly symmetrical and winsomely self-contained, they often pair themselves (in the original manuscripts) with other sonatas in similar keys, and there are even a few instances of the sonata-triptych. Essentially a miniaturist, Scarlatti nevertheless gave the eighteenth-century world of music a new language that was grafted imperceptibly and idiosyncratically on to the old.

The work of an Italian, Giovanni Picchi, appears on one page of the *Fitzwilliam Virginal Book*, a famous anthology of late Tudor and early Stuart keyboard music almost entirely devoted to secular compositions. Sweelinck finds a place there too, but it may not be inferred that the English virginalists were greatly indebted to their continental contemporaries. For the most part, they pursued their own remarkable way, combining prodigious feats of virtuosity with examples of simpler, almost child-like composition, decorated by fanciful names foreshadowing the polished miniatures of Couperin. Yet this school of virginalists left only a meagre handful of followers, and Orlando Gibbons and Thomas Tomkins were the only ones, apart from Byrd, who continued to write in the old vein when the new century was well advanced.

Interest in organ music slowly revived after the Commonwealth, but the harpsichord was not given the importance it deserved until Purcell wrote his energetic and resourceful suites. There are eight of these, and the general pattern is a four-movement group beginning with a prelude and continuing with three contrasting dances. Other music by Purcell, including arrangements of some of his incidental music for the theatre, was published in *The Second Part of Musick's Handmaid*. John Blow left very little in the way of harpsichord music, but the next generation brought with it an unusual contribution, a book of *Suits or Lessons* by Thomas Roseingrave, who was much influenced by Scarlatti and managed to reflect something of that master's mercurial quality in his own harpsichord style. Handel's Suites were written for his royal pupils, but soon became part of the staple diet of London's musical populace: they respected Handel's unique blend of German solidity and Italian verve, and they welcomed music that was not too difficult to play.

3. Other Solo Instruments

THE growing popularity of the harpsichord during the seventeenth century was due mainly to two features: its harmonic independence, and its long-tested links with ordinary staff notation. Although the lute was also harmonically independent, its reliance on tablature eventually became something of an embarrassment in an age that witnessed increased acceptance of a comparatively simple form of mensural notation, freed at last from its medieval bonds. Yet lute music was published and played up to, and even beyond, the time of Bach and Handel, both of whom included the lute in sacred and secular works. The reason why this vast repertory is almost unknown today emerges clearly from a comparison between the number of lutenists now active and the number of harpsichordists. For every one of the former there must be one hundred of the latter.

The guitar, with its simpler technique and tablature, gained ascendancy over the lute in Spain and Italy, but France, Germany, and to a lesser extent England, remained strongholds of lutenists and lute-music. In the earliest French anthologies (Besard's *Thesaurus harmonicus* of 1603 and Vallet's *Secretum musarum* of 1615) preludes, fantasias, and dances were freely intermingled. By the middle of the century, when the Gaultier family was active, it had become customary to group individual items into some semblance of logical order, and the suites contained in *La Rhétorique des dieux* (Denis Gaultier, 1597–1672) display a fairly constant pattern whose most remarkable feature is the stress on one particular dance, the courante, of which there are usually several, each with its own variation or *double*. Gaultier's elaborate ornamentation, his arpeggic formulae, and his preludes in free rhythm influenced contemporary harpsichordists for many years, as well as shaping the compositions of non-French lutenists (Example 52). Esaias Reussner (1636–79) left outstanding examples of suites after the French manner (allemande – courante – sarabande – gigue) in his *Deliciae testudinis* (1667) and *Neuen Lautenfrüchte* (1676). Sylvius Leopold Weiss was an almost exact contemporary of J. S. Bach, and Bach's flowing and expressive counterpoint seems to pervade many of the Weiss suites and sonatas.

Gaultier *Tombeau*

52

Genuinely solo compositions for the violin and cello were at first somewhat rare. The thousands of *sonate a violino solo* published in Italy were always for violin and continuo, but in 1689 Domenico Gabrielli wrote several *ricercari* for solo violoncello. The German school of violinists, among whom the most brilliant were J. J. Walther and Heinrich Biber, contributed much towards the exploitation of quasi-polyphony on a mainly melodic instrument, and Biber's fine *Passacaglia* for violin alone, together with a suite by Telemann, point the way to Bach's unaccompanied sonatas and partitas and those of the Swedish composer J. H. Roman. The essays (*Assaggi a violino solo*) of Roman bear out his cosmopolitan upbringing, but they cannot seriously compare with the depth and intensity of Bach's music for violin and cello, where free fantasy and complex fugal structures exist in perfect artistic balance.

4. Ensemble Music

THE fantasy, or fantasia, beloved of the Jacobean composers
for viol consort stood its ground in England until Purcell's
time, and though incapable of little intrinsic development of
its own it sent more than a mere surface ripple across the
apparently smooth sonata and suite. A notable feature of the
fantasy was its multipartite structure, and contrasting tunes
and tempi contributed much to the general impression of
loosely organized instrumental polyphony. Many fantasias,
however, are skilfully balanced artistic structures in which
tonality – together with contrast of mood and movement –
plays its part in unifying what seems to be diverse and inconsequential. Fantasia-like movements in suites and sonatas
owed a great deal to the example of such early masters as
Henri Le Jeune in France and Orlando Gibbons in England.

The viol consort was slow to yield to the violin in England,
although for some time the old and new instruments co-
existed peacefully enough. In the *Royal Consorts* of William
Lawes, violins play the two upper parts while bass viols express
the two lower ones. Both are supported by a thorough-bass
provided by theorboes which could be doubled by other
continuo instruments. In his *Harp Consorts* the harp serves as

a harmonic envelope for the ensemble, both supporting the bass and supplying ideas for the treble (Example 53).

Purcell's Fantasias for Strings stand as a musical monument to the instrumental polyphony of the preceding age, and they serve as a reminder that instrumental music, no less than vocal, could draw forth from the composer a vein of lyricism and harmonic colour rarely surpassed in any land. Purcell's recognizably English vein is here in abundance, and it matters little whether the music is played on viols, violins, or a mixed consort: almost any group can reveal the startling range of colour, the unique melodic contours, and the deeply expressive qualities which modern audiences now know to be a significant part of Purcell's artistic personality.

John Jenkins (1592–1678) followed Lawes and Coperario in offering what were virtually suites for one or two violins, bass viol, and continuo, the usual order of movements being Fancy, Almaine, and Air. The final air frequently recalled the spirit of the galliard, so that these early suites, with their stately introductions and light-hearted finales, foreshadow the classical form of the suite established towards the end of the century.

At first the suite for small ensemble, usually two violins and continuo, consisted of heterogeneous collections of dances which could be played in any convenient order according to the whim of the musicians. The titles sometimes betrayed the exact nature of the dances, as in Martino Pesenti's *Correnti, Gagliarde, e Balletti* (1645). Set out in the first instance for a keyboard instrument, the composer made it clear that strings could join in, playing from the same single volume of music. Mauritio Cazzati, in his *Trattenimenti per camera* of 1660, provides separate part-books for the two violins, spinet, and double-bass (or archlute), and there is a recognizable pattern in the sequence of dances, each *ballo* being followed by its *corrente*. At the end is a chaconne and a capriccio 'on twelve notes'. Later still, there are examples of Italian publications grouping the dances under common headings rather than dispersing them into ready-made suites: Marco Uccellini's *Sinfonici concerti* (1667) are neatly set out under four headings: *sinfonia, brando, corrente*, and *ballo*.

Fashion was of prime importance throughout the seventeenth century, and dictated many of the apparently illogical and extraordinary schemes adopted by composers in their attempts to satisfy a fickle and largely unknown public. Italian music-books were eagerly bought in countries far distant from Italy, and the buyer's influence on the publisher can therefore have been beneficent but not in any way absolute. The wave of publications, on the other hand, exerted considerable powers of attraction for composers in Germany, France, and England, and all three at some time experienced strong tendencies towards Italianization. Violinists from Naples, Brescia, Bologna, and Venice travelled to many of the courts of Europe, and added virtuosic lustre to the already fashionable suites and sonatas of their countrymen.

Court audiences proved to be connoisseurs of these dance-suites, and in Germany especially there was an attempt to rationalize the often arbitrary sequence of movements. The court sonata, or *sonata da camera*, made an early appearance as a balanced and crystallized unit in one of Johann Rosenmüller's publications (1667) and the general pattern there is *sinfonia – allemande – corrente – intrada – ballo – sarabande*. The actual term *sonata da camera* was used in this instance, and in due course Corelli and other Italians adopted the same pattern, or something akin to it. There were no hard-and-fast rules to follow: each composer could choose for himself the sequence of movements best suited to each publication. It is just this flexibility in suite and *sonata da camera* that makes the repertory of the age so fascinating. The reader is never really sure of what he will find.

Attempts have been made to distinguish between the *sonata da camera* and *sonata da chiesa* on the grounds that the former contained dance-movements and the latter did not, but in fact the distinction was by no means as clear as this. The *sonata da chiesa*, so called because it was often used as an optional adjunct to the available liturgical music, could and did contain movements not far removed in style from the sarabande and gigue. Even as late as Corelli, the third movement hints at homophony and triple metre, while the fourth often bears at least the trace of a gigue, if not the dance itself. Strictly speaking, the church sonata made its initial impression by means of a solemn *adagio*, following this with a movement in fugal style. The two remaining movements, usually an *adagio* and an *allegro*, were to some extent appendages to an accepted pair, yet this scheme rapidly became accepted throughout Europe. Purcell acknowledged his indebtedness to the Italian vein in one of his prefaces, while Couperin, although he gallicized the term to *sonade*, paid constant homage to Italian forms and styles from his earliest works to those of his final maturity. More typically French are Rameau's *Pièces de Clavecin en Concert*, in which the performer is offered a useful choice of instrumentation.

Thousands upon thousands of sonatas poured from presses all over Europe once the demand had become obvious and continual. Although there are exceptions, most of them conformed to one or other of the main patterns, which Brossard and others defined early in the eighteenth century. By far the majority were for two violins and continuo, although composers of all nationalities found it expedient both to reduce this to the solo sonata and enlarge it, often for ensembles of five or six instruments, so that the boundary between sonata and concerto, between chamber music and orchestral music, begins to crumble and eventually gives way entirely. In prefaces, notes to the players, and theoretical works there is often a broad hint that works written for a large ensemble will sound perfectly well if reduced to trio-sonata dimensions, and conversely trio-sonatas can be augmented and played by a group of ten or twelve musicians. This is the Baroque sonata in its most flexible form.

As opposed to the true equality of parts in genuine chamber music, the virtuoso element existed in the sonata from its earliest beginnings. The violin was the solo instrument most exploited initially, although cello sonatas by Jacchini and dall'Abaco display remarkable feats of bravura at a time when most cellists were content to play along with the figured bass. Outstanding players influenced composers then as they have done in more recent times, and in many cases the composer

was also the virtuoso. Veracini and Tartini were both violinists
of agility and ability, but they were closely rivalled by the
elder Matteis (who spent some time in England) and by
Johann Jacob Walther in Germany. Walther's *Scherzi da
violino solo* contain a multitude of remarkable technical effects
considering their early date (1676), and the polyphonic
writing, especially, brought forth succulent fruit in the works
of Kühnel and Biber (Example 54). Heinrich Biber wrote one

set of exceptional interest since, by its very title, it attempts to
break down the sharp distinction between church and chamber
(or court) sonatas: *Sonatae tam aris quam aulis servientes* (1676).
These compositions, apt for altar and court hall, are richly
scored, sometimes in as many as eight parts, and they may be
considered examples of the orchestral sonata.

In France, a pupil of Lully – Jean-Féry Rebel – produced
sonatas that combined the flare and fire of the Italians with the
wisdom and gentleness of the French. This, at least, was the
considered opinion of Lecerf de la Viéville, who was never slow
to speak up for Parisian composers. François Duval wrote
seven books of sonatas between 1704 and 1720, and a younger

contemporary, Joseph Marchand, mixed suites and sonatas in such a way that the sonatas appear to function as overtures to the suites. François Couperin was one of the first in France to use ornamental titles for his ensemble music: *La Pucelle*, *La Visionnaire*, *L'Astrée*, and *La Sultane* are all early yet impressive examples of his highly sympathetic feeling for music of an intimate and delicate kind. The solo sonata interested him hardly at all, yet he poured into the mould of the Italian trio sonata a musical alloy that made his *Apothéose de Lulli* and *Apothéose de Corelli* two of the most delightful and diversified suite-sonatas of their time.

In the preface to *Les Nations* (1726), a group of suites drawing on several of the earlier sonatas, Couperin explained how it was that he first won success as a composer of instrumental music. Admiring Corelli almost without reserve, and at the same time unsure of his own youthful powers, he decided to write a trio-sonata on the Corelli model and give it a fictitious Italian name formed from an anagram of his own. Thus Couperin became 'Perucino' or some appropriately Italianate surname, and the sonata was launched before a Parisian audience who had been led to believe that this 'new Italian work' had come to them via a relative of Couperin's in the service of the King of Sardinia. The ruse was successful, and Couperin was encouraged to write and publish further trio-sonatas under his own name. Like the Jacobean composer John Cooper (who found that the name Giovanni Coperario brought him more renown among his own countrymen), Couperin used an innocent camouflage to good effect, conditioning his audiences for home-made products every bit as attractive as the prototypes which had inspired them.

5. Orchestral Music

THE borderline between chamber music, or music for small ensembles, and orchestral music such as the Italian *concerti* and *sinfonie*, was throughout the seventeenth century a conveniently movable affair which enabled composers and performers to make the most of small resources as well as to provide material for larger groups. Many are the prefaces that tell the reader to add or subtract inner parts at will; and even as late as 1701 Muffat, in the Foreword to his *Auserlesene Instrumental-Music*, stresses the flexibility of his orchestration with almost commercial gusto. If string players are in short supply, his concertos can be performed with first and second solo violins, a small (French) double-bass, and a harpsichord. Should there be two violas available, these can usefully supply the two inner parts, which are not, however, indispensable. Muffat's tonal edifice progresses with additional violins, who are assigned to the first and second *ripieno* parts, and a large double-bass 'to make the harmony of the bass more majestic'. More violas can be added, and the bass enriched by theorboes and harps, but on no account must the solo (*concertino*) parts be doubled. Giuseppe Torelli, in the preface to his Concerti Grossi, Op. 8 (1708), is equally insistent on this point, for if ignored it will cause major confusion.

The words *sinfonia* and *concerto* were often used in Italian publications of the first half of the seventeenth century (Monteverdi's seventh book of madrigals was entitled *Concerto*) but the contents of the volumes rarely resembled anything remotely orchestral. Uccellini's *Sinfonie boscareccie* (1669) were primarily intended for solo violin, but the composer and his publisher supplied part-books for second and third violins in case the harmony and sonority might need to be increased. Giovanni Bononcini's *Sinfonie* (1685) were on the other hand conceived for a large and varied group of instrumentalists: four violins, two violas, two cellos, double-bass or theorbo, organ, and two trumpets. This set was dedicated to Giovanni

Paolo Colonna, Musical Director of San Petronio in Bologna, which boasted at that time one of the finest orchestras in Italy. Although a later set of *sinfonie* by Bononcini called only for string orchestra, he was careful to label it *Sinfonie da chiesa a quattro*, thus reminding his public that the music was really meant for use in churches. Its function there was to provide pleasant pendants to both musical and spoken parts of the services, much as Mozart's 'Epistle Sonatas' did in a later age.

The sinfonia also found a place in the opera-house, not only before the opera began, but sometimes between acts (the *entr'acte* or *intermezzo* served as later alternative terms) and even though the music rarely reached publication it was often of considerable complexity. One of the first composers to perfect the Italian overture was Alessandro Scarlatti (1660–1725) whose Neapolitan triumphs had made him the envy of Western Europe, and the teacher from whom all desired to learn. It was due to Scarlatti that the overture became a work of artistic importance rather than a purely functional call-to-order in a crowded theatre, and he not only helped develop this new form but also linked it with the concerti grossi written by his contemporaries. He called his set of twelve symphonies *Sinfonie di concerto grosso*, thus stressing the dual nature of the compositions and their place midway between the overture proper and the stock concerto grosso of Corelli and his followers.

The name of Archangelo Corelli will always be of prime importance in the history of the concerto grosso. But the contributions of others must not be neglected. Alessandro Stradella, Giuseppe Torelli, and Tommaso Albinoni all made very valuable contributions to the development of the concerto grosso, and they were aided by minor figures such as Taglietti, Gregori, and Bononcini, with the result that this form soon became the most popular kind of concerted music in the Continent of Europe. It was taken up in France by Aubert and Leclair, in Germany by Telemann and Bach, and in England by Handel and Boyce. Geminiani, who studied with both Corelli and the elder Scarlatti, made first-rate contributions to the concerto repertoire.

Perhaps the most prolific composer of all was Antonio Vivaldi (*c.* 1678–1741), a violinist who had at his daily disposal an excellent orchestra at the Ospedale della Pietà in Venice. An English traveller who visited the city in 1720 tells us that

Every Sunday and Holiday there is a performance of music in the chapels of these Hospitals, vocal and instrumental, performed by the young women of the place, who are set in a gallery above, and are hid from any distinct view of those below, by a lattice of ironwork. The organ parts, as well as those of other instruments, are all performed by young women.

It is in many ways unfortunate that the organ is omitted in modern performances and recordings of these concertos, for the weight it adds to the *tutti* passages helps to bring out the necessary contrast between these and the solo passages. To quote Muffat once again:

By observing exactly this opposition or rivalry of loud and soft, the fullness of the concerto grosso and the delicacy of the little trio, the ear is ravished by a singular astonishment, as is the eye by contrast of light and shade. Though this has often been mentioned by others, it can never be said or enjoined sufficiently.

The emergence of the solo concerto occurred quite naturally in the first decade of the eighteenth century. Torelli's Op. 8 was a set of twelve concerti grossi, but although they were so styled on the title-page they were in fact divided into two groups of six concertos. The first six are for two solo violins, which with the solo cello make up the normal *concertino*; the last six are however for solo violin. An unusual pattern of a related kind can be seen in Vivaldi's Op. 3 (*L'estro armonico*) whose twelve concertos are divided into four sets of three: each group of three begins with a concerto for four violins, then comes a concerto for two, and finally a solo concerto. Vivaldi's vast output includes solo concertos for flute, oboe, bassoon, mandoline, and cello; but it was left to Bach (who greatly admired his work and transcribed some of it for other instruments) to produce the first keyboard concertos.

Bach's journey to Berlin in 1719, to try out and bring back to Cöthen a new harpsichord, is generally accepted as the inspiration of the Fifth Brandenburg Concerto, and of the other concertos for two and three keyboard instruments written a few years later. Odd as it may seem, Bach – who was a virtuoso organist – wrote no organ concertos, whereas Handel (no mean exponent of the harpsichord) left no specific concertos for this instrument among his considerable collection of instrumental compositions. Both Bach and Handel kept to the Italian system of writing works in sets of six or twelve, and both broadened the content and orchestration of their concertos by extending the number of movements and making use of instruments other than strings.

Quick to realize the importance of the rapidly growing consumer market for Italian concertos, Handel wrote two superb sets which were enthusiastically welcomed in his own day and still retain their popularity in ours. The earlier set, Op. 3, is usually thought of as a set of six concertos in which strings are joined by woodwind – mainly oboes and bassoons – and conversely Op. 6 (which contains twelve concertos) is normally associated with a string orchestra pure and simple. The autographs of Op. 6 show, however, that two of the concertos were originally intended to be performed with a pair of oboes, or even a group of oboes firmly anchored by attendant bassoons. The printed versions give the string orchestra scoring only, though the various editions prove not only that the later set was very much in vogue among amateur orchestral societies but also that Handel wanted, if possible, two continuo instruments – an organ for the *tutti*, and a harpsichord for the concertino.

The three sets of six organ concertos were written for Handel's own use, since it was hardly possible for a new oratorio to be given without one or more interludes whose major feature was an organ concerto with Handel as soloist. There is evidence that these works were sometimes written in great haste, for the organ parts are seldom written out in full as Handel himself would have played them. Nevertheless they serve to demonstrate the immense skill which he brought to bear on his own modification of Italian concerto principles, as well as his sensitive balancing of the virtuoso element with purely formal considerations. His musical strength depended on this balance, which lesser lights were often unable to achieve.

Handel saw fit to borrow various movements from an important German publication of 1733, the *Musique de table* of Georg Philip Telemann, a composer even more prolific than Vivaldi, but with more than a hint of gallic grace in his musical style. The three sets of 'table-music' were so arranged as to follow a unique pattern devised by Telemann himself, and making use of both orchestral and chamber groups. First came a Suite for strings and *obbligato* wind instruments, the various movements often bearing French titles. Then followed a Quartet, a Concerto, a Trio, a Solo (with, of course, continuo), and, to end with, a Finale scored for the same combination of instruments as the Suite. Although this might be classed as eighteenth-century light music in view of its title, there is much evidence of a lively musical mind as well as a happy blend of French and German artistic elements such as are found also in the music of Muffat.

In France, the resistance to the sonata was almost paralleled by the mistrust of the concerto, yet in due course both came to be accepted after a century of orchestral music almost entirely restricted to ballet, opera, or church music. Yet much of this music is of admirable quality, especially when the composer was himself able – and willing – to write the inner parts. Lully did not always do this, and his musical secretaries were not noted for their musical invention. But it is clear from the work of a giant like Marc-Antoine Charpentier (1634–1704), and even from the humbler creations of a court musician such as Étienne Nau, that good and genuine five-part string writing can be one of the most satisfying of orchestral textures. The concertos of Leclair lean to some extent on the principle of the four-square *ritornello* standardized by Vivaldi, but they also present undeniable French traits in their slow movements, often cast in the form of an *air tendre*.

Features of French and Italian music helped to nourish the early orchestral work of the young Henry Purcell (1659–95) who left no formal concertos and symphonies but instead a number of impressive overtures and *ritornelli* in stage works and court odes. It was Handel who did most to interest the English musical public in the concerto grosso, and his Op. 6 enjoyed widespread fame among professionals and amateurs alike. The overtures and concertos of William Boyce and Charles Avison provide satisfactory evidence of the English ability to imitate without doing so slavishly.

Boyce often uses an almost Purcellian lyricism as a leavening for the solid Handelian characteristics which he doubtless admired and unconsciously imitated. His concerti grossi are classical in their adherence to the trio-sonata type of concertino, contrasting in brilliance and virtuosity with the four-part sonority of the *tutti* sections; yet in their choice of movements they sometimes give evidence of a more modern approach. Solemn adagios and vigorous fugues find him at his very best, though he can often relax in a final gavotte or minuet suffused with a gracious touch hardly equalled by the best of his contemporaries. Avison favoured a lighter texture in general, and his melodic ideas are more epigrammatic than those of Boyce, who was happiest in well-developed paragraphs and leisurely sentences. But if Avison's concertos are slight, they are nevertheless full of charm and spontaneity, constituting an effective and useful foil to the gravity of Boyce and Handel.

Books for Further Reading

I – II · THE EARLY AND LATE RENAISSANCE

Apel, Willi, *The Notation of Polyphonic Music*, Medieval Academy of America, 1953.

Besseler, Heinrich, *Die Musik des Mittelalters und der Renaissance*, Athenaion, 1931.

Bukofzer, Manfred, *Studies in Medieval and Renaissance Music*, Dent, 1951.

Davison and Apel, *Historical Anthology of Music*, vol. 1, O.U.P., 1949.

Einstein, Alfred, *The Italian Madrigal*, Princeton, 1949.

Garvie, Peter (ed.), *Music and Western Man*, Dent, 1958.

Grout, Donald J., *A History of Western Music*, Norton, 1960.

Harrison, F. Ll., *Music in Medieval Britain*, Routledge & Kegan Paul, 1958.

Hughes and Abraham (eds.), *New Oxford History of Music*, vol. 3, O.U.P., 1960.

Lang, Paul Henry, *Music in Western Civilization*, Dent, 1942.

Pirro, André, *Histoire de la musique de la fin du XIVe siècle à la fin du XVIe*, Laurens, 1940.

Reese, Gustave, *Music in the Middle Ages*, Dent, 1941.
  Music in the Renaissance, Dent, 1959.

Schering, Arnold, *Geschichte der Musik in Beispielen*, 1957.

Stevens, Denis (ed.), *A History of Song*, Hutchinson, 1960.

Stevenson, Robert, *Spanish Music in the Age of Columbus*, Nijhoff, 1960.
  Spanish Cathedral Music in the Golden Age, University of California Press, 1961.

Strunk, Oliver (ed.), *Source Readings in Music History*, Faber & Faber, 1952.

III – V · THE BAROQUE ERA

Bontoux, Germaine, *La Chanson en Angleterre aux temps d'Élisabeth*, 1936.

Bukofzer, Manfred, *Music in the Baroque Era*, Dent, 1947.

Davison and Apel, *Historical Anthology of Music*, vol. 2, O.U.P., 1950.

Garvie, Peter (ed.), *Music and Western Man*, Dent, 1958.

Grout, Donald J., *A History of Western Music*, Norton, 1960.
  A Short History of Opera, Columbia, 1947.

Haas, Robert, *Die Musik des Barocks*, Athenaion, 1928.

Hutchings, Arthur, *The Baroque Concerto*, Faber & Faber, 1961.

Laurencie, Lionel de la, *L'École française de violon de Lully à Viotti*, Delagrave, 1922.

Newman, William S., *The Sonata in the Baroque Era*, Chapel Hill, 1959.

Parrish, Carl, *A Treasury of Early Music*, Faber & Faber, 1959.

Schering, Arnold, *Geschichte der Musik in Beispielen*, 1957.

Stevens, Denis (ed.), *A History of Song*, Hutchinson, 1960.

Worsthorne, S. T., *Venetian Opera*, O.U.P., 1954.

Blume, Friedrich, *Renaissance and Baroque Music*, Faber & Faber, 1969.

Discography

RECORDED music covering the time-span of this volume is altogether too vast to be listed here even briefly. There are more than 1,000 discs of Bach's music to choose from, and although few of his predecessors are represented on so generous a scale as this, there must be enough records from Dunstable onwards to treble or even quadruple this figure. Anthologies such as the H.M.V. *History of Music in Sound* and the Deutsche Grammophon *Archive Production* will be found to contain many of the works discussed in the foregoing pages. Music by individual composers, both famous and otherwise, may be found by consulting *The Long Playing Classical Record Catalogue* (published quarterly by *The Gramophone*), and – in North America – the *Schwann Long Playing Record Catalogue* (published monthly by W. Schwann Inc., Boston, Mass.)

Index

INDEX

THE PELICAN HISTORY OF MUSIC

Edited by Alec Robertson and Denis Stevens

Volume 1: Ancient Forms to Polyphony

The '1066' of our music lies somewhere in the Middle Ages, when the Western tradition seemed to spring, fully armed with tonality, harmony, and rhythm, from the head of medieval man. It is easy to forget that musical languages had been evolving, both in the East and the West, for at least five thousand years before music in Europe began to assume the laws we are tempted to regard as perfect and unalterable. This first volume in the *Pelican History of Music* traces the story of music from the earliest known forms as far as the beginnings of the polyphonic period in the first half of the fifteenth century. A full section on non-Western music indicates how our tradition is linked with or has evolved from the forms of music prevailing in other parts of the world.

Volume 3: Classical and Romantic

This volume is mainly concerned with the eighteenth and nineteenth centuries, but works by Mahler, Bloch, Bax and others are discussed in a coda.

Even in the age of enlightenment a patron's 'good taste' was something that composers had to contend with and the so-called *style galant* forms the background to the achievement of C. P. E. Bach, Mozart and Haydn. But Beethoven scorned conventional taste, and the great classical works of later eighteenth-century composers owe their boldness to the *style bourgeois*.

Nineteenth-century romantic composers, such as Wagner and Verdi, were aware of the enormous material expansion and adventure of their age. And unlike previous composers they were conscious of their kinship with writers and painters; some of their greatest musical triumphs are to be found in opera.